FL!P

FL!P

How to Succeed by Turning Everything You Know on Its Head

PeterSheahan

HarperCollins*Publishers*

HarperCollins*Publishers*
77–85 Fulham Palace Road,
Hammersmith, London W6 8JB

HarperCollins' website address is: www.harpercollins.co.uk

First published in Australia in 2007 by Random House Australia
This edition published in 2008 by HarperCollins*Publishers*

1 3 5 7 9 10 8 6 4 2

A catalogue record of this book is
available from the British Library

ISBN-13 978-0-00-727598-4
ISBN-10 0-00-727598-6

Printed and bound in Great Britain by
Clays Ltd, St Ives plc

TO ALL YOU FLIPSTARS OUT THERE TRYING SOMETHING NEW,
TAKING A RISK AND PUTTING IT ALL ON THE LINE. KEEP YOUR NERVE!

contents

FL!P

introduction:
GETTING FLIPPED!

> **Flip:** A shift in mind-set and thinking; often a counterintuitive approach that reflects the hard reality of the business landscape as it is today, and not as it used to be.

Business today requires new perspectives on strategy, operations, customers and staff. Most of all it requires a level of flexibility that has previously been considered a weakness in some organizations. To navigate in an increasingly complex environment and zig when the competition are all zagging, you must flip repeatedly between different perspectives and paradigms. And you must do so in real time and on demand.

Flip provides a foundation and guidelines for developing and employing that flexible mind-set. It stimulates a way of thinking – an approach to business and life – that will remain relevant regardless of the changes that will occur at an increasingly rapid pace in coming years. It does not replace one rigid set of rules with another that will soon be outmoded. To *flip* is to turn conventional wisdom on its head, whether it be the wisdom of 1987, 2007 or 2027.

This book will, I hope, be a tonic for many readers. Daily I meet people who are struggling to keep their heads above water, crippled by their desire to always be "right" and to have an answer about what will happen in the future. But you can't know this, nor do you need to. You just need to notice what is and isn't working, and then be willing to *flip*.

The complexity of the current business climate means there is no single right way forward. There are many ways, and the most successful companies and leaders will try them all at one time or another. They will keep flipping. This is what Toyota is doing with the Scion and with hybrid technology throughout the Toyota and Lexus brands. It is what Apple is doing with the iPod. It is what Richard Branson does in virtually every industry he touches. And it is what Wal-Mart is doing in becoming a leader in environmental sustainability. Flipping, you are about to discover, is what the world's most effective organizations and individuals do to distinguish themselves from the competition.

· · ·

There has never been a more exciting time to be in business. Things are changing faster and faster, new opportunities and new markets are opening up every day. In order to profit from these new opportunities and markets you first need to understand exactly what is changing, and

MIND-SET FLEXIBILITY, NOT PROPRIETARY EXPERTISE OR RESOURCES, WILL DEFINE THE SUCCESSFUL BUSINESSES AND LEADERS OF THE FUTURE.

what impact this is having on your existing business. Then you need to *flip*. Flip from the perspective that has governed your business and competitive strategy into new perspectives and strategic directions tomorrow and the day after tomorrow. Mind-set flexibility, not proprietary expertise or resources, will define the successful businesses and leaders of the future.

This book will show you how seemingly upside-down thinking creates straight-up success. That thinking begins with understanding that we have seen the end of an *either/or* world. Conventional business models are built on choices between mutually exclusive options. That's a non-starter in a world where few, if any, options are truly mutually exclusive. For the foreseeable future, you must *Think AND, Not OR*.

Consider the following statements:

- The world is getting smaller every day.
- The world is getting bigger every day.

Both statements are true. The world is getting smaller all the time because people, things and ideas move from one place to another in greater and greater numbers at greater and greater speed. And the world is getting bigger all the time for the same reason; all those people, things and ideas in motion create an ever-increasing number of possibilities and options. Concentrate on one of these statements at the expense of the other and you will miss crucial possibilities and options and cripple your decision-making ability.

The need to "Think AND, Not OR" will pop up throughout

IF YOU LEARN TO FLIP, YOU WILL FUTURE-PROOF YOUR ORGANIZATION AND YOUR CAREER.

the book. It is the overarching context for six major flips I will explore:

- *Action Creates Clarity* – to move forward you must act in spite of ambiguity. Your action will create the clarity you're looking for.
- To keep pace with rising expectations, you can't just be fast, good or cheap, or even any two of these. Instead you must recognize that *Fast, Good, Cheap: Pick Three – Then Add Something Extra* has become the price of entry in every industry.
- To keep *ahead* of rising expectations and develop competitive advantage, you must *Absolutely, Positively Sweat the Small Stuff.*
- To satisfy customers' needs for engagement and contact – spiritual, emotional, physical – remember that business is not business, *Business Is Personal.* One thing that has not changed in a globalizing economy is that people want to do business with people they know, like and trust.
- To win mass-market success, *Find It on the Fringe.* The way to separate yourself from the competitive herd is by being courageous and creating new market space.
- *To Get Control, Give It Up.* You cannot command and control customers or the talented staff you need to reach them. Instead you must empower others to create, dream and believe for you.

Within each of the major flips there will be more subtle ones. I hope as you read this book you will begin to see opportunities to flip in all parts of your business and life, and each chapter includes suggestions of things to do when you finish reading it. More than specific examples of upside-down thinking, *flipping* is a philosophy. To be a *flipstar* like Richard Branson, Steve Jobs and Rupert Murdoch, to name a few, is to embrace the need for mind-set flexibility. To understand that what was right for yesterday may not be right for today and will probably be dead wrong for tomorrow. If you learn to flip, however, you will future-proof your organization, your career and ultimately your ability to live life to the fullest.

THE FOUR FORCES
OF CHANGE

I hope everyone knows that the world is changing. Pundits in every field talk incessantly about the constant change we are experiencing, to the point that "change agent" has become one of the biggest clichés of our time. But what specifically is changing? And why does it feel so pervasive?

Allow me to introduce you to the four forces of change that are completely redefining the way you compete in the marketplace, attract and reward staff, and even live your life. And then, through a series of flips, allow me to help you deal with these four forces of change (the latter being more important). This is not a book about the fact of change, it is a book about how to handle and profit from change. First, however, it is essential that we identify succinctly what is changing, because only then can we get more specific about what to do about it.

Here are the four forces of change I will be referring to throughout the book:

THE FOUR FORCES OF CHANGE

expectations   compression

YOU

accountability   complexity

1. increasing compression of time and space
2. increasing complexity
3. increasing transparency and accountability
4. increasing expectations on the part of everyone for everything

These forces are squeezing organizations and individuals alike. If you want to, you can see them as enemies, as the Four Horsemen of the Apocalypse that are ending business as you know it. Or you can welcome them as allies that are indeed changing the nature of business in challenging ways, but that also have the potential to accelerate your success and help you achieve competitive advantage.

None of the four forces is new. They've been around in one form or another at least as long as human beings have been creating complex societies. But there has been a dramatic shift in how the four forces affect our daily lives. They've never been

IF YOU AND YOUR COMPANY LEARN TO RIDE THE WAVE OF CHANGE, YOU STAND TO REAP MASSIVE WINDFALLS.

in as tight and immediate a feedback loop as they are today. That's why the pundits can't stop talking about change and change agents. That's why organizations and enterprises all over the world are freaking out about these shifts. And that's why you and your company must get on the front foot and learn to ride the wave of change – you stand to reap massive windfalls. Just think of Toyota and the car-industry-shifting Prius, or Apple and iTunes leading to the phenomenal sales of the iPod.

Let's take a look at these four forces.

1. INCREASING COMPRESSION OF TIME AND SPACE

Outside of science fiction and the thought experiments of theoretical physicists, it is not actually possible to compress time or space. However, our perceptions of both are certainly malleable.

Compression of time

Human beings have always been impatient. Today we expect things to happen faster than ever before. And not just a little bit faster, but over the last few years a lot faster. The quicker something can be done, the quicker we expect it to happen, whether it's the movement of goods by overnight courier companies such as DHL, TNT and UPS, the movement of people on flights from one side of the world to the other or the movement of digital information from anywhere to anywhere via broadband internet (something that merits fuller discussion below). They all feed our insatiable need for speed.

Staffan B. Linder's book *The Harried Leisure Class* notes that as economic growth and affluence increase, "the pace is quickening, and our lives are in fact becoming steadily more hectic". This has formed the basis of a commonly discussed sociological concept: as affluence increases, so does pressure around time. Ask yourself, are you feeling a little bit of pressure around time? Consider the following example.

I was discussing this idea of compression around time with the partners of a leading law firm. Afterwards the CEO told me how only a decade or so ago, as a young lawyer, he typically spent an hour dictating a letter to a client. Then he reckoned on half a day for the letter to be typed and returned to his in-box for signature before being put in the post, two days for it to reach the recipient, two days for the recipient to draft and send a reply, and two more days for the reply to reach his desk – more than a week for a single exchange of business letters. To-day, as CEO of his firm, he types and sends his own e-mails, or a short message text on his BlackBerry if he's travelling, and he expects an answer later the same day, if not within the hour.

And this CEO is not some "young twentysomething" exhibiting the impatience of youth. Increasingly we begin our work-days not fully rested, because we got to bed so late the night before, whether from trying to get overdue work done or to have a bit of social life in the midst of all our other commit-ments. When the alarm first goes off we hit the snooze button and go into what a friend of mine calls "mathematician mode", calculating the last possible minute we can get out of bed and not be late. Then we race to catch a train or bus to the office. Whether it's a blessing or a curse, technology frees us from the need to interact with anyone as we board. When we arrive at work we mill about restlessly, waiting for the express lift. Then we spend the day responding to the hectic demands of colleagues and superiors. We have two-minute noodles for lunch. And when we get home we pop our instant dinner in the microwave and stand there thinking, *Come on now, I have not got all minute.*

An exaggeration, perhaps, but I'm sure most people will agree it's only a slight one.

Unless you want to go off into the hills and be a hermit there is no escape from the nearly instant communication and feedback loops represented by e-mail, text messaging and mobile phones. Whether we're talking about countries, companies or individuals, events that happen on the other side of the globe can and do have an immediate impact on our daily lives.

This is only half the story. It is not just that we want what we want faster, but that we change our minds about what we want more quickly. Con-

IF THE LATE TWENTIETH CENTURY WAS ABOUT DOING MORE WITH LESS, THEN THE EARLY TWENTY-FIRST CENTURY WILL BE ABOUT DOING MORE WITH LESS, FASTER!

sider that the average time from concept to product in the US motor industry is down from between five and seven years (about ten years ago) to around two years today. And what is ironic about this is that the US motor industry is considered to be among the least innovative and slowest to change on the globe. It is competing with companies such as Toyota, which brings entire vehicle ranges (Lexus and Scion) and new value propositions (hybrid engines) to market while most of their rivals are still trying to digest the fact that there might be a significant near-term profit opportunity in mid-priced luxury cars, customizable cars for Generation Y or eco-friendly engines.

Back in 1979, when the Walkman, not PlayStation, was its

signature product, Sony went from product inception to product launch in under four months – remarkable for the time. Just recently, however, the PlayStation 3 cost Sony millions because of delays associated with its launch. It was shown to the public at the E3 games convention in May 2005, but didn't hit the shelves until November of the next year. By the time the PS3 got to market, its competition, the Microsoft Xbox 360, had shipped almost 10 million units, and Sony, a company that was once famous for its speed to market and relentless pursuit of first-mover advantage, lost almost $2.3 billion because of the late entry.

In summary, increased affluence and rapidly developing communications technology are compressing our expectations around time. If the late twentieth century was about doing more with less, then the early twenty-first century will be about doing more with less, faster!

Compression of space

Compression of the way we view space is shrinking the world. People no longer see geographical distance as a barrier to the way they do business. The world is the new market, especially in light of an increasing number of international free-trade agreements.

Distances have always been relative to the time it takes to travel them. In our grandparents' youth, the other side of the world was weeks away. Now it is one day away by plane, or one second away given communications technology that makes it less and less likely that we actually need our flesh and bones to be on the other side of the globe.

My own business is an example of this. Daily, thousands of

people from all over the planet log onto www.petersheahan.com and some buy products – some of which are digital and can be downloaded instantly – or subscribe to a free RSS feed that will help keep them on the cutting edge of new markets and trends. The point here is not to plug the "Peter Sheahan Live" section on my site (although I am glad to do so), but to point out that neither time nor geography poses any barrier to these trans- actions of value. I get visitors from countries I have never been to and make sales to people I have never met. I am able to complete transactions, even

COMPRESSION OF DISTANCE MEANS THERE ARE NEW MARKETS TO BE SERVICED, AND NEW WAYS TO SERVICE EXISTING MARKETS.

though neither I nor any other human is there to service the cus- tomer.

Compression of distance means there are new markets to be serviced, and new ways to service existing markets. It also means there are more competitors – the most dangerous of whom may be a twenty-year-old at her computer in Sydney, San José, Seville or Seoul, who in less than a decade could dominate your market.

Now, it is important to put the current status of this change in the proper context. Some economists argue that in many ways globalization is overstated. Consider that, for instance, of all the phone calls made in the world only 10 per cent are inter- national calls. And of all the investment in the world today, again only 10 per cent is foreign (international) investment.[1]

But even if the direct international component of business holds steady at around 10 per cent, we are now competing against international benchmarks. In an increasingly connected world, customers are increasingly exposed to global trends and fashions. The customer's sense of what the local business can do has irrevocably changed. Although people will always prefer to do business with people they know, like and trust (see Chapter 5, "Business Is Personal"), they expect those people to deliver at a global standard of excellence, not a local one. There is no escaping the need to position your business today to compete – in real time and on demand – in the increasingly globalized world of tomorrow. Flips are the future-focused way to achieve this.

2. INCREASING COMPLEXITY

Increasing compression of time and space produces increasing complexity. Businesses are being hit from all directions – from above, as they are saddled with dense and complex regulatory regimes; from inside, with the challenges posed by the adoption of sophisticated new technologies and the explosion of information networks; and from below, with the diversifying and intangible new demands of consumers.

COMPLEXITY BRINGS UNCERTAINTY AND COMPLEXITY THAT CAN PARALYSE INNOVATION AND POSITIVE ACTION.

The uncertainty and ambiguity this complexity brings can induce paralysis that prevents innovation and positive action, and may in turn force the downfall of once-great companies and careers.

Increasing complexity is being driven by, among others, the following six things:

- Rapidly interconnecting networks of ideas and people – from motorways, planes and

containerized shipping to the information
superhighway of the internet.

- Disruptive technology – innovations in product and
process almost always have unintended consequences
that challenge our ability to adapt, and reward those
with the flexibility to flip into new modes of acting and
thinking.
- Explosion of choice – in a globalizing economy, no one
has a monopoly on any product or service for long, and
the consumer's biggest problem is often choosing among
apparently identical offerings.
- Increasingly intangible desires of the market – rising
affluence shifts the business imperative from supplying
customer needs to meeting customer desires for
emotional fulfilment, no matter how mundane the
product or service.
- Increased sophistication of technology, systems, and
processes – complexity begets complexity.
- Legislation – whether it's financial transparency, safety,
the environment or human rights, the world's
governments are regulating it.

Rapidly interconnecting networks of ideas and people

I've already mentioned increasing flows of people, goods and
data, but there's more to the story. Think of every person in the
world as a node in a vast information system. Each node has
different perspectives, ideas and desires from the other nodes
in the system. Some differences are slight; others are large.
And a slight difference in one context may loom large in another.

Now connect those nodes by all the networks – physical and virtual – that link them together: text message, e-mail, landline phones, mobile phones, express delivery, container shipping and transport networks for people comprising motor vehicles, trains, ships and planes. These links crisscross the developed and the developing world, and more of them are overlapping all the time. Traffic on all these networks is constantly increasing, most notably in the form of digitized words, images and numbers moving at the speed of light.

A senior executive at Google shared some interesting statistics with me when I spoke to a large group of managers at Google's headquarters in Mountain View, California. Did you know, for example, that 20 to 25 per cent of daily searches on Google are unique? They have never been searched before – 25 per cent! This is not so surprising when you realize that 25 to 30 per cent of the Web is new *all the time*. We are generating content – opinions, survey results, perspectives, ideas, or just pointless garbage – so fast that at any one time more than a quarter of the World Wide Web is brand new. According to *Time* magazine, the world produced 161 exabytes (161 *billion* gigabytes) of digital information in 2006. That's more than three million times the amount of information contained in all the books ever written.[2]

This ongoing, explosive content creation challenges us to assimilate greater and greater amounts of often conflicting information, increasing the complexity, ambiguity and uncertainty in our lives. This rising noise puts a premium on what I call *confusion management,* which is without a doubt the most important asset for a leader today. Confusion management means dealing with ambiguity, contradiction and uncertainty while still retaining the ability to function. More on how to do this later, but for now back to the challenge it represents. Separating the wheat from the chaff in the information pouring in on us, recognizing when two or more apparently conflicting ideas must be used in tandem and accepting that new ambiguities will constantly arise are exactly what will distinguish winners from losers.

Disruptive technology

Add to this immense creation of knowledge (a generous label for much of what is online) the fact that the world has always been and always will be unpredictable because of unanticipated consequences. New technologies in particular have a history of creating unintended consequences, and nowadays new technologies enter the market faster and more frequently than ever before.

Take, for example, the diminishing impact of a thirty-second television commercial. Once a guaranteed way to drive sales, this form of media and advertising has become much less effective, especially with younger people, since the growth of the internet, or more specifically of massive multiplayer online games, social networking sites and greater access to broadband connections. Imagine what it is like for the forty-year-old advertising account director advising the fifty-five-year-old consumer-goods brand manager that the market requires entirely new messages delivered in entirely new formats through entirely new media. You'll definitely have confusion and ambiguity in the mind of a once-unstoppable executive. Perhaps you *are* that forty-year-old executive, or your industry's equivalent. Oh, and just when you've worked out what that new message and media should be, the fickle consumer has moved on to even newer things.

Whenever technology changes rapidly, actions you took yesterday may have a different effect today. These unintended consequences make planning difficult, and they constitute yet more new information that eventually joins the crowded flow of data you must digest and evaluate. This book will help you do just that. I will speak in later chapters about the need to unlearn and relearn at a much faster rate in order to stay in step with not just this but the other three forces of change as well.

> WHENEVER TECHNOLOGY CHANGES RAPIDLY, ACTIONS YOU TOOK YESTERDAY MAY HAVE A DIFFERENT EFFECT TODAY.

Explosion of choice

More information, more knowledge and more options ultimately mean more choices. Yet too much choice can actually paralyse. This is both a challenge and an opportunity.

The opportunity is for a business that can make itself "easier" for customers to choose and interact with. The challenge is that it is not just the customer faced with more choices, but the business as well. In an increasingly global economy with more and more sophisticated technology, there are not only more markets you can serve, but more ways you can serve them with a greater array of offerings.

"The paradox of choice" is now a fact of business throughout the world as companies re-examine which products and services to specialize in, which markets to serve, and how best to design, create and deliver a growing selection of offerings to increasingly broad and diverse markets.

Increasingly intangible desires of the market

Not only are the markets we serve more diverse and more demanding in terms of choice, they are also increasingly looking to intangible qualities to differentiate between one offering and another. The truth is most businesses are operating in oversupplied markets, where customers can choose between multiple products with the same functional value. In such markets, customers inevitably base the decision to buy one product over another on previously "superficial" features, a subject I'll explore in detail in Chapter 4, "Absolutely, Positively Sweat the Small Stuff".

Increased sophistication of technology, systems and processes

The technology, systems and processes that you and your competitors use to access and service the market keep becoming more sophisticated. It is commonplace to buy things such as a server, laptop or software, only to find that the tool requires an update – or even worse is completely obsolete – before you have even integrated it into your existing business processes and trained your team to use it.

To share a personal example, I have spent serious money and time configuring my own business systems so I could get the information I need from the database whenever and wherever I want. I can't tell you how challenging it has been to get members of my team to understand how the technology works and also to get me the exact information I need. Just when I thought I had my finger on it, online customer-relationship management (CRM) programs like Salesforce.com may have gathered enough momentum and critical mass to make my locally stored data a business process of the past.

This both excites me and hugely frustrates me. I'm sure you have had similar experiences.

Legislation

It is not just new technology, new choices and empowered staff and consumers that are leading to increased complexity. It is legislation as well. Consider the following two examples.

Enacted in the aftermath of the Enron, WorldCom and other business scandals, the Sarbanes–Oxley Act of 2002 (SOX), named after its key sponsors in the US Congress, places new demands on corporate financial reporting. Because of the global reach of the US economy, SOX has serious global impacts. For example, its strict guidelines on independent auditing of financial results have greatly complicated matters for both non-US and US companies, especially in terms of their relationships with the four major global accounting firms.

And this is to say nothing of the complexity of tax legislation around the world, especially for multinational companies with operations that span the globe. I read recently that the US Internal Revenue Code is 7,500 pages and contains 3,500,000 words.

MANAGING CONFUSION IS USUALLY A CASE OF DOING MORE, NOT LESS, AT LEAST INITIALLY.

The second is a more grassroots example of a takeaway restaurant I visited the day after attending a friend's wedding. Still recovering from the previous evening, I went to buy a kebab to try to settle my stomach. When I asked them to cut my kebab in half, they said they were not allowed to do so because of hygiene regulations. They even pointed out a sign they had posted to that effect. I told them they were off their rockers and wondered if it wasn't just an excuse to avoid extra work. But a week later I was doing some consulting for the Institute of Environmental Health and I related my experience to a former chief food inspector, who suspected, but could not say for sure, that cutting the kebab in half wasn't forbidden. Now, if a former chief food inspector doesn't know for sure, I obviously can't blame the restaurant proprietor for interpreting the law as he did.

All of this bureaucracy and complexity tends to lead to paralysis. In the face of the confusion, you do less. But taking less action is often counterproductive. Managing confusion is usually a case of doing more, not less, at least initially.

3. INCREASING TRANSPARENCY AND ACCOUNTABILITY

As my reference to Sarbanes–Oxley may suggest, the flip side (I couldn't resist) of the increasing volume and complexity of information flow is greater transparency and accountability. The digital communications revolution has put global information in the hands of literally billions of individuals, who can then share that information with one another at will. I have talked about the expanding exchange of knowledge and ideas, and how much additional complexity it creates for companies as they try to manage their databases. Even more important, information technology puts the power to obtain and share data in the hands of the individual.

The constant upswell in information, misinformation, complexity, ambiguity and confusion thus does not increase opportunities to hide your mistakes and misdeeds. It actually has the opposite effect, subjecting you to increasing transparency and accountability.

You would think that people have enough to do, given how

busy everyone is, and how overloaded they are with information, without worrying themselves about your actions. Again the opposite seems to be true. There are always people ready to catch other people's mistakes with today's information technology. When they find mistakes, or what they think are mistakes, the very same technology allows them to spread their knowledge and opinions to literally the whole world. There is a good chance they are in the cubicle outside your office, bored out of their minds and looking for something more interesting to do.

Accountability is being forced onto businesses in three interconnected ways:

- *Top-down accountability.* This is where legislation such as Sarbanes–Oxley and government oversight are being introduced to make businesses more accountable for their behaviour. In the near future, legislation on new behaviours such as carbon offset trading will shed an increasingly bright light on companies' environmental impacts.
- *Lateral accountability.* The existence of competitors in your marketplace gives customers the ability to "talk with their feet" when they don't feel as though you are meeting their increasingly intangible and constantly changing desires.
- *Bottom-up accountability.* A grassroots movement (be it word of mouth or mouse) can have a big impact on your reputation because of a positive or negative experience people have had with your brand.

Let me give you an example of these three elements playing together. A bottom-up movement has led to a growing awareness of issues related to climate change and the impact business has on the environment. This growing awareness creates an opportunity for a company to differentiate itself (or for a consumer to discriminate against a company) based on its level of "greenness". Take Westpac's "every generation should live better than the last" campaign and its joining nine other global banks in signing the "Equator Principles" in 2003, promising not to finance projects that endanger local communities or the environment. It was the only Australian bank to do so. A consumer may now keep competitors of Westpac accountable by not doing business with them, because they have not been as transparent and "green" in their behaviour.

Or consider the example of McDonald's. Once upon a time if you had a good experience in a restaurant you might tell two or three people. If it was a bad experience you might tell ten or eleven. These days if you have a bad experience you can tell many times that number. You type an e-mail, put up a blog post, and click – a viral public relations attack!

I followed with interest the move by McDonald's to post a series of short videos on YouTube under the theme of "the McDonald's you don't know". On a recent visit to YouTube, I found the most popular of the McDonald's-produced videos had received 1,746 views. What intrigued me was that a video directly above this one had been viewed 387,747 times. It was not a video about how "great" the Golden Arches are, according to the company, rather it was a frame-by-frame video of how McDonald's had allegedly inserted its logo into the programming of the popular US TV programme *The Iron Chef.* This may sound perfectly normal, except that the alleged logo allegedly appeared for only one frame, long enough to be processed subconsciously but not long enough for the viewer to realize what has just happened, a very sneaky way of manipulating the viewer. It is an example of how companies can be held accountable in the public's mind for their actions – or even their alleged actions.

4. RISING EXPECTATIONS

The fourth force of change results from the other three and in turn feeds back into them: rising expectations for faster, better, cheaper products, for more varied options, and for greater transparency and flexibility in response to customer needs and wants. Let's consider the following product time line.

Twenty years ago it was standard to have two or three keys for your car – one to open the door and start the ignition, one to open the boot, and perhaps another for your petrol cap. This evolved into just one key, with buttons inside the car for access to the petrol cap, boot and bonnet.

In an attempt to further improve the user experience, luxury-car manufacturers decided to save drivers the immense effort required to stick a key in a lock and offered remote keyless entry, allowing the driver to press a button to unlock the door. Then they would need to put that remote key into either a traditional ignition and turn the car on, or more recently hit the start button.

Now even this is too much, and you don't even have to take the key out of your pocket. The car automatically senses the key in proximity, and when you place your hands on the door handle the car unlocks instantly. Then, leaving the key in your handbag or pocket, you hit the start button and the engine starts up. Not only that, but some leading cars will automatically reconfigure the seat and mirror settings based on the programmed owner of the key. To top things off, keyless ignition moved in the space of a few months from a luxury-car feature to one available on mass-market cars such as the Nissan Altima.

A "SATISFIED NEED" NO LONGER MOTIVATES. ONCE A NEED IS MET WE MOVE UP OUR HIERARCHY AND START DESIRING MORE AND MORE OF LESS AND LESS PRACTI- CAL THINGS. THINGS THAT WERE ONCE A DESIRE RAP- IDLY BECOME A NECESSITY.

What's next is guesswork, but perhaps it will be fingerprint or voice recognition only, no need for a key. Or, wackier still, your car will know what you smell like and open and start upon sensing your uniqueness. (That is probably not a visualization you needed just now.)

The point is that what we are satisfied with today, we will not be satisfied with tomorrow. A "satisfied need" no longer motivates. We move endlessly up our hierarchy of needs and start desiring more and more of less and less practical things. Things that were once a desire rapidly become a necessity. Or, in business terms, features that once differentiated your product in the market fast become the price of entry, as competitors rip off, copy and enhance your own innovations.

In the autumn of 2006 the Pew Research Center, a non-profit, non-partisan "think tank", reported on the per centage of people who consider various items a necessity in life. Not nice to have, but a necessity. Here are a few selected items from that report:

- car, 91 per cent
- home air-conditioning, 70 per cent
- mobile phone, 49 per cent
- television, 64 per cent
- cable television, 33 per cent
- high-speed internet, 29 per cent
- flat-screen television, 5 per cent
- iPod, 4 per cent[3]

High-speed internet is barely a decade old, and it has only had a critical mass of users for less than five years, yet already just under 30 per cent of people surveyed in a random sample said it was a necessity for their life. At first glance you may think the 5 per cent who call a flat-screen television a life necessity should join the real world, but if you do this survey again in five years, as no doubt Pew will, it will be more like 25 per cent saying a flat-screen television is essential, and 5 per cent saying one in each room. Expectations keep rising higher and higher.

The way you treated your customers and staff up until today will not be good enough tomorrow. You need to keep getting better, and with the compression of time you had better start getting better a whole lot faster, too.

In closing this chapter I will say again, *change is not new*. Hopefully now you have a clear understanding of exactly what is changing, and are beginning to see the impacts these changes are having on your business. Within this context, let's now explore the *flips* and how to turn them to your advantage.

FIVE THINGS TO DO NOW

1. Hold a solo brainstorming session and write a list of all the ways the compression of time and space affects your business.

2. Think about complexity. What impact does it have on your business? More important, what impact does it have on your customers? Now think about strategy: How can you alleviate some of that complexity by simplifying existing services, or offering entirely new products and services?

3. Nominate someone from your team to become a red-tape renegade. Give them six months to cut as much bureaucracy and complexity from your internal communications and the interactions you have with your market as possible.

4. Ask yourself, "What do we currently do for our customers as an added bonus that may become the 'price of entry' in our market in the next few months or years?" Start thinking about how you can add new value to the same market.

5. Present the findings of the above four activities to your boss, or better still the executive team, and make some recommendations for the business.

ACTION CREATES
CLARITY

There is nothing more important in business today than an action orientation. If you take nothing else from this book, take this: you can't plan your way to greatness. There is nothing more valuable for your business (and for your life and career) than to do away with your commitment to microplanning everything and to let loose with some bold and courageous action.

This does not mean planning and strategizing are unimportant. Of course, having a plan remains vitally important. Although some pundits have declared "the end of strategy", I think that is far from the truth. But the big changes happening in the world mean that your plans must be shorter and more flexible. They must be built on the fundamentals of the most impressive human characteristic, behavioural flexibility. Most important, you must let your strategy and vision be refined, crystallized and improved by the feedback you get from the actions that you take.

As you read your way through this book, you're going to be confronted with some pretty challenging suggestions about the things you must do to stay competitive in the face of the changes that are occurring in the marketplace. The overarching lesson from the ferocious rapidity of all of these changes is that you can't possibly understand them *all* before they happen, nor can you predict precisely what those changes might look like tomorrow.

So the worst thing you can possibly do is sit down and try to factor every suggestion and every change into your next project plan. It would be time poorly spent. The *best* reaction you could have is to put this book down and *do something*. Trust me when I say the feedback you get will be more valuable than any plan you ever fashion.

Consider this book itself as a case study. As I was struggling to gain traction with this book, a mentor asked me, "Pete, how's *Flip* coming along?"

"Great," I replied.

"How many words have you written?"

"None. I am still doing research."

"How long have you been talking about this book? Two years? Isn't one of the chapters about how action creates clarity, or something like that?"

"What's your point?" I asked.

"Nothing really ..."

It is always a little aggravating when someone gives you your own advice. We teach what we most need to know, the saying goes. I had taken two years to get to this point. Thorough and well researched, perhaps; slow and delayed, *yes*! I had employed a full-time researcher, and even sponsored a PhD. project on related themes. Despite all of this work, until my mentor's question I had nothing to show for it.

Perhaps this sounds like the logical way to approach writing a book or accomplishing any major task. Given that this is my fifth book, I would like to suggest that it is not. It is in fact the opposite. Your best work does not happen when you are planning. Your best work happens when you are in the flow. On a plane, in a coffee shop or locked in your office late at night. It happens when you are taking action. Certainly, you need planning time, but at some point you have to stop thinking, stop planning and just *do something*. Anything!

Counterintuitively, the clarity I was so desperately trying to find before I started writing came only *after* I started writing. The point is, of course, that only through taking action, and the more the better, I say, will your strategy reveal itself (and rarely in one fell swoop) and the clarity you seek will be gained. Not only is the potential upside of this action orientation great, the downside of overplanning and overanalysing can be worse than merely being confused. In a market being squeezed by constantly rising expectations, less client and customer loyalty, and a compression of time, distance and required effort, inaction means you will probably miss the opportunity you were planning to exploit.

AT SOME POINT YOU HAVE TO STOP THINKING, STOP PLANNING AND JUST *DO SOMETHING.* ANYTHING!

What are you procrastinating about, as you plan and plan and plan?

It is like the young couple (or singles nowadays) saving for their first house during a property price boom. House prices keep increasing faster than their ability to put together a sizeable deposit. They effectively "save" themselves out of the market. The longer they "save" the further they are from their goal. A *flip,* no less. It can be the same in business. When we delay our action we deny ourselves the intensely valuable feedback that comes from putting the product to the test in front of a real consumer (or employee), who spends real money and uses it in real life situations. Life and business move and change so fast that the longer we procrastinate the more we put ourselves at a competitive disadvantage.

It is small wonder that David Vice, CEO of Northern Telecom, says, "In the future, there will be two kinds of companies: the quick, and the dead."

What about you? Have you ever had an idea that someone else made a squillion on? You know, you had it in the back of your mind, shared it with friends, even made some preliminary notes about it, only to mess around thinking about it for so long that one day you read a two-page profile in a magazine about someone half your age who did what you wanted to do and made millions doing it.

Or worse, have you ever knocked down an idea that someone in your team came up with, by saying it was "a good idea, but the market would never want it or be prepared to pay for it", only to see your competitor nail you to the wall with it the following year?

You get the drift. If you want to develop a better business strategy, and a more compelling and achievable vision, then act first, and plan later. *Action creates clarity!* If you want a successful career, do the same. Stop trying to find the perfect answer, the perfect job or the perfect product or business idea. Move! Do something! Anything! The action you take will generate clarity. From the clarity you will gain clearer vision on what you want to achieve, and the feedback you will receive will let you rejig your strategy to focus on the activities that are actually working as opposed to what you think might work. I call this "strategy on the go".

STRATEGY ON THE GO!

Strategy on the go is not the same as having no strategy at all. Dispensing with strategy altogether would be downright foolish, and even though some pundits have declared the end of strategy, this is not what I think nor is it what I am suggesting. I am, however, suggesting that we need a newer, more modern approach to strategy, an approach built on the fundamentals of behavioural flexibility and rapid decision making. It is time we let go of our obsession with detailed strategy, built on time frames of five, ten or even twenty years. It is no longer possible to begin with point B in mind and reverse-engineer the result until you get back to point A with a detailed, step-by-step plan for achieving what you want.

YOU NEED TO HAVE A BROAD VISION THAT COMPELS YOU TOWARDS A BETTER FUTURE.

Instead, you need to have a broad vision, or what I call a trajectory, that compels you towards a better future. It should be flexible enough to absorb changes in market conditions and completely new technologies and products. The key is to map out how you are going to get there only in the broadest of strokes.

Imagine telling this to some of the Japanese companies. To

think that some of them still speak of fifty-year plans! There is a good chance that many of us will be dead in fifty years. How on earth are we supposed to know what the marketplace will want in fifty years, or what technology will be available, let alone what it will mean for our industry or our companies? Don't get too excited right now, as you laugh off the fifty-year plans, knowing you have a rock-solid five-year strategy. Perhaps even your five-year strategy is a little absurd. First, it is not rock solid. Second, in the current business climate a five-year plan could be just as dysfunctional as a fifty-year plan.

Meg Whitman of eBay could not have said it better when she observed, "Forget about five-year plans, we're working on five-day plans here." It's not that Whitman doesn't look five years into the future. She didn't pay $2.6 billion for Skype without thinking long term. But she and her colleagues are not following a detailed master plan; they're working out the plan as they go.

In an increasingly compressed and complex world with constantly shifting expectations, an obsession with planning and detail can be more of a hindrance than a help. It can wed your teams and business units to plans of action that are not working in the marketplace, and that are not reflective of how your business has changed. It is no different in your career. Be flexible in your approach, prepared to unlearn and let go of what no longer supports your ability to move towards your vision, and learn new skills and behaviours quickly that will take you to your goal.

Rupert Murdoch is doing the same. He paid a huge sum for MySpace without a clear and proven business model for how he would generate revenue from the site. MySpace gives us insight into a multinational company and its CEO taking action without a fully developed strategy. Rupert Murdoch is a flip-star! Here is what he said about MySpace and similar News Corporation ventures:

> The precise business model for sustained
> profitability from our digital investments is still
> uncertain at this point. Consequently, in some ways,
> we are embarking on a period of trial and error.
> – News Corporation Annual Report,
> December 2006

I have met Mr Murdoch, having worked with News Corp in the United States and having had the pleasure of dining with him in Los Angeles. The man is very impressive. He was a few days shy of his seventy-sixth birthday when we met, and he was as sharp as any twenty-six-year-old. He knew the MySpace purchase could be profitable, and the signs so far indicate that he is well on the way to being right, even if, as the quotation above shows, there are still some uncertainties.

News Corp's Fox Interactive Media division bought MySpace in July 2005 for $580 million. Barely more than a year later, in August 2006, Google and News Corp signed a deal under which Google will pay News Corp at least $900 million, assuming web traffic targets are met, to be the search and advertising provider for MySpace and some other Fox Interactive Media websites. At the time the deal was announced MySpace was adding 250,000 users a day, suggesting that the web traffic targets would have to be very high indeed to be out of reach. (In April 2007 they registered *thirty-one billion* unique page views.)

Flash-forward another seven months, to March 2007, when News Corp and NBC Universal, the news and entertainment media division of General Electric, announced the creation of the largest internet video-distribution network yet assembled. With initial distribution partners AOL, MSN, MySpace and Yahoo, the network, hulu.com, will reach an unprecedented 96 per cent of the US internet audience. And I am sure internet portals in other countries will soon be added to the mix. At the time of the announcement, Cadbury Schweppes, Cisco Systems, Esurance, Intel and General Motors had signed on as charter advertisers.

There's a flipstar time line for you. Spend roughly half a billion dollars with no definite idea of how to make it back, and eighteen months later monetize returns at roughly a billion dollars and counting.

The MySpace deals beautifully illustrate the overarching flip principle, "Think AND, Not OR". In the first place, the new video-distribution network signals that exploiting intellectual-property rights and giving the public free access to copyrighted materials on the internet are not mutually exclusive concepts. Flexibility distinguishes flipstar organizations from their competitors. Instead of relying on business as usual in the television and film business, News Corp and NBC Universal are seizing the opportunity to make the internet a fully fledged, advertiser-supported entertainment medium.

FLEXIBILITY DISTINGUISHES FLIPSTAR ORGANIZATIONS FROM THEIR COMPETITORS.

Second, note that in the August 2006 deal Google and News Corp are partners, whereas hulu.com, the News Corp/NBC

Universal video-distribution network, takes dead aim at Google's YouTube as a competitor. Likewise, outside the new internet video network, NBC Universal and News Corp's Fox television, film and internet divisions are themselves competitors rather than partners. Change partners and dance with your rival. It's obviously complicated and will no doubt sow confusion along the way, but Google, NBC Universal and News Corp – three of the most successful companies on the planet – recognize that the way forward is to "Think AND, Not OR", that "Action Creates Clarity", and that "confusion management" is now an inevitable cost of doing business. You can resent these facts if you like, or you can learn to love them and join the flipstars.

Take Burger King for another example. Burger King led the corporate charge into MySpace – a messy, ambiguous and ultimately foreign situation – with action. They created a funny and personable profile, and the page took off. Burger King now has 134,000 "friends" (and probably a lot more by the time you read this), many of whom regularly post funny notes or even suggestions for burgers or promotions.

Fox itself is plunging in to promote the company's own products. Their brilliantly conceived MySpace profile for *X-Men: The Last Stand* has attracted almost three million friends. It is impossible to quantify how much the MySpace profile for *X-Men: The Last Stand* contributed to the movie's record-setting $120 million opening four-day holiday weekend release (the Memorial Day weekend) in the United States, but it surely didn't hurt. The previous Memorial Day weekend record gross was *The Lost World: Jurassic Park*'s $90.2 million in 1997. And *The Last Stand*'s Friday gross of $45.5 million trailed only 2005's *Star Wars: Episode III*'s record first-day take of $50 million.

MySpace is messy, but you need to learn to love the mess, to take some action without the clarity you desire. Others are choosing to sit on the sidelines and wait to see what, if anything, works.

Wired asked Rupert Murdoch how News Corp was going to weather the cold dawn of a world in which traditional media are besieged by bottom-up, user-driven content: " 'We'll figure it out,' he says, with a cheeky grin, scratching his head. 'You want to learn from MySpace,' he muses. 'Can you democratize newspapers, for instance? What does it mean for how we do sports or politics? I don't know – no one does. I just know we'll figure it out.' " [1]

This is what I am talking about. I love his new strategy, which strangely looks a little bit like: "I am not sure whether this will work or how I am going to go about it, but let's have a crack anyway. We have some bright people, we will pay to retain the bright people who started MySpace, and we will find out."

Even with the $900 million Google deal and the new internet video-distribution network, it is still unclear whether News Corp's internet properties will pay off as they should. But Rupert Murdoch and his colleagues act anyway. They learn to manage the confusion and accept the risk.

There's no detailed master plan. What News Corp does have is a broad trajectory. They know the media business. They know that people, particularly the younger generations, are consuming media in new and different ways, and they know they want News Corp to be a major player in the new media channels. MySpace is a leader of the so-called new media and Murdoch wants a piece of the action. Rather than try to reinvent the wheel and outspend some of the sites that have grown organically, he buys one of the most visited sites on earth. Then instead of doing what I reckon plenty of other media conglomerates would have done – namely, rebrand and integrate the website into its other media properties – he leaves it as is.

There's not a pixel of News Corp presence on MySpace. "Obviously MySpace is a world unto itself," *Wired* quotes News Corp COO Peter Chernin. "There's never been a second when we said, "How do we put our stamp on it?" We'd be crazy to interfere."

It is possible that I may end up eating my words on this, and News Corporation shareholders eating their losses, but it is exactly the willingness to take risks based on a broad vision for the future, in spite of some ambiguity in the present, that the most successful leaders nurture in their executive teams. And you will need to embrace the same openness to risk in your career as well.

For another example, consider the Lonely Planet travel guidebooks. In 1973, after meeting on a park bench in Regent's Park, London, and later getting married, Maureen and Tony Wheeler spent their honeymoon travelling overland across Europe and Asia to settle in Australia. They weren't planning on writing a travel book, but when they told friends about their experiences, and these friends told their friends, they began to be besieged for advice. So they wrote up their experiences and self-published *Across Asia on the Cheap,* which they stapled together on their kitchen table in Sydney and sold for $1.80 a copy.

They sold 1,500 copies the first week, and a new business was born. For their follow-up guidebook, the Wheelers travelled throughout Southeast Asia in 1975. At this time the fires from the Vietnam War were still smouldering, and tourist travel in the region was almost unheard of. Yet *Southeast Asia on a Shoestring* proved another immediate success. Go forward thirty-plus years and the Lonely Planet guides have inspired imitators like the Rough Guides travel books and have carved out a large slice of the travel-book market. Lonely Planet now employs over 500 people and has annual revenues of more than $100 million. In September 2007 the BBC's publishing division acquired it in a deal that put a lot of cash in the Wheelers' pockets (the exact sum was not disclosed) and still left them holding a 25 per cent stake in the company.

Tony Wheeler is not a reckless man. Nor, with an MBA from the London School of Economics, is he the pot-smoking hippie some may expect. At the same time, says Tony (I've had the pleasure of meeting him, and he is an inspiring person), "We knew nothing about publishing." The Wheelers simply took action based on their own experiences, the eagerness of friends and acquaintances to learn from them, and their gut instincts.

Not that financial success came overnight. For a time they were so broke they would steam unpostmarked stamps off incoming letters and reuse them. That's creative recycling for you. This is the kind of hunger we need in our bigger organizations. A get-down-and-dirty-and-make-it-happen kind of attitude. Imagine what you could do with that desire and the money that so many of our bigger businesses have access to. Some months things were so bad that the Wheelers would go to dinner with their friends, pay by credit card, and collect their friends' share of the bill in cash to get them through the month.

Go and find someone who is boot-strapping a new project or prototype in your business, and help get it off the ground. Tell their story to everyone in your company. Celebrate this kind of internal entrepreneurialism.

So many businesses have started just this way. Anita Roddick's Body Shop chain is another great example. This is how strategy gets done. Through action we get clarity.

> GO AND FIND SOMEONE WHO IS BOOT-STRAPPING A NEW PROJECT OR PROTOTYPE IN YOUR BUSINESS, AND HELP GET IT OFF THE GROUND. TELL THEIR STORY TO EVERYONE IN YOUR COMPANY. CELEBRATE THIS KIND OF INTERNAL ENTREPRENEURIALISM.

If you have never watched the TV show *House,* then you should. It is a crash course in twenty-first-century strategy. Dr House has a worldwide reputation as a brilliant diagnostician. In the medical profession, prescription in advance of diagnosis is generally considered a form of malpractice. Yet when he is confronted with patients whose ailments fit no obvious pattern, House boldly acts on the belief that prescription *is* diagnosis. He acts on his best hunch and, assuming the patients survive, adjusts their treatment according to their reaction to the first treatment.

Now I know it seems a little crazy to use a TV show as an example, but I can assure you the metaphor is powerful. Dr House takes only the most complicated cases, for which he is the last resort. The more ambiguous and confusing the patient's symptoms, the more interested he is. He takes the seemingly unsolvable cases and solves them. He does it by acting on the best information he can get at the time of diagnosis, without knowing for sure if he is right, and he treats the patient as though he is right. His reasoning is that if he is right then great, the patient will get better. And if he is wrong, not only will he now rule that educated guess off his list of possible illnesses, but the patient's response to the treatment will give him a better insight into what is wrong. Or said another way, action enhances clarity.

I was having a conversation recently with one of Australia's leading equity traders, who was mortified when I suggested that action creates clarity. As an equities trader, he always wants to make as informed a decision as possible before investing millions of dollars of clients' money. (Equally, despite using the *House* example above, there is no way I am going to suggest that physicians should go and prescribe drugs to patients on a whim.) However, there is still an element of doubt when he makes that investment. There is always a risk. He can use many inventive financial plays to mitigate that risk, but never completely. In a way he is taking action without complete clarity every day, even if he would never say this out loud.

You can't let the presence of risk, or the absence of clarity, prevent you from taking action. Whether that action be an investment, an attempt to ask someone out on a date or, more seriously, an attempt to cure a patient suffering what at first seems like an incurable disease.

DECISION MAKING ON THE MOVE

It may seem like a bit of a stretch, but human beings have been doing strategy on the go throughout the course of time. From as far back as studies have looked into, the early hunter-gatherer lifestyle conditioned human beings to be opportunistic foragers in a constantly changing environment. That required decision making on the move. Where is the best place to look for food today? How are we going to work together to find food as the weather changes day by day and season by season?

This lifestyle naturally stimulated our creativity and problem-solving skills, and as societies evolved and became more complex, these skills were honed in ever more challenging environments.

In this sense, it is very strange that we have become geared against, rather than towards, change. We arrange our organizations around command and control instead of around what has worked for most of time: change and adapt (*flipping*). Weekly I work with organizations with structures, reporting lines and cultures that are against the very notion of flipping, and are for consistency and predictability. Even though at some level the organizations know this is dysfunctional – otherwise they wouldn't have asked me to consult with them – they resist hearing the fact and acting on it.

> IT IS AS THOUGH THE PHENOMENAL SUCCESS OF BUSINESS IN THE LAST CENTURY, AND ESPECIALLY THE LAST FEW DECADES, HAS CREATED A SORT OF ARROGANCE THAT WE CAN PREDICT THE FUTURE.

Human success at adapting to changing conditions periodically lulls us into thinking that we've got it all worked out. Then we start developing and trusting long-term plans, which sooner or later – usually sooner – are exploded by a changing world. It is as though the phenomenal success of business in the last century, and especially the last few decades, has created a sort of arrogance that we can predict the future. I think it is fair to say we are increasingly feeling that confidence shaken as the four forces of change come to bear on us daily.

In what area of your business have you become overconfident? What do you assume to be immutable today that may become irrelevant tomorrow?

The truth is human beings are always much better off and much more productive when they abandon the desire to command and control things and accept the need to change and adapt to them. While the industrial age lent itself to systemizing and efficiency, that is not the case with the knowledge age, creative age, or – as I like to think of it – the relationship age. We think better on our feet, as Mihaly Csikszentmihalyi documented in his classic book *Flow: The Psychology of Optimal Experience,* and as Malcolm Gladwell also shows in his more recent examination of our capacity to make quick decisions in *Blink: The Power of Thinking Without Thinking.*

Of particular importance to this point are the studies Gladwell reports that demonstrate that we actually learn and adapt much faster than we think we do. We have a reliable ability to make decisions on the spot that are every bit as accurate as those over which we deliberate for months. We make *excellent* decisions quickly.

One study into the "adaptive unconscious", as it is known, used two decks of cards – one was stacked with cards that made it hard to win, one with cards that made it much more likely that you would win. Over time, test subjects gradually altered their behaviour to draw more cards from the winning deck. But *more* interestingly, players actually altered their behaviour *before* they reported that they had consciously detected a pattern. They were physically learning faster than they thought they were.

Gladwell argues, based on this and a whole host of other evidence, that "decisions made very quickly can be every bit as good as decisions made cautiously and deliberately". One of many possible examples of human beings' ability to make accurate judgements quickly is a 2006 study showing that people can accurately predict the result of political elections after seeing just ten seconds of footage of the candidates.

It is true; every action is a gamble, and that's scary. But as I said, we're evolved to thrive on taking lots of hunter-gatherer gambles every day. So stop complaining, because the time has come to ...

BUILD A BRIDGE AND GET OVER IT!

We're all scared. Seriously. We do our best to pretend we are not, but even the most senior executives I meet are freaking out. They worry that new ideas might not take off. Will they meet budget? Will the stock market hammer that less-than-double-digit growth this year? Will they lose their jobs? And so on. This fear compounds, and is fuelled by, the complexity of the world, especially as we try to plan further and further out into the future. This can often result in a paralysis of inaction.

Consider the photographic industry in recent times. It is well known that this industry has been thrown into turmoil by the digital electronics revolution. Recently I worked on the issue with the Photo Marketing Association of Australia, and Konica Minolta. Midway through a project for helping their retailers – mostly baby-boomer mum-and-dad operations – to promote and market digital products, Konica Minolta completely withdrew from the digital camera market globally, doing so literally overnight. One day we were working on a strategy of short-term actions to get better penetration in the market using their retail distribution network; the next day, nothing. Never mind, Sony stepped in to continue the work.

The problem was that Konica Minolta left its foray into the digital camera market too late, not releasing their first attempt, the Minolta D Image EX-1500, until 1998. They were aware of the technology, and even aware of competitors like Sony making gains in this market, but they waited as they tried to gauge the market better, searching for better information on consumers' responses to digital technology before they acted.

WHAT DECISION HAVE YOU BEEN PUTTING OFF? MAKE A DECISION *NOW*! TRUST YOUR INSTINCTS, AND GO WITH IT.

When they finally realized that digital technology was not only here to stay, but was already the dominant medium in consumer photography, it was too late. They had missed the early adopter's advantage. Instead of acting, they wasted time planning a response they never made to the biggest market opportunity to hit their industry in decades.

What decision have you been putting off? Make a decision *now*! Trust your instincts, and go with it.

Kodak and Sony were both pioneers of digital technology, dating as far back as the mid-1970s, but it was not until the mid-1990s that digital cameras met the market requirements of fast, good and cheap at the price. Kodak started the digital trend with their DCS 100 camera in 1991, but they were almost crippled by the "disruptive" technology they introduced. Perhaps this is because the adoption of digital happened so fast that they were not ready for the change, because film was their primary product.

They seem to be back on track, and now have the number one US market share in digital cameras and photo printers. They are still struggling to achieve their old levels of profitability, but at least they're on trend. The analogue camera share of the market is fast falling to about 10 per cent, and probably lower.

Sony got in fast enough, but only just, with their CyberShot in 1996. They had been playing in the digital space for two decades, and still they almost missed the boat. They had the same incomplete information and the same technological resources as Konica Minolta, and they faced the same ambiguity. Fortunately for employees and shareholders, Sony chose to act first and refine their planning second. Before you write Konica Minolta off, consider that they are now focusing on selling printing paper to be used for printing digital photographs, which to date is a very popular activity.

When digital cameras first came on the market, no one anticipated how quickly consumers would embrace them. But the nature of modern consumers is that they act *fast*. Either you move fast as well, or you lose.

After I spoke about the digital-camera revolution and its implications at a conference on behalf of my client Sony, a small-business owner named Jack approached me for some advice. Three years before, he had owned half a dozen photo-developing shops, with net positive cash flow of $250,000 each. On that basis he was making a lot of speculative investments and planning to retire in eight years.

When he came to me, Jack was down to one shop, which was barely breaking even. He no longer owned the freehold on the shop, but had been forced to sell it to service the debt on his speculative investments, which crashed when the technology stock bubble burst. To top it all off, his wife had left him.

As this example should make clear, when I talk about the need to stop planning and start acting, I'm not talking about acting blindly. Jack wanted to believe that his plan was foolproof, and he resisted looking at the accumulating evidence that it was not. While he was busy doing his wishful thinking, his smart competitors were beginning to offer digital photography lessons, digital photo frames, online photo-album and scrapbook design, and other value-added services, using market feedback to find out what customers wanted most. Also, making speculative investments is not really the same as strategy on the go.

After brainstorming with me, Jack has now begun to offer similar services. In effect he is transforming himself from a commoditized printer to a provider of customer experiences. He no longer sees his business as a simple and easily replicated transaction (printing photos for a fee) that the consumer could get down the road. He sees himself as a partner and mentor for his customers as they capture the memories of their lives. Through lessons and coaching, he is helping customers to adapt their own photography habits to the new digital world. His remaining shop is back on track, and he has a chance to return to the profitability he once enjoyed. If he'd had the guts to listen to the market and act on what it was telling him, instead of remaining loyal to an obsolete plan, he wouldn't have as much lost ground to make up. At any rate, I'm glad I could help him with his business.

Let's step back and look at the larger market again. When digital cameras arrived, most of the businesses that lived on selling traditional film and traditional film printing feared the end of printing photos and went into a state of denial. A few snapped out of denial and accepted reality fairly quickly, but most did not. Deep down Jack knew he was in denial, but he couldn't face up to his wishful thinking. He was hoping traditional film would hold on long enough for him to complete his detailed plan to retire in luxury in eight years.

In fact digital photography did not mean the end of printing photos at all. It meant that consumers no longer had to print their photos to look at them, but it also meant that consumers could easily take and store many more photos than ever before. The per centage of captured images that were printed might go down, but over the long term the total number of images printed would keep going up. One important reason for this is that most consumer photo printing is done by women, who are not content with storing pictures on a personal computer or the Web and who like to share prints with friends and family. The companies that acted in step with the market positioned themselves to profit from this, whether or not they saw the underlying dynamic clearly. The companies that bided their time to plan a response lost their place at the table.

THE ONES WHO WILL COME OUT ON TOP WILL BE THOSE WHO ACT IN SPITE OF THEIR FEAR.

Again I say: move! Do *something*. Whatever fear you are feeling, trust me, everyone else is freaking out about the same things. The ones who will come out on top will be those who act in spite of their fear. It will be those willing to expose themselves to the market (job or consumer market), be aware of the result and adapt their behaviour accordingly (think strategy on the go). I am constantly surprised at how few organizations want to do this.

AVOIDING REGRET

The saddest words in the English language are *if only*.

Ask yourself now: What opportunities are open to me, my career, my life, my business that are potential if-onlys tomorrow? What path of action do you think is worth taking a bet on now? Take it!

ASK YOURSELF NOW: WHAT OPPORTUNITIES ARE OPEN TO ME, MY CAREER, MY LIFE, MY BUSINESS THAT ARE POTENTIAL IF-ONLYS TOMORROW? WHAT PATH OF ACTION DO YOU THINK IS WORTH TAKING A BET ON NOW? TAKE IT!

You don't want to go through life continuing to pile up if-onlys. You want to say "if only" less and less, as you become smarter, more confident and more successful. And the only way to do that is by getting comfortable with risk.

This takes on a new and even more potent twist when you delve into the psychology of the way humans process and experience regret. Many people will not act because they fear they will regret their action. Most people also operate under the assumption that they will regret foolish actions taken more than smart actions not taken. This is, interestingly, false.

Echoing commonsense wisdom, psychologist Daniel Gilbert, in *Stumbling on Happiness,* says, "In the long run, people of every age and in every walk of life seem to regret *not* having done things more than they regret things they *did*." This is borne out by a number of academic studies over time – and if you're interested, the most common regrets include "not going to college, not grasping profitable business opportunities and not spending enough time with family and friends".[2]

Despite this, the four driving forces of change seem to have made a lot of companies and CEOs risk averse. It is not surprising really. With the average tenure of a CEO these days barely five years, so many just try to get through it unscathed. The average tenure of a chief marketing officer is far less, and it is not surprising that this is the area most in need of some innovation. Paralysed by fear of failure, risk-averse organizations and leaders try to plan their way to a secure future. The result is that they plan and procrastinate their way straight into the arms of the failure they want to avoid. Think of the major American motor companies, for example. They failed to move towards small cars over the last several decades, and hybrid engines in the last decade or so, and watched both Japanese and European carmakers steal their market share.

Today's most successful organizations and people are risk happy. They embrace the messy ambiguity and confusion in the marketplace and the fact that you can't hide your mistakes, and they turn these forces into allies by continually taking chances and trying new things.

This earns them credit with customers, because in oversupplied markets people want their brands to show leadership and courage. They love Nike for phasing out and updating an Air Max style before it's reached the height of its potential sales curve. They become even more loyal to Toyota's Scion when the company limits production in the face of increasing demand so that its hip young brand keeps its edge for the long term and doesn't get oversold in the short term. Meanwhile the business-as-usual brands like Dunlop and Ford can't even get customers' attention.

Risk-happy companies also attract the best staff. It used to be the case that companies that offered stable, long-term employment were more attractive. But these days the average tenure of people aged twenty to twenty-seven at a single job is less than two years. Companies are finding that the best and the brightest young people are generally not interested in long-term stability and want to leave after a year because they're bored.

GE CEO Jeffrey Immelt worries that his company is not attracting enough young hunter-gatherers, because gas turbines are not as cool as iPods and search engines. "If we can attract the best twenty-two-year-olds," he has said, "then we can double, even triple in size. If not, then we are already too big." Not content with that, Immelt has challenged GE to achieve 8 per cent organic growth, exactly the kind of action-oriented move that will keep GE an exciting place to work. It is not the action of a CEO who is afraid to fail, and GE's continued success is testament to the effectiveness of this approach.

IS YOUR ORGANIZATION WORKING ON PROJECTS SO EXCITING THAT THE BEST AND BRIGHTEST IN YOUR INDUSTRY ARE BANGING THE DOOR DOWN TO COME AND WORK FOR YOU? IF NOT, WHY NOT?

Is your organization working on projects so exciting that the best and brightest in your industry are banging the door down to come and work for you? If not, why not? What could you get off the ground in the next thirty days that will excite not just the people who work for you but the talent that works for your competitors, too?

Do you think the people who are scrambling to work for Google (they get 7,000 unsolicited applications each day) want to settle into a predictable routine governed by a detailed, long-term plan? These are some of the brightest and most talented people in the world, and they are dying to work for Google precisely because it is impossible to predict what the company will look like in five years' time. Sure, Google has vision, but it acts on its vision in short-term instalments, rolling out new concepts and products fast, abandoning what doesn't work, and moving on to something else in a heartbeat. At a recent conference in Los Angeles I got to spend some time with Laszlo Bock, the head of HR at Google. He was asked what he thought the Google workforce would look like in five years. He almost laughed as the question was being asked, and explained that their business changes so fast, as it adapts to the market, that they only really thought in detail about two years out from a workforce-planning point of view.

A risk-taking, action orientation isn't just a good business decision from an innovation and market-penetration point of view, it is also highly desirable from a staffing perspective. Ambiguity and confusion may scare you as a business leader, but bright and talented employees – the ones you really want and need – love the high-paced, high-energy environment that an action-oriented company creates.

THE SUREST ROUTE TO FAILURE IS NOT TO TAKE RISKS.

Risk-averse companies and people misunderstand one of the basic facts of life: the surest route to catastrophic failure is not to take any risks. Ice hockey great Wayne Gretzky famously said,

"I miss all of the shots I don't take." If you want to succeed at anything, you've got to take a lot of shots. You've got to throw plenty of mud against the wall and see what sticks and what doesn't. You've got to develop your risk tolerance by taking lots of small- to medium-size risks. In so doing, you develop your recovery ability, and you shrink risk. You also shrink your fear of failure and learn to make big risks manageable.

This is a key element of confusion management, the number one skill of a good leader in the flipped world. I am about to explain how to manage confusion, but first I must make a very important point.

It is vital that we do not confuse action creates clarity with speed to market. Speed to market can be very important, but putting something on the market and giving it to consumers before it is ready can have disastrous consequences – it can sometimes be enough to kill a company. This is not what I am trying to say. What this chapter is about is making sure you can have speed to market without compromising what you put out there.

For example, Atari was first in video games, but it was Nintendo, a fast follower, that survived to do battle with Sony's PlayStation and Microsoft's Xbox. Likewise Apple, a frequent flipstar example in these pages, brought the Newton PDA to market before it was ready, and saw the Palm Pilot become the first truly successful PDA.

CONFUSION MANAGEMENT

There is going to be more confusion in the business world
in the next ten years than in any decade, maybe in history.
– Steve Case, former AOL Time Warner Chairman

I've already referred to confusion management. The best definition I have ever heard for confusion management came from a good friend and client of mine, Sheryle Moon, who at the time was a director of Manpower (the recruitment company), when she said the key to being a successful manager today is the ability to deal with ambiguity and still take effective action day to day. Here are my thoughts on what it takes to be a good confusion manager.

KEEP MOVING

It goes without saying that step one is to keep taking action. Action creates clarity, so take plenty of it. You may like to look at it in the following ways:

EXPERIMENTATION

Look at your work, your project, as an experiment. Allocate a reasonable amount of time each week to try new things. At Google, software engineers spend 20 per cent of their time on projects of their own interest. Although the founders credit this idea to their experiences at Stanford, where PhD students are encouraged to spend one day a week on something besides their officially sanctioned thesis topics, companies like 3M with their 15 per cent rule have been doing the same for decades.

These ideas generally do not need to be approved by management. They are usually the ideas of the scientists themselves. From these little experiments came the Post-it notes at 3M, and Google News, Google Earth and Froogle, among others, at Google.

Could your business implement something like 20 per cent

time? What about one day a month dedicated to new-idea generation?

GUERRILLA TACTICS

I have met my share of potential flipstars who are caught inside very traditional and unexciting companies. They don't leave because they love the product they make or sell. My advice to them (and you) is to start little hidden experiments. Your company may not give you 20 per cent time, but take some of it anyway. Use the company's resources to get a working prototype of the service or product you are envisioning up and ready for demonstration. You may get your backside kicked, but who cares.

DEDICATE ONE DAY A MONTH TO NEW-IDEA GENERATION.

First, you probably don't even like your manager, and second, it is easier to apologize than to ask for permission.

These little behind-the-scenes activities are like guerrilla tactics. Here are some extra ideas for all you hidden flipstars:

1. Recruit a champion. Find someone high in the organization who you think is a closet flipstar as well. Recruit them for your project. Stop them in the foyer, stalk them at lunch if you have to. Tell them what you are up to, tell them that it is undercover, and ask first that they make some suggestions on how to further the idea, and second that they help you to get your new idea a hearing at the level of the organization where things can actually change.
2. Recruit some helpers. If you are bored, I can guarantee some of your fellow workers are, too. They probably don't have the rebellious energy required to start a guerrilla

project themselves, but I am willing to bet they would happily work with you on yours.

3. Make sure it works. Don't be all self-righteous just because you are doing something. Although I think you have a right to feel great about your risk taking and orientation to action – I have been writing about it non-stop in this chapter – it won't get you anywhere in your organization by itself. No one can argue with results. Get your prototype up and running, make sure it can work, crunch some numbers, and then show people. Not the other way around.

4. Move on. Your little experiments will often fail. Get over it. Start another one.

As Richard D'Aveni of Dartmouth University's Tuck School of Business puts it, "This is not the age of castles, moats and armour. It is rather an age of cunning, speed and surprise." Your career is no different. You can contemplate your navel all you wish, searching for your soul's purpose, the perfect job, the foolproof strategy, the most innovative product or the grand unified theory of everything, but you won't find it there. You will find it by taking action, by trying something – damn near anything, I say. And the combination of wins and losses, successes and failures, and everything in between will deliver back to you the clarity you need to fine-tune those actions and strategies to make you more effective, and to generate the results you desire.

WHAT GUERRILLA PROJECT COULD YOU PERSONALLY KICK OFF? EVEN IF YOU ARE A VERY SENIOR EXEC, GET SOMETHING COOL STARTED. TODAY!

What guerrilla project could you personally kick off? Even if you are a very senior exec, get something cool started. Today!

DECIDE ON A TRAJECTORY

You really do need to have some idea of where you are going. We live in times of too much opportunity, rather than a time of not enough opportunity. The greatest challenge a flipstar will face will be to decide what to focus on. But decide you must.

WE LIVE IN TIMES OF TOO MUCH OPPORTUNITY, RATHER THAN A TIME OF NOT ENOUGH OPPORTUNITY.

The beauty of the trajectory model is it leaves plenty of room for serendipity. It is more about where you are heading, not necessarily exactly what you will be doing to get there. Being the leading bank will probably mean something vastly different in fifteen years from what it means today, but it is still a worthy goal. The best real estate company in twenty years might be one dominated by property management rather than by sales.

Cirque du Soleil has a trajectory that does not limit it to the production of circus events. Their trajectory is to "evoke, provoke and invoke imagination". It sounds a little trite, I know, but they certainly have done this with their stage shows to date. This is not all they are doing. They are looking deeply into establishing Cirque du Soleil resorts, as well as staging stadium-size productions. I think there is huge potential for them in corporate training. This is on top of Cirque du Monde, which is a not-for-profit venture that travels into third-world countries and teaches juggling and other such imagination-building skills.

Cirque du Soleil's strategy would actually include all of the above items, but as you can see, their actions are quite varied, yet still fit into their broader vision.

While on the topic of imagination, I would like to encourage you to use some. It is the companies who in recent times had far-reaching imaginations that we celebrate today, companies that were able to see outside of their narrow sphere and imagine a bigger and brighter future. Think big! Dream, even. Only this will inspire intelligent people to join you on your quest to create something that is bigger and better and faster than whatever is currently available.

Confusion management requires that we balance activity and big-picture thinking. Replace your detailed strategy for the long term with a basic trajectory, a direction you want to head in, within which you will have the flexibility and agility to change quickly as you respond to changes in the external and internal environment that will alter the landscape you will be competing in. And allow the ambiguity that comes with it to excite you rather than scare you.

Focus your strategy and planning on the shorter term, which I will outline in a moment.

I am using business-focused language here, but your career is exactly the same. I meet very few successful people who knew from a very early age what they wanted to do. Sure there are the Tiger Woods and Eminem style examples, but in reality they are few and far between. People may have known they wanted – for example – to be an entrepreneur, but did they know it would be in the specific industry they are in today? Probably not.

The chances are they would not even have been certain that they wanted to be an entrepreneur. In fact they may not even have known what the word meant when they got their first job. I certainly did not. I did not know that there were jobs even remotely like what I now do.

The trajectory is a powerful thing when the market changes in your direction. Google began at Stanford with Sergey Brin and his PhD supervisor, Rajeev Motwani, as a data mining project. There is no way in the mid-1990s, when they were getting very interested in this topic and how it applied to the newborn internet, that any of the MIDAS (Mining Data at Stanford) crew, which included among others Google co-founder Larry Page, could ever have imagined how valuable internet search tools would become. As the project evolved and Brin and Page got more and more committed to it, they decided that no matter what, they would focus on better search functions. This remains at the core of the Google trajectory and all of their very powerful and valuable tools, and their skyrocketing revenues come from all things related to search.

Google could easily rest on the success of their AdWords business and choose to consolidate rather than aggressively pursue new applications for search technology. The millions of AdWords clicks, most only worth a couple of dollars each, are where Google gets almost all of its revenue – $3.66 billion a quarter and rising in 2007.

But instead of sitting back and counting the cash, Google keeps developing new opportunities and new services built around search capability.

They are also expanding into other areas: for example, taking Microsoft on in the business-software market, looking to replicate the success of Microsoft Office with a suite of online alternatives such as Google Spreadsheets under the banner of Google Apps.

CONNECT WITH THE FUNDAMENTALS

Some things never change. Seriously! In fact what we do actually changes very little over time. It is *how we do it* that changes far more often. Never lose sight of what you are trying to do. For example, the customer should be at the centre of everything that you do. The new strategy for the Commonwealth Bank is built around this fundamental idea. Here is a 30,000-plus-people organization that dominated the banking sector for many years. Under the leadership of David Murray, they embarked on a deep and widespread cost-cutting rampage. Most industry pundits agree that this was essential for the bank to generate better profitability and increased efficiency. The problem is they seem to have done so at the expense of quality customer service.

I don't think the banking sector is all that complicated. Of course the products, multitude of choices and other such things can make it seem very complicated, but in reality all banks are offering the same sorts of products and services. The competitive advantage, then, will be very simple. Those who offer these products and services in the fastest, easiest and, dare I say it, the most helpful and the friendliest way will win. Good customer service, among other things, is a fundamental in this industry. Stay connected to it, no matter what else changes. Certainly, the way you deliver that customer service can change, using things like the internet for example, and customer expectations of quality will continue to rise, but customer service will still remain a fundamental in the provision of banking products and services.

What are the fundamentals in your business? How are you performing in these areas? Are you staying abreast of new developments and rising expectations in these areas? If not, why not? What could you do now to get started?

WHAT ARE THE FUNDAMEN-
TALS IN YOUR BUSINESS? HOW
ARE YOU PERFORMING IN
THESE AREAS? ARE YOU
STAYING ABREAST OF NEW
DEVELOPMENTS AND RISING
EXPECTATIONS IN THESE
AREAS? IF NOT, WHY NOT?
WHAT COULD YOU DO NOW TO
GET STARTED?

If you are running a large organization, you will obviously be delegating the accountability of the fundamentals to key people. Do so, but monitor them like a hawk.

Getting back to the Commonwealth Bank for a moment, their new CEO, Graeme Murray, who has successfully turned around the Commonwealth Bank's sister bank in New Zealand, ASB, and also Air New Zealand, has said publicly that business is much simpler than we make it out to be. There are some basics that are not negotiable and you must execute on these flawlessly. I am backing Murray to do this successfully at the Commonwealth Bank.

LOOK, LISTEN, AND UNLEARN

It is essential that we keep our eyes and ears open. The reason people and the businesses they run fall behind is that we as individuals are not paying attention to the changes taking place. We are not looking for them, we are not reading about them, and sometimes we notice them but refuse to listen to the lessons they give. Sure, you can trundle out any one of hundreds of excuses about being too busy, underresourced or restricted by upper management (or the board and shareholders if you are upper management), but in reality these are all just excuses.

To be a flipstar you need to have high sensory acuity. That is, you must notice the nuances of change that occur around you daily and see what is happening. You must begin to act on the fact that more of your customers mention they visited your website before calling you, or that increasingly people get confused when you tell them what you do. The point is you won't be able to change and adapt if you do not know what is going on.

If you take repeated action that is not pushing in the right direction and you are not using this feedback to infer how you may need to change, then this is not intelligent behaviour. It has been referred to colloquially as the definition of insanity; that is, doing the same thing over and over again and expecting a different result. Not all feedback is good in the first instance. The faster you move through denial, through believing that all is rosy when it is actually not, and make some changes, the better. First, you have to notice that all is not rosy.

And it is not just noticing things about your individual business and industry. It is said that the disposable aluminium drum invented by Canon that revolutionized the copier market was inspired by a can of beer. I know, I know. That particular engineer really needs to get a life. Thinking about photocopiers while having a beer. But in reality, this is how many such things actually happen.

Step one – keep moving. This will create plenty of feedback for you to observe. Go beyond this and look to what your competitors have done that has and has not worked.

Look to other industries for what they have done. How could you do something similar? I was with a large healthcare provider recently. The biggest challenge they have is finding nursing staff for their many hospitals. Skills shortages are rampant, and filling rosters is a nightmare. One of the members of the board had been a consultant for an airline and was responsible for implementing systems that would allow them to get the maximum out of their staff while cutting their numbers (and costs).

She was able to explain the rostering system the airline used – which mostly consisted of a staff bidding system, with the hard-to-fill shifts paying more money, and the traditionally desirable ones less – and show that it could meet the health company's needs. The board and senior managers adopted the same approach across multiple sites and are saving tens of thousands of dollars every month in a tight labour market. This is an example of listening to someone with the right expertise.

I would like to reiterate here that no matter how much information you gather, you will still be confused. In fact, the more you discover, the more confused you may become. Again, celebrate the confusion. Rather than dig deeper and deeper and run the risk of growing more paralysed, revel in the ignorance and see it as an opportunity to try something new.

A groundbreaking piece of work by David Gray at BCG Strategy Group, published in the *Harvard Business Review,* argues that embracing "nescience" (the opposite of knowledge) is actually enormously beneficial. Too much knowledge can constrain thinking and limit you to acting within the confines of what you "know" to be true.

WHAT KNOWLEDGE OR PRACTICES DO YOU HOLD ON TO THAT ARE NO LONGER EMPOWERING? WHAT BEHAVIOUR THAT ONCE DROVE YOUR SUCCESS DO YOU AND YOUR TEAM NEED TO UNLEARN?

The beauty of being a flipstar is you can always do the opposite of what the world suggests. People say knowledge is power. Perhaps knowledge is not power. Maybe ignorance is. David Gray even mourns the loss of ignorance:

> Unlike knowledge, which is infinitely reusable,
> ignorance is a one shot deal: Once it has been
> displaced by knowledge, it can be hard to get back.
> And after it's gone, we are more apt to follow well-
> worn paths to find answers than to exert our sense
> of what we don't know in order to probe new
> options. Knowledge can stand in the way of
> innovation. Solved problems tend to stay solved –
> sometimes disastrously so.[3]

Two thousand years ago people "knew" the universe was created in a week. A thousand years ago humans "knew" the sun moved around the earth. Five hundred years ago people "knew" the earth was flat. Imagine what you will "know" tomorrow.

What knowledge or practices do you hold on to that are no longer empowering? What behaviour that once drove your success do you and your team need to unlearn?

MAKE UP YOUR OWN MIND

The most powerful way to work out the right answer is to ask yourself what you think. I know this sounds ridiculously simple, but I can assure you it is very powerful. Ask yourself: What do I think? You will come up with new answers – answers that make sense, and that are based on all the experience that has brought you to where you are today.

Great leaders and managers must be prepared to make decisions about their business, and for that matter their lives. Often these decisions will be based as much on intuition and educated guesswork as on predictable data and knowledge. The flipstar makes the decision anyway. Why?

- *Decisions lead to action.* When you finally make up your mind about something, it usually leads to action. There is no need at this point to say why this is a good thing.
- *Decisions create momentum.* The action that follows your decision will give you the clarity that was preventing you from making the decision in the first place, and now you are off on a positive upward spiral. Action, clarity, confidence, decision, action, and so on.
- *Decisions create confidence.* The decision gives not just you a sense of confidence but also those around you. If you are to get your team or, if you are a CEO, your whole bloody company moving in the direction of your stated trajectory, you had better instil some confidence. Decisions create that confidence.

In reality you have no choice but to make up your mind. If you ponder too long you will become irrelevant faster and faster. Sure, a decision usually requires some change and some risk, but the risk of not deciding and not taking action is, of course, much higher.

To be a flipstar you will need some degree of delusional self-confidence, a willingness to believe in your opinions and ideas even if the whole world says they are crazy. John Chambers, CEO of Cisco Systems, says, "You have to have the courage of your conviction."

Let's get real about it. We spend so much of our lives pretending we know what we are talking about, trying to appear in control in front of those we are supposed to lead. But as I want to emphasize again, the reality is we are all throwing mud at the wall and hoping some of it sticks. Business texts and conventional wisdom suggest this is reckless and unintelligent behaviour. I say it is just the reality of a global business world.

Now, don't stop pretending. This is an essential part of what you as a leader need to do. You must instil a sense of optimism in those you attempt to lead. Your team and colleagues will be attracted to confidence. An air of certainty must surround the leader. You can be honest about the confusion in the market, but you must remain certain that the business can pull through it, and that you are the one to lead them through.

I would suggest that without this blind faith it would become impossible to lead. The belief that tomorrow can be better than today makes the pain of the hard work bearable. The belief that your product is going to be a hit makes the late nights and inevitable setbacks tolerable as the promise of something great tomorrow keeps you going.

You must make a decision, and *move*.

GO CRAZY!

By this point you should have a good idea of what is working and what is not. If you have been continually taking action, observing the results and taking new action based on that feedback, you are ready to make a decision and bet the bank on it. There comes a time when your little experiments need to become full-scale attacks.

Whether you choose to do this through rapid evolutions or full-scale revolution is up to you. Either way, a rapid, full-blown effort is the only way change happens.

Bain & Co. conducted a study of twenty-one recent "corporate transformations" (large-scale management consulting projects involving massive company overhaul, mostly the CEO firing all of upper management). In every case where the transformations led to positive benefits for the company, the changes happened in two years or less. For the companies that changed fast and enjoyed quick and tangible results, their stock prices rose on average 250 per cent a year as they revived.[4]

This kind of commitment creates energy. And energy is what we need. An apathetic staff is worse than an angry staff. An angry staff can have its energy redirected when an organization is ready to move in a positive new direction. Apathy is far harder to budge. Consider from the same study quoted above that 90 per cent of people with heart problems that required invasive heart surgery never change their behaviour after surgery, even though it is likely to kill them. The same lazy habits that got them into this mess are likely to keep them in this mess.

> BUSINESS IS NO DIFFERENT FROM A PRE-SCHOOL PLAYGROUND. IN ORDER TO PROGRESS ALONG THE MONKEY BARS, YOU NEED TO LET GO.

IBM has not treated its reinvention as a global services company lightly. They actually sold an important part of their hardware business – their entire PC division, including the ThinkPad laptops – to Lenovo in

China. Although IBM continues to manufacture mainframe computers (the latest is the Enterprise z9), jettisoning the part of the brand that had become most familiar to ordinary consumers was not a half measure. Of $91.4 billion in 2006 revenues, IBM got $20 billion from its systems-and-technology division, which manufactures mainframe computers and designs server processors and computer chips, and $47 billion from services. Who knows, maybe one day Apple will execute a similar flip and become a full-scale music business.

Business is no different from a pre-school playground. In order to progress along the monkey bars, you need to let go.

RAPIDLY DEVISE SHORT-TERM PLANS

Strategy on the go requires that you do have a strategy – it just requires that it be shorter term not longer term, and that you allow yourself the requisite degree of flexibility within your longer-term plans.

This is a vital point. Long-term planning is built on your capacity to accurately predict not only the environment of the future but also the outcomes of each of your steps along the way. The problem we face is that the four compounding forces of the changing world make long-term prediction nigh on impossible. Prediction, as an activity, is getting harder and harder.

Consider this point, made by Daniel Gilbert: "All brains – human brains, chimpanzee brains, even ordinary food-burying squirrel brains – make predictions about the *immediate, local, personal future*. They do this by using information about current events ('I smell something') and past events ('Last time I smelled this smell, something big tried to eat me') to anticipate what will happen next ('A big thing is about to –')."[5]

But the more complex a system becomes, the less likely it is that past results are going to be accurate predictors of future outcomes. Think about this in terms of something we try to predict all the time: You can predict what the weather in your immediate vicinity will be like in the next ten minutes, but it becomes much harder to make an accurate prediction if you expand the time span and you increase the complexity of the system.

As both time span and complexity increase so does the margin for error when predicting the future. The preceding steps are an attempt to minimize the complexity you face, so add to that a reduction in the time span for which you are attempting to plan and you will reduce your margin of error.

This kind of short-term planning approach requires genuine speed. You must be able to devise and communicate your plan rapidly, and repeatedly, as you go.

CHANGE AND ADAPT

At a conference recently I heard the mountain climber Tim Macartney-Snape speak. He is one of the few people in history to climb Mount Everest without the assistance of oxygen. He said that the hardest thing about climbing Everest, apart from the lack of oxygen and the cold, is that the mountain "makes its own weather", Apparently, even the best climbing technology can't predict the weather patterns at that altitude. It reminded me of the marketplace. It makes its own weather; you either adapt and flip to stay on the mountain or you resist and get blown off it.

At the end of the day, you need to be flexible. You must be able to change and adapt your actions and strategy in order to more effectively propel your business, your career and your life in the direction you desire, not just in little ways but in big ways. Sure, you may have a whole lot of personal or business capital invested in doing business a certain way, but if the world changes, so must you. This is true regardless of the infrastructure you have in place, the degrees you have or the business models that have made you profitable.

When I first started my business, I wanted to work with students in schools. I wanted to teach them how to make a smooth transition from the classroom to work, and to give them the inside scoop about résumés, interview skills, employment expectations and – most of all – about the changing career landscape. I thought a one-week course would be perfect. How wrong I was.

The mistake was not in the idea. There was a lot of support for the content I was intending to teach. It was the format of a one-week course that was wrong. But even this was not the mistake. There is nothing wrong with "guessing" what will work. In many ways this is what we do when we strategize (we hate to admit it, but it is all just educated guessing). The mistake was spending a year perfecting my guess before I opened myself up to the feedback of the market.

Month after month I worked on what I would say, on what day in the one-week programme I would say it, and what activities I would get the students to engage in to drive their learning. Then, in less than a week, the market made it very clear that this was not what the schools could use. They could not afford to

ACTION MUST HAPPEN NOW – RISKS MUST BE TAKEN: CALCULATED, INTELLIGENT AND HIGH-PAYOFF RISKS.

release students from class for that long. Even though it would provide a good learning opportunity, it was simply not practical. They wanted short (as quick as one hour), sharp sessions with simple take-home tip sheets for their students. Had I started earlier, had I committed before I was ready, had I acted in spite of my early confusion, I would have gained more clarity faster. I would have saved a year!

Action must happen now – risks must be taken: calculated, intelligent and high-pay-off risks, but risks nonetheless. You can change and adapt. You must believe it is possible.

FAST, GOOD, CHEAP: PICK THREE – THEN
ADD SOMETHING EXTRA

A friend of mine had a successful business in Sydney, manufacturing point-of-sale materials and displays out of Plexiglas. Walk into a shoe shop looking for Nikes or Reeboks anywhere in Australia, or a consumer electronics shop looking for a new camera, and you would probably find a product in that shop made by my mate. At least that was the case a decade or so ago.

He had a good thing going until one day when everything started to change. That's when Plexiglas made in China first began to trickle into the market, and then suddenly flooded in.

As I sat with him having a coffee in his office towards the end of this tumultuous period, he said to me, "Peter, I just don't get it. What am I doing wrong?"

He probably meant it as a rhetorical question. But I stood

up and walked to the wall behind him, where he pinned up family photos, cartoons, inspirational quotes and that kind of jazz. In the middle was a piece of traditional workplace wisdom, a sign that said in block capital letters, FAST, GOOD, CHEAP: PICK 2.

My friend thought the sign was funny, but it also expressed a business philosophy that had served him well over the years. Perfection's not possible, and as Mick Jagger sang, you can't always get what you want. If you try hard, you can get what you need, as long as you don't ask for too much.

I took a red marker, crossed out the "2" and replaced it with a "3". That was my way of saying, "Getting what you need is yesterday. Today is getting what you want. And too much is never enough."

My friend had built his business by making good-quality products and responding promptly to his customers' needs. Compared to the Chinese imports, his products were not cheap, but he thought he had a quality advantage and could match anyone on efficiency and speed of delivery (at least initially anyway). As it turns out, many of my friend's customers thought his quality advantage was superfluous. The Chinese goods were made well enough to last through their normal span of use in a fast-changing sales environment, where customers are eager for the next new thing, and merchandisers replace their displays and point-of-sale materials frequently.

Behind my friend's wrong assumption about his quality advantage was a mistake about time and the pace of market change. It was two errors, really. One mistake was thinking the greater durability of his product was actually an advantage for most of his customers, rather than being increasingly irrelevant given how fast market trends change. The second mistake was in thinking he was a fast enough manufacturer and supplier to hold his market share. The Chinese manufac- turers turned out to be much faster than he was as well as much cheaper, and were good

GETTING WHAT YOU NEED IS YESTERDAY. TODAY IS GET- TING WHAT YOU WANT. AND TOO MUCH IS NEVER ENOUGH.

enough on quality to rapidly erode his market share. Not only that, but over time the Chinese imports arguably began to match the quality on which he once built his market position.

My friend's mistake wasn't unusual. It was business as usual. The standard advice in business textbooks is that you can't lead your league on fast, good and cheap, so you should concentrate your efforts to excel and establish competitive advantage in one category, be average or good in a second category, and don't worry too much about lagging in the third category.

But remember, today's customers increasingly "Think AND, Not OR". In a world of global oversupply, global under-demand and non-stop technological change, they get more of what they want faster and faster all the time. In the case of some of the most profitable businesses of our time (think of success-ful product launches such as the Apple iPod, Nintendo Wii, Toyota Scion or the latest Nike shoe), customers get more of what they want before they know they want it.

The four forces of change I discussed in Chapter 1 – especially the fourth: rising expectations – are the cause of this change. The bottom line, as you can see from my mate's example, is that the more variety, the better quality and the faster service cus-tomers enjoy, and the more comparative information that is available to them about you versus the competition, the more finicky, demanding and impatient they become. In that context, competitive advantages quickly turn into competitive necessities that rivals can copy and adapt for themselves.

COMPETITIVE ADVANTAGES QUICKLY TURN INTO COM- PETITIVE NECESSITIES THAT RIVALS CAN COPY AND ADAPT FOR THEMSELVES.

For you as a businessperson, that situation desperately requires you to flip on its head any notion that fast, good, cheap: pick two is sufficient in today's market. Genuine competitive advantage requires a minimum of all three, plus something above and beyond these necessities.

In order to really grasp this flip and implement it into your day-to-day operations you must understand:

- To compete in any market, being fast, good and cheap is the price of entry. To achieve competitive advantage, you must lead the league in at least one category and be industry standard in the remainder.
- You must commit to a perpetual cycle of innovation. Fast today is not fast enough for tomorrow. Good today is not good enough for tomorrow. Cheap today is not cheap enough for tomorrow.
- Customer satisfaction sucks! If you're ever going to move beyond satisfying customer needs to fulfilling customer wants, which is where the big profits are, you've got to be fast, good, cheap and *more*!

When I tell executives, "Customer satisfaction sucks!", they look at me as if I'm crazy. If anything is accepted business wisdom today, it is that customer satisfaction is paramount.

Yes and no. Bear with me while I split a very important hair.

My cable-television provider recently called to ask if I was satisfied with my new package. Well, the service does what they promised it would do, but I'm not going out of my way to tell people how great it is. Instead of five television channels with nothing on that I want to watch, there are more than a hundred. I need digital-television service if I'm going to get the most out of my high-definition flat-panel television. But I don't want lots of channels. I want one that shows what I want to watch.

Lots of channels satisfied my need, but they didn't fulfil my want. The cable-television industry as a whole is a classic example of company needs and wants being out of alignment with customer needs and wants. New digital-video services such as TiVo are going some of the way to addressing this disparity, as are cable-television packages offering you the ability to choose your dominant programming such as football, films or some other genre that interests you. The programmers, the television networks and the cable-television providers prefer to aggregate hundreds of channels into tiered services that only seem to fulfil customers' desire to watch what they choose when they choose.

That's the subscription model the industry wants. And some customers are probably perfectly happy with it. But other customers aren't going to be happy until they get à la carte pricing that enables them to pick and choose only the channels they really want to watch, or perhaps until they can freely choose high-definition video from millions of sources streaming over the internet. Over the next few years, as YouTube continues to grow and more households opt for digital-video recorders like TiVo, I suspect many customers will want to program their own television viewing rather than settle for the cable-television industry's programming packages.

This will, of course, happen not only as technology gives customers more choices outside the traditional television providers' control, but also as peer-to-peer networks allow users to get recommendations from people they know and trust so they can sort through the limitless choices efficiently. The internet video distribution network from NBC Universal and News Corporation, in collaboration with AOL, MSN, MySpace and Yahoo, anticipates that future and represents a savvy response to the popularity of YouTube.

The NBC Universal–News Corp network is a brilliant flip on the entertainment business as usual, and I have more to say about it in Chapter 7, "To Get Control, Give It Up". The general point I want to make here is that customer satisfaction measures your ability to deliver what you have conditioned the customer to expect, not what he or she really wants. And that leaves you vulnerable to a competitor who will supply that want with a positive, memorable, mind-blowing customer experience, something that exponentially raises the standard on fast, good and cheap, and instantly creates a whole new level of customer expectation.

GREAT YESTERDAY, GOOD TODAY, BAD TOMORROW

Once you recognize the "Fast, Good, Cheap: Pick Three – Then Add Something Extra" dynamic at work, you begin to notice it everywhere. I want to point you to some of the best current examples of it among the world's leading companies. But first let me tell you what happened to my friend's Plexiglas business.

When I crossed out the "2" in his FAST, GOOD, CHEAP: PICK 2 sign and replaced it with a "3", my friend got it instantly. He had been flipped, and he knew it. So without any detailed plan (he is the kind of person who showed me that action creates clarity) he began to act differently.

He stopped trying to stem the losses from his broad old customer base, and he began to concentrate on serving only the most profitable customers. This quickly led him to a much more specialized focus serving specialty and high-end retailers and letting the Chinese imports have the mass market. In effect, he evolved his business model via action, without too much planning (he was desperate), to one in which key accounts were all that mattered. This is a strategy that Noel Capon of Columbia Business School has shown to be a crucial component of success for many of the world's top companies, such as IBM, Xerox and Citibank (see Professor Capon's *Key Account Management and Planning* for a great primer on this subject).

In my friend's Plexiglas business, the result has been to boost margins. He can now continue to charge more for his products than the Chinese imports cost, while delivering faster service and better quality than ever before. This may sound like he has picked *fast* and *good*, but still not *cheap*. No, he has picked cheap – cheap at the price. The customer's sense of a product's cheapness can be expressed by the ratio of value to price. Customers feel a product is cheap at the price, not when they pay the lowest possible price, but when they feel that they received great value and a good deal on all measures, including price.

My friend's customers pay a premium for his products, but they get exactly what they want. What they need is just a properly sized and shaped piece of Plexiglas. What they want is getting that from someone with a deep understanding of their needs and the ability to fine-tune the product offering to their specifications. Together these factors make my friend's premium pricing a bargain in the minds of his most profitable customers. He is indeed fast, good and cheap.

His next challenge, if he really wants to be a flipstar, is to "Think AND, Not OR", and to work on selling a large volume of high-margin products. Because who says there needs to be a trade-off? Apple, after all, sold millions of iPods at a 30 per cent price premium to other MP3 players. How? Well, as you will learn in Chapter 4, "Absolutely, Positively Sweat the Small Stuff," £300 is a bargain if the item makes you feel cool.

Before moving on, I would like to give you an excellent example of how "Fast, Good, Cheap: Pick 2" has become "Fast, Good, Cheap: Pick Three – Then Add Something Extra". The original brand identity of McDonald's was fast and cheap. Of course the food had to be good enough to satisfy customers' needs for a meal, but it also had to be served in good-enough surroundings, which simply meant that the restaurants were clean and neat, and it had to be available at lunch and dinner. For a long time that was all McDonald's needed to be, and it grew to become one of the world's dominant brands simply by adding more and more locations in the United States and other countries.

CUSTOMERS FEEL A PRODUCT IS CHEAP AT THE PRICE, NOT WHEN THEY PAY THE LOWEST POSSIBLE PRICE, BUT WHEN THEY FEEL THEY RECEIVED GREAT VALUE AND A GOOD DEAL ON ALL MEASURES, INCLUDING PRICE.

In 2002, however, McDonald's posted its first-ever quarterly loss because of declining margins and year-to-year same-store sales. Since then the company has pursued a strategy of "better, not just bigger", adding only fifty to a hundred restaurants per year in the United States compared to hundreds a year in the 1990s. McDonald's looked at a new competitive landscape that included Starbucks, Burger King, Wendy's and Dunkin' Donuts, among others, and it looked at changing customer behaviours, especially eating more meals on the run outside traditional mealtimes. Then McDonald's responded aggressively by encouraging franchisees to stay open later than the traditional 11 P.M. closing time (in 2002 only 0.5 per cent of McDonald's restaurants in the United States were open 24/7; in 2007 that figure was 40 per cent and rising) and to redecorate restaurants (many now include casual seating areas with flat-screen televisions as well as playrooms for children and other amenities). The company also increased investments in its test kitchens to develop new customer favourites like the McGriddle, first offered in 2003, and the Snack Wrap, first offered in 2006. And to position itself against Starbucks in particular as the customer's "third place" of choice, besides home and work or school, it launched the McCafé concept, which is proving successful in both the United States and foreign markets.

The result of recognizing that being fast, good and cheap means meeting constantly rising customer expectations is that the first-ever quarterly loss in 2002 may be the only one McDonald's ever experiences. It is enjoying an unbroken streak of sales increases, and profit margins are up for both the company and its franchisees.[1]

McDonald's showed great flexibility in changing the hours of operation, décor and menu of its US restaurants. It showed equal flexibility in adapting its rebound tactics to different regional markets around the world. To remain fast, good and cheap in the perceptions of Australian consumers, for example, McDonald's had to convince them that its version of "good" included healthy food. The breakthrough came with "Salads Plus", which drove hundreds of thousands of new customers into McDonald's restaurants in Australia, and increased same-store sales nearly $1 million per year in many instances. Of course, the new customers did not eat only salads. They also bought lots of soft drinks and fries and burgers. More recently, in addition to introducing the McCafé concept which is also working in the United States and other markets, McDonald's in Australia has secured the Heart Foundation of Australia's seal of approval on a number of menu offerings. All in all, McDonald's regional market flexibility is a superb strategy from a very proactive company and a model for other global brands.

Throughout its lacklustre period, McDonald's never lost sight of the need to stay fast. In fact, McDonald's has always been the fastest restaurant company in the fast-food business. As I said, to achieve competitive advantage, to have the best market share and the best profitability in your market segment like McDonald's, you have to lead the league on at least one of fast, good and cheap, and be industry standard in the others. What McDonald's has successfully done is come up to standard as consumers' definition of "good" changed, while still remaining fast enough and cheap enough.

Another example of an industry constantly hammered by the need to be faster, better and cheaper is the automotive fuel industry, especially in the context of dramatic changes in automotive technology. Traditionally the petrol station was also a service station, which sought extra profit margin and brand loyalty by offering car maintenance and repairs as well as fuel. But today's cars are more reliable than older cars, and they're filled with computer chips for diagnostics and vehicle systems control that the average service station can't fix.

In other words, the service-station business is obsolete, or quickly becoming so. That has led to a new business model in which petrol stations are linked with convenience stores or other retail operations that sell drinks, snacks and basic grocery and impulse items. The profit margin on convenience-store items is much greater than that on fuel. According to A.C. Nielsen, 25 per cent of household grocery purchases are "convenience" purchases and are not price driven.

For example, ExxonMobil created a new franchise of On the Run stores behind the petrol pumps at Exxon and Mobil stations, and the other major petrol brands made similar moves. The popularity of filling stations in combination with convenience stores inevitably attracted the interest of retailers that had never sold petrol. In effect, fuel sales, although modestly profitable in themselves, served as a "loss leader" to drive higher-margin retail sales. For the same reason, there are now petrol pumps at many supermarkets in the UK.

Well-established retailers such as Tesco can make low-priced fuel sales profitable both because the petrol-buying driver who stops to fill up at a Tesco petrol station is likely to buy other things at their shops, and because they are big and powerful enough to negotiate favourable pricing from petrol wholesalers and refineries. Discount petrol prices complement their existing reputation for delivering good value to customers.

Let's see what sense "Fast, Good, Cheap: Pick Three – Then

Add Something Extra" can make of this. Filling up the tank takes the same amount of time wherever you do it. Maybe you save a little time by stopping at the first station you see, or maybe you lose a little time by looking for a favoured brand or a cheaper price. You may have a favourite brand, but the reason won't be because you like their petrol. For the vast majority of drivers, there is no quality difference between different brands of petrol. Assuming equivalent octane ratings, one brand is as functionally good as any other brand in the customer's eyes.

So if you're in the business of selling petrol to drivers, how are you going to differentiate your brand from other brands, when one fuel-buying experience is more or less as fast, good and cheap as another? As these examples show, you "Think AND, Not OR". You combine two previously distinct retail sales categories into a new value proposition that offers customers who feel intense time and opportunity pressure throughout their lives a faster, better, cheaper way to buy petrol and other daily essentials at one go. It's a value proposition tailored to increasingly affluent customers who rate the low fuel price per gallon and time savings plus extra cost per item of quickly buying a few necessities and impulse items as better overall than taking the time to drive to a major supermarket, park in a large car park, walk from the car and through the aisles to find what they want, pay for their purchases and walk back to their car.

> FAST TODAY IS NOT FAST ENOUGH FOR TOMORROW, GOOD TODAY IS NOT GOOD ENOUGH FOR TOMORROW, AND CHEAP TODAY IS NOT CHEAP ENOUGH FOR TOMORROW.

The companies selling fuel to drivers have to meet the challenge of "Fast, Good, Cheap: Pick Three – Then Add Something Extra" on two levels: the fuel itself, and the fuel in combination with a higher-margin sales channel. Within this mix they can emphasize fast, good or cheap, but to stay in the game they also have to be industry standard on the other two. Tesco may emphasize cheap, but they must also be fast and good enough to keep attracting a profitable share of customers. Likewise, ExxonMobil's highly profitable On the Run stores, in the USA may emphasize convenience, but if they seek too high a profit margin on things like milk that are available in many other places, they won't be able to sustain and increase their market share.

But remember that "Fast, Good, Cheap: Pick Three – Then Add Something Extra" is both a moving target and table stakes, the price of entry into any market. To build significant competitive advantage you've got to offer something else, an X factor that will really differentiate you positively in customers' eyes. That's the subject of the next chapter, "Absolutely, Positively Sweat the Small Stuff."

As both the McDonald's and consumer petrol examples show, fast today is not fast enough for tomorrow, good today is not good enough for tomorrow, and cheap today is not cheap enough for tomorrow. Three areas where we can see this are fashion, cars and telecommunications.

FAST IS NOT FAST ENOUGH

We always notice when products and services take an increasing share of our wallet. But the increasing time pressure we all feel today makes us increasingly sensitive to the time that products and services take. We also have less and less patience for anything other than instant delivery of those products and services. We repetitively hit the "close" button on lifts, when no one is racing to join us inside, because the five seconds it takes for the average lifts door to close is unbearably, excruciatingly long. We do this even though we know that the lift system will not respond any quicker, no matter how many times we press the button.

We do it because technology is speeding up the world and making just about everything but the closing of lift doors happen faster and faster all the time. The result is that, especially for the youngest customers (and the youngest staff, too, when it comes to the pace of their careers), no demand on speed of delivery feels unrealistic or exorbitant.

Few industries operate at as rapid a pace as the retail clothing business. As fashions constantly change, the ones who profit are the ones who can quickly and efficiently provide styles, colours and fabrics that appeal to the key demographic of young customers, who in turn set the trends for other demographic groups. Three retail clothing chains – Zara, H&M and Uniqlo – now perform that fast, good, cheap hat trick better than any others, and Zara is perhaps first among equals in delivering fresh, exciting apparel to young consumers.

The Zara chain is owned by the Spanish company Inditex, which has 70,000 employees and counting (they added 11,000 employees in 2006), 3,131 stores in sixty-four countries and counting (they added 439 stores in 2006), and net 2006 sales of 8.1 billion euros (an increase of 22 per cent over the year before). Practising what it calls a "fast fashion" system, Zara can design and distribute a fashion forward garment in fifteen days. Some Zara styles resemble the latest couture offerings, albeit in less expensive fabrics. Others beat the luxury fashion houses to market with Zara designers' fresh takes on the clothing trends of urban youth around the world.

Equally significant is the number of styles and variations Zara retails every year. Three teams of designers for women's, men's, and children's lines generate 40,000 or more designs a year, and about 10,000 of these make it into actual production of five to seven sizes and five to six colours per garment. That means Zara's supply-chain management must smoothly handle around 300,000 new stock-keeping units (SKUs) per year.

The final flip – or should I say wrinkle? – is that Zara produces each garment in very limited quantities. Most clothing companies try to milk the most popular styles and sell them in high volume, which inevitably creates lags in inventory supply and turnover, and at the end of most selling seasons triggers unprofitable discounting to move inventory that no longer excites customers. Instead, Zara says, so to speak, "We love stock-outs" (the retail term for being out of stock on a requested item).

The speed with which Zara changes garment styles and colours encourages impulse buying and more frequent store visits. Customers know that if they see something they like at Zara, they'd better buy it right then and there, because it won't be available later. They also know that whenever they enter a Zara store, they're going to see new things. Thus, for example, Zara's London stores attract an average of seventeen store visits per unique customer per year, whereas their competitors attract an average of only

EVERYTHING ABOUT ZARA'S ORGANIZATION EXPRESSES THE BELIEF THAT THEY CAN NEVER BE FAST ENOUGH.

four visits per unique customer per year. Zara's strategy makes its customers so curious to know what new clothes are on the racks that the company spends only 0.3 per cent of sales on advertising against 3 to 4 per cent for most of the competition.

Everything about Zara's organization expresses the belief that they can never be fast enough, and that there is also no excuse for forgetting good and cheap while they're at it. Instead of isolating design, production, and marketing staff in separate silos, Zara's offices, shops and other facilities are laid out to encourage the fast, free flow of information, with designers working in the midst of production and marketing so that feedback on new styles, production glitches, quality problems and customer behaviour becomes virtually immediate. This also sends a message to Zara's staff that no one is "cooler" than anyone else, or to put it another way, that everybody in the company is as cool as the design team.

Likewise, design and production move quickly thanks to an intensive use of computer-aided design (CAD) and just-in-time supply-chain management. The stores themselves are integrated into this blindingly fast feedback loop through daily PDA and weekly telephone communication on how customers are reacting to different offerings. The result is that whereas most competitors are hard-pressed to vary 20 per cent of the order mix in any one selling season in response to customer behaviour and other factors, Zara can adjust 40 to 50 per cent of the order mix without strain.[2]

Zara's "fast fashion" system would break down if customers didn't think the clothes were of high enough quality or affordable enough, and the company could easily serve as an example of "good is not good enough" or "cheap is not cheap enough".

The same could be said of both H&M, which is based in Sweden and has 1,300 stores in twenty-nine countries, and Uniqlo, which is based in Japan and has more than 730 stores in Japan, China, South Korea, Hong Kong, the UK and the United States.

In the "Fast, Good, Cheap: Pick Three – Then Add Something Extra" mix, H&M might be said to emphasize good. It delivers what the company website calls "discount high-end fashion" through special one-season-only collections from prominent designers such as Karl Lagerfeld and Stella McCartney, or in association with trendsetting personalities such as Madonna and Kylie Minogue.

Uniqlo (a name formed from the words *unique* and *clothes*) might be said to emphasize cheap. Despite a persistent economic downturn, between 1999 and 2002 Uniqlo opened 200 new stores in Japan, selling "recession chic" so cheaply that some Japanese business commentators and many competitors accused it of causing deflation. (Sounds like sour grapes to me.)

All the same, "fast is not fast enough" rules the fashion industry. H&M's name-brand designer- and celebrity-connected offerings deliver up-to-the-minute, trendsetting quality at a discount price. And Uniqlo's business DNA derives from its parent company, which is named Fast Retailing Company, because young customers would never buy clothing that is not fashion forward, no matter how cheap it might be.

GOOD IS NOT GOOD ENOUGH

One of the great flipstars of modern business is Toyota. The only car-maker that is consistently gaining market share in all product categories in all market regions, Toyota has an enviable reputation for product quality. Scores of articles and several books have been written about the efficiency and speed of the Toyota Manufacturing System, which made just-in-time inventories a global business trend.

Toyota's quality advantage underpins a number of other strengths. It spends the least amount of time to make a vehicle of any car-maker and has been the least vulnerable to costly vehicle recalls (although it has had some lately). It also spends the least amount of promotion money per car sold, and its vehicles spend the least amount of time on dealers' forcourts. To top this all off, Toyota has the highest per-unit profitability of any volume or luxury-car maker.

Over the past few decades Toyota has shown a greater commitment than any other car-maker to the idea that good is not good enough, without ever forgetting the need to be fast enough and cheap enough in customers' eyes as well. Segment by segment, Toyota has leveraged its quality advantage from economy cars to mid-size family saloons, luxury cars, sports cars, 4×4s and utility vehicles. The most dramatic example of that remains the Lexus and its quick ascent to become the world's number one luxury car.

The more economy cars Toyota, Honda and Nissan sold in the United States – the world's biggest car market – the more they wanted to expand the range of vehicles they sold there. All three sold luxury cars in Japan, and Honda was actually first to market a luxury car brand in the United States with its Acura range. There is no question that Acura has been a success, but there is also no question that Lexus quickly overtook it and left it a good distance behind.

When Toyota looked into entering the US luxury-car market, it saw two things. First, there was a gap in what might be called mid-price luxury between normal cars and luxury automobiles from the likes of Jaguar and Mercedes-Benz. Second, most luxury cars were unreliable and very costly to maintain. Toyota therefore set out not only to build a luxury car of high quality at an attractive price, but also to deliver a total customer experience that would be second to none.[3]

After Toyota launched the Lexus in 1989, managers in the company followed up with all new buyers to confirm that they were happy with their cars and to offer to fix anything that was wrong. They not only fixed every mechanical problem, but they also returned the car freshly washed and with a full fuel tank. Toyota didn't rest with building a luxury car that matched or exceeded Mercedes-Benz and BMW in quality; they also made sure that their customer service was nothing short of mind-blowing.

Another Toyota flip of special interest here is that "Fast, Good, Cheap: Pick Three – Then Add Something Extra" does not necessarily mean lowest- or low-priced. Remember my friend the Plexiglas manufacturer. Cheap is not only an absolute measure of price, but a relative measure of value perceived and received. Toyota's products are cheap at the price, because a Lexus, say, works exactly as it should, retains value against the competition over its life span and is supported by industry-leading customer service. Throughout its range, Toyota maintains a premium pricing advantage over its Japanese, Korean, European, Australian and American competitors.

Having steadily grown to overtake DaimlerChrysler and Ford along the way, in the first quarter of 2007 Toyota displaced troubled General Motors as the world's number one car-maker. To remain at the top it must continue to be fast, good and cheap at the price in customers' eyes. In other words, it must continue to innovate, offering appealingly designed, user-friendly and dependable vehicles.

CHEAP IS NOT CHEAP ENOUGH

Over the past two decades the telecommunications industry has alternately been the darling and the favourite whipping boy of the world's stock markets. Deregulation of telecom monopolies, mergers and acquisitions and the growth of mobile-phone use have redrawn the telecom map several times. Throughout that process there has been steady downward pressure on pricing and margins.

The latest upheaval in the telephone business has come from the ability to bypass both landline and mobile networks and offer phone service via the internet. Start-ups in the US market such as Vonage, internet service providers such as Earthlink and cable-television providers such as Time Warner that offer broadband internet connections through their cable networks have all got into the business of selling VoIP (Voice-over internet Protocol) telephone service.

Although these companies have seized a new channel for reaching and serving customers, they are all still practising business as usual, selling phone services for fees billed on a monthly basis. These services are fast and good, and can be much cheaper than those of the established phone companies (although the latter have fought back on price). Having tried VoIP, I am convinced that the service is almost cheap enough, but it is definitely not yet good enough for the low price to be compelling.

I tried VoIP in my business and found the quality substandard, unless I upgraded not only my plan but my broadband connection, too. Fast and cheap are not enough. The product also needs to be good if it is going to get mainstream support. From what I understand, big companies are getting excellent results with VoIP, but not without significant investment. One of the major advantages it offers is that it taps into existing network infrastructure and allows a lot more flexibility than traditional phone lines.

Vonage is the most prominent of the VoIP providers in the US market. They seemed headed for as glorious an IPO and subsequent rise in share price as Google. But by the time Vonage did go public, the air was already leaking out of its balloon, thanks to an even bolder newcomer called Skype.

Skype's business model abandoned fast, good, cheap for instant, excellent, free at the entry level of service, which is all many customers will ever use. Two or more Skype users can communicate with crystal-clear digital sound quality on their broadband connections for absolutely no additional cost. And if they want to include someone on a traditional landline phone, that costs about 1p per minute. After eBay bought Skype for $2.6 billion, the two-cents-per-minute charge to call a normal phone was waived in North America for several months in order to build usage.

Instant, excellent, free: what kind of business model is that? But if you wonder how Skype will ever make enough profit for eBay to justify paying $2.6 billion for it, you're missing something. Sooner or later the technology that Skype used to create its service was bound to be exploited in a similar way by someone. Once that technology existed, the genie was out of the bottle. Not only that, but as with Google's purchase of YouTube and News Corps of MySpace, the value was in the network and the relationship the brands have built with their customer base. (More on this in Chapter 5, "Business Is Personal".)

Skype's founders were willing to act first and strategize how to exploit the technology as they proceeded. The enthusiastic response of customers all over the world made Skype the gold standard of internet calling and created several revenue streams, including calls between Skype users and regular landline and mobile phones, business tele- and videoconferencing, and business phone services. For eBay there is the chance not only to grow the Skype brand in those areas, but to grow its core e-auction and e-commerce business by plugging Skype telephony into the eBay network along with PayPal's financial transaction service.

No one can be certain yet if this is going to pay off at a level that justifies a $2.6 billion purchase price, but I love Skype for trying, and eBay for trying harder (or should I say for paying). An indicator that Skype will ultimately be profitable for eBay, in my view, is the growing universe of third-party products made specifically for use with Skype. Before the iPod there were many MP3 players on the market, but none generated the add-ons from third-party vendors that are now available for playing the iPod in a car, on a portable boom box or in a home entertainment system. Likewise there are other VoIP platforms, but only Skype is generating products from third-party vendors such as the Skype-ready WiFi phones from Philips, Netgear and Belkin.

When eBay released its first-quarter numbers for 2007, first-quarter net revenues for the entire company rose 27 per cent to a record $1.77 billion, and net income rose 52 per cent to $377 million. First-quarter net revenues for Skype rose 123 per cent to $79 million. CEO Meg Whitman said of Skype, "This is a very young business growing very fast."[4]

The picture admittedly looked less rosy on 1 October 2007, when eBay announced a $900 million one-time write-down on the $2.6 billion purchase of Skype. Critics of the company immediately released statements on eBay's overpaying for Skype. But there is a solid chance that eBay will eventually profit handsomely from Skype. Two weeks after eBay's announcement, MySpace and Skype formed an alliance that enables MySpace users to make phone calls and send instant messages via Skype. And at the end of October 2007 the British telecommunications provider 3 announced that it was releasing a Skype-ready mobile phone for use in the UK, Australia, Denmark, Italy and Hong Kong. These are not the signs of a failing brand. There are inevitably stumbles in any new venture, but on balance it looks as though eBay has reason to feel good about Skype's long-term prospects.

Vonage has very clever ads that say it is "leading the internet telephone revolution". But again, Vonage is a half-way revolutionary, trying to use a cheaper channel to conduct telephone business as usual. They are caught between the established phone companies' ability to match or nearly match them on price, on the one hand, and Skype's ability to profit by providing the same or better service for free, on the other. In Vonage's case the market has responded by making its heralded IPO and subsequent share price lacklustre, to say the least.

Skype's challenge to the telephone business as usual does

not mean that you have to give away your products and services for free, even at the entry level of a tier of products and services. My point is instead that Skype shows you can't take the customer value of your pricing for granted. If I'm going to be on one side of the change outlined above for the telecommunications industry, I want to be on Skype's side, not Vonage's. I want to be so fast, good and cheap at the level that customers are uncomfortable with how much they are paying for something that they willingly pay me a premium for what I deliver on top of that. That's the formula eBay is following with Skype.

• • •

Sooner or later, somebody or something is bound to come along and yank the price floor out from under your entire industry. Flipstar Richard Branson has made a career doing just that. His most notable achievements in this regard are taking on the European, transatlantic and Australian airline industries with his Virgin Express, Virgin Atlantic and Virgin Blue airlines. The result was a substantial reduction in the price of airfares in all three markets. In August of 2007 Branson finally succeeded in launching Virgin America (for air travel within the United States) after hitting regulatory brick walls over the airline's ownership structure, which had to conform to US laws that require US airlines to be controlled by American citizens and at least 75 per cent owned by American companies.

In any case, remember that cheap today is not cheap enough for tomorrow. Virgin Express

SOONER OR LATER, SOMEBODY OR SOMETHING IS BOUND TO COME ALONG AND YANK THE PRICE FLOOR OUT FROM UNDER YOUR ENTIRE INDUSTRY.

opened the door for Ryanair and other low-cost air-travel competitors in the European market. And Tiger Airways, backed
by the founder of Ryanair, and Jetstar are both giving Virgin
Blue a run for the low-cost air traveller's money in Australasia,
which has always been a very cutthroat market.

FAST, GOOD, CHEAP AND MORE!

The price of entry in every market today is undeniably "Fast,
Good, Cheap: Pick Three". But because a satisfied need no
longer motivates and expectations keep rising, the price of entry will soon be "Fast, Good, Cheap: Pick Three – Then Add
Something Extra".

The ante to get in the game keeps rising, the table stakes
keep getting bigger, because of the feedback loop between increasing compression of time and space, increasing complexity
and ambiguity, increasing transparency and accountability for
actions that have to be performed in conditions of high uncertainty, and increasing customer expectations. You can't escape
that challenge. You can only flip it to your advantage by meeting it sooner than your competition. You can attune your behaviour to the psychology of human expectations in a time of
constant technological development, or you can be left by the
side of the road.

If "Fast, Good, Cheap: Pick Three" is not yet the price of
entry in your market, it soon will be. And if you want to top
the standings when that happens, you must not only ensure
that you are fast enough, good enough and cheap enough for
today and tomorrow, you must also offer customers something
else as well. With that in mind, let's look closely at the flips that
are needed to create the value customers want in addition to

fast, good and cheap, beginning with the fact that you must *"Absolutely, Positively Sweat the Small Stuff"*!

FIVE THINGS TO DO NOW

1. Get five of your smartest people in a room and put the following scenario to them. You have to speed up your service delivery, or out-of-the-box performance, by 20 per cent in the next three months. Ask them to work out how you could do it.

2. While you have your best and brightest in the room, you should also ask them to give you two possible quality improvements that would leave your competitors for dead. Then give someone the project of working out how you could do them as cheaply as possible

3. Using some creative thinking tools, develop at least three potential Skype-like scenarios that, even though your industry dare not consider the possibility, would completely rip the margins out of your business.

4. Purchase your product or service, or at least pretend to, from your own business. Then ask yourself, was that fast, good and cheap at the price?

5. Conduct a round-table discussion with your team, the more senior the better, and discuss the potential changes in the demands of your customers and staff over the coming years. Remembering that what is good enough, fast enough and cheap enough today won't be tomorrow. What challenges would these changes present your business?

!

ABSOLUTELY, POSITIVELY
SWEAT THE SMALL STUFF

Companies have to do more to win customers than offer a dependable, good-quality, reasonably priced product or service. That's what lots of ordinary companies do. Extraordinary companies do something else, and so do extraordinary career-minded professionals. These flipstars do the little things. They realize that in an oversupplied market competitive advantage will increasingly be built on elements once considered superficial. You know, the small stuff. Flipstars sweat the small stuff. Big-time!

FLIPSTARS SWEAT
THE SMALL STUFF.

FAST, GOOD, CHEAP, X-FACTOR: PICK FOUR

Doing the little things right is all about figuring out how to fulfil customer wants, not just satisfy customer needs. Customer satisfaction is fleeting at best. You could invest your time and energy in meeting customer expectations only to have those expectations rise before you get there. Even if you met the expectations before they increased, it would not give you an advantage in the marketplace. The money will be in giving customers what they want, even when they don't yet know what that is.

People need fast, good and cheap. Faced with the four forces of change, people want things to be simpler, easier and more beautiful, among other qualities, and they want to feel good about the products, services and experiences they consume.

It sounds a little ridiculous to say that fast, good, cheap is a need. It is! The ability of the market to turn features and standards that were once a luxury into a necessity in the competitive landscape is nothing short of fascinating. Remember the research discussed in Chapter 1, which shows that 29 per cent of Americans today consider fast broadband a necessity. And 5 per cent said the same thing about flat-screen televisions.

In that same survey 4 per cent of American consumers said an iPod is a necessity. This is their reality, and over the coming years the per centage of people who feel that an iPod is a *need* not a *want* will increase markedly. Ask yourself, what feature or standard of service do you currently offer that was previously an added luxury that may have become commoditized without you even realizing? I can think of keyless entry for cars, as discussed in Chapter 3. Or what about same-day service from a courier company? internet banking for some. The ability to pay with a credit card. Or maybe you are a little spoiled and it is your home-delivery-and-pickup dry-cleaning service.

Purchasing decisions are rarely based on rational thought processes. Time and time again customer research has shown that emotions drive our decisions and behaviour. According to the *Advertising Research Journal,* research has found that emotions are twice as important as any other consideration in customers' decisions about what to purchase. And not just purchasing decisions but all decisions we make in life. Only after making the decision emotionally do we call upon our cognitive processes to rationalize our behaviour.

It is amazing how powerful our minds are at rationalizing some of the objectively insane decisions we make. In fact, we *automatically* rationalize everything we do. Psychologists and marketers refer to the cognitive bias we demonstrate after buying something as "post-purchase rationalization" – the willing self-delusion about the quality of a recent purchase. Even when we know we've made a terrible decision, we can convince ourselves it was worth it.

It will often be the smallest things that we grab on to to rationalize our emotionally driven behaviour. This is why it is necessary to "Absolutely, Positively Sweat the Small Stuff", and why even with regard to utilitarian products and services:

- Style is substance.
- Fashion is function.
- Feelings are the most important facts.
- The soft stuff is the hardest stuff, and the hardest to get right.

Later in this chapter we'll look at these factors in terms of what I call the "total ownership experience". For now let's continue the discussion by looking at some of the most powerful X-factor positions you can take to market.

Fast, good, cheap + green

The X factor could be any number of things. Being green is popular right now, as environmental issues become ever more urgent. Innovating far ahead of the competition, Toyota has staked its new millennium play on being fast, good, cheap and green. Starting with the Prius and then extending its hybrid technology through the rest of the Toyota and Lexus brands, Toyota has offered time-stressed, upwardly mobile, increasingly affluent customers the opportunity to control their personal contribution to the world's pollution. At the same time it has relieved them of guilt as conspicuous consumers, decreasing their sense of stress in that way as well. Toyota is not merely satisfying needs here. It is fulfilling wants.

Other companies that are defining themselves as fast, good, cheap and green include Siemens, L'Oréal, and even what you might think of as old-industry Alcoa, which has staked out a position as the cleanest and most high-value-added company in the metals business, with large revenues coming from high-premium alloys and packaging and fastener expertise that extends from aluminium drinks cans to plastics. In a highly publicized speech in May 2007, Rupert Murdoch, a real flip-star, declared that the News Corporation will go green.

One of the most widely reported examples is Wal-Mart. Undoubtedly one of the most successful companies of the last twenty years, Wal-Mart grew to enormous size by being the best combination of fast, good, cheap that customers in retail had ever seen. But having made fast, good, cheap the price of entry into their industry and spawned copycat behaviour from a host of competitors, and with same-store sales down in 2006 for the first time in the company's history, Wal-Mart has had to look for something new to sustain growth.

At first they tried to be fast, good, cheap and hip. But Wal-Mart has had trouble convincing customers that they should look to its stores not only for the cheapest deal, but for designer clothing and high-margin products like flat-screen televisions. In December 2006 Wal-Mart seemed to lose its nerve for this effort, firing the cutting-edge marketers whom only a year earlier it had hired with fanfare. Where it has not lost its nerve is in a determined effort to be green.

Long criticized for low wages, inadequate health-care coverage, gender discrimination and a devastating impact on small local businesses Wal-Mart regularly faces a negative public relations picture. A number of American communities have lobbied successfully to keep Wal-Mart from opening a store in their vicinity. CEO Lee Scott admitted that when Wal-Mart began to explore an environmental sustainability agenda in 2004 it was simply "a defensive strategy".

Since then Wal-Mart has embraced sustainability with a passion, and Scott told *Fortune* magazine, "What I thought was going to be a defensive strategy is turning out to be precisely the opposite." Wal-Mart's environmental goals include a 25 per cent increase in the efficiency of its truck fleet within three years, and a 100 per cent increase within ten years; a 30 per cent decrease in store energy use; and a 25 per cent reduction in solid waste. Wal-Mart now sees sustainability not only as good public relations but as good for Wal-Mart, both in terms of millions of dollars saved in lower energy, packaging and other costs and in terms of heightened morale and productivity on the part of employees, who have a new reason to be proud of where they work.

Wal-Mart is such a big company – fiscal-year 2007 revenues were almost $349 billion; there are 1.8 million direct Wal-Mart employees; and 176 million unique customers visit its more than 6,700 stores every week – that its decisions have a huge ripple effect. With a supply-chain network of 60,000 suppliers around the world, Wal-Mart can shift many markets towards greater sustainability. For example, it has made a commitment to sell salmon only from sustainable fisheries, and Wal-Mart now has fourteen "sustainable value [supplier] networks" for everything from chemicals to food and paper products. One of its biggest recent successes with customers, organic cotton clothing, has helped to grow global organic cotton production by over 20 per cent since 2001. Wal-Mart's flip into a green brand identity is now being emulated by North America's second largest retailer, the Home Depot, which is branding thousands of the products it sells with an "Eco Options" label.[1]

• • •

BP is an interesting case study in the pros and cons of offering a "green" alternative to the oil business as usual. In 1998 BP (at the time the company's legal name was its original one, British Petroleum) acquired the Amoco Corporation, an American business. To make the deal palatable in the United States, it was presented as a merger and the company temporarily became BP Amoco. In 2001 Amoco was dropped from the name, and the company once more became BP. Only now BP no longer stood for British Petroleum, it was simply an "initialism" that company marketing presented in advertising as standing for "Beyond Petroleum". Along

PEOPLE WANT TO BE SEEN AS GREEN, AND THEY WANT TO WORK FOR AND BUY FROM COMPANIES THAT THEY SEE AS GREEN, TOO.

with this came a new logo, a green-and-gold disc representing Helios, the Greek God of the Sun.

No longer trading as "British Petroleum" was useful because it sidestepped long-standing criticism of corporate colonialism in BP's traditional market strongholds in ex-British colonies in Africa and elsewhere. But no doubt more important, especially in markets such as the UK, the United States and Australia, was the desire to appeal to public concern about the environment.

In this regard, BP's former CEO John Browne showed remarkable prescience. In 1997 the company withdrew from the Global Climate Coalition, an oil-industry organization dedicated to promoting climate-change scepticism, with Browne commenting that "the time to consider [global warming] is not when the link between greenhouse gases and climate change has been conclusively proven, but when the possibility cannot be discounted and is taken seriously by the society of which we are a part. We in BP have reached that point." This was the first time an oil-industry executive had spoken out in support of doing something about the climate. Oil company or not, BP deserved some kudos for this.

In 2002 Browne gave a high-profile speech saying global warming was "real and required urgent action", and he was one of the most vocal industry advocates of signing the so-called

Kyoto Accords on international action to combat global warming. In 2004 BP started making low-sulphur diesel fuel, and they are creating a network of hydrogen fuelling stations in California. In 2000 BP purchased Solarex and became a leading producer of solar panels. BP Solar, to be renamed BP Alternative Energy, accounts for 20 per cent of world photovoltaic (solar panel) production.

All this was to the benefit of the company's image and its bottom line, and I am sure it is a viable strategy for the long term. But BP will face increasing pressure to make its operations as green in fact as its marketing is in spirit. This task will fall to Andy Hayward, the designated successor to John Browne, who resigned in 2007 in large part because of criticism of BP's environmental record.

BP's "Beyond Petroleum" play is a great strategy, if future reality matches present marketing. The marketing has been so successful that I believe it has won the company significant leeway with customers to get things right. In seminars on employment branding I flash a slide with the logos of the biggest oil companies in the world, and BP gets the most favourable response. It is mixed, of course, with some very cynical reactions, but all in all the BP campaign has been successful. Almost unanimously audiences say that, all other things being equal, they would accept a job at BP first. Some people even insist that "Beyond Petroleum" is actually BP's legal name.

One of BP's billboard and print ads reads, "BP: Solar, natural gas, hydrogen, wind. And oh yes, oil. It's a start." I agree. Now BP must execute and finish the job of "greening" itself, or a competitor will hijack the strategy and the customer goodwill that it has temporarily won.

An article entitled "Green Is Good" in the *Bulletin* cited the following companies for doing good in the green space:

- Continental Airlines spent $16 billion to upgrade the efficiency of its aircraft, including fuel-saving winglets that have led to a 5 per cent reduction in emissions.
- British Airways will sell customers offsets for their share of the carbon emissions generated by the flights they take. Sadly only one in 200 consumers has stuck his hand in his own pockets for carbon offsets, but the trend is growing among affluent, socially conscious consumers. Even if the big impact from carbon offset trading will no doubt be on the part of multinational companies driven by regulatory pressure and general public sentiment, this offer effectively brands British Airways as green among a much wider customer demographic than the relatively small group who buy a per-flight carbon offset.
- Tesco has biodiesel delivery lorries and offers loyalty card points to customers who bring in their own shopping bags.
- HP will take back any of its own machines from customers for recycling and has started to audit its suppliers for their recycling practices.

Companies are beginning to make serious money from investments in being "Fast, Good, Cheap+Green". Consider the following examples cited in the same edition of the *Bulletin* in April 2007:

- Goldman Sachs invested $1.5 billion into cellulosic ethanol, wind and solar, a gamble that has more than paid off.
- Swiss RE, the Swiss insurance giant with revenues over $24 billion, pioneered derivative-based products to hedge against the risks of climate change.
- DuPont, once a poster child of environmental mismanagement, now receives $5 billion of its $29 billion in revenue from green end-use products such as chemical coatings for solar panels. It is developing a green replacement for nylon called bio-PDO, produces genetically engineered corn to make ethanol, and has partnered with BP on a new fuel called biobutanol.
- GE wind turbines are selling faster than they can produce them.

There is one final example that I like. I had an opportunity to work with Google in Silicon Valley, and was astonished to hear that if a Googler buys a Prius or any other hybrid-engine car, the company will contribute $5,000 towards the purchase, with some conditions around staying at the company and not selling the car the next day, of course. It is behaviour in perfect alignment with Google's mission statement: "Don't be evil."

Fast, good, cheap + responsible

Not being evil is also the order of the day, and not a moment too soon. Corporate social responsibility, which includes both environmental and ethical issues, is proving to be important for both society and the bottom line. It is not just how you treat the communities you operate in, but also how and where you source your raw materials and labour.

One of my favourite clients is the Commonwealth Bank Foundation. Born out of unclaimed savings accounts, the foundation is dedicated to helping Australians, especially the younger generations, improve their financial literacy skills. They run seminars, have websites, and basically invest millions of dollars in this social initiative. Commonwealth Bank refuses to allow any product information to be included in such activities, so it is not a hidden sales pitch. This does not mean, however, that the bank is not proud of its achievements in this area over quite a few decades, and, as you would expect, it uses its foundation activity to help attract the best staff and the most profitable customers.

IT IS NOT JUST HOW YOU TREAT THE COMMUNITIES YOU OPERATE IN, BUT ALSO HOW AND WHERE YOU SOURCE YOUR RAW MATERIALS AND LABOUR.

Some companies have built their entire brands on being responsible. The Body Shop is an excellent example. In her brilliant book *Business as Unusual*, flipstar Anita Roddick told the story of how she built the Body Shop on a reputation of social and environmental activism. As far back as 1986 the Body Shop formed an alliance with Greenpeace on the "save the whales" campaign. The Body Shop actually promoted the fact that its products were banned in China because Chinese law required animal testing of cosmetics and skin-care products.

Roddick insisted that Body Shop marketing reflect a "values-based company". Shareholders even complained that maximum profits were not being achieved because profits were being funnelled into social projects. But this is the drawing card of the company. Marketing along these lines, the company achieved phenomenal growth, expanding at a rate of 50 per cent annually from its opening. When its stock was first floated on the Unlisted Securities Market in London in 1984 it was listed at 95p. Eighteen months later the stock was valued at 820p. After a patchy performance period in the early 2000s (not due to a failure of marketing, but due to a manufacturing outsourcing bungle and some internal turmoil), the company was valued at roughly $1 billion at the end of 2005.

In March 2006 the Body Shop's positive reputation for social and ethical responsibility was tested by its sale to cosmetics giant L'Oréal for £652 million. Because of the sale, *Ethical Consumer* magazine dropped the Body Shop from 11 out of 20 on their "ethical rating" system to only 2.5 out of 20. Whoops! The sale (or sell-out, as some have called it) has been seen as a bit of a betrayal of the company's ethical and unique roots. An index that tracks thousands of consumers in the UK (the daily BrandIndex UK) saw the perception of L'Oréal slump by almost *half*.

So important is no animal testing to the Body Shop's core customers that some of them actively promoted a Body Shop boycott, because L'Oréal has not banned animal testing of its products. Dame Anita Roddick, who died in 2007, swore to give away the £130 million she made from the sale, but this did not stop the cry that she had "sold out".

On the flip side, the Body Shop boosts L'Oréal's image among socially conscious investors and customers. And despite the backlash of hard-core Body Shop fans, L'Oréal grew sales in key Body Shop lines 9.7 per cent like-for-like in the year ending 31 December 2006, compared with 6.4 per cent for all L'Oréal brands. Twenty-five new Body Shop stores opened in 2006, bringing the total to 2,290. The stores in Canada, Japan, and Russia performed particularly well, with US stores lagging somewhat.

More broadly in the cosmetics industry, the Campaign for Safe Cosmetics lobbying group says that more than 500 cosmetics and body-care producers have joined its campaign, pledging to eliminate toxic ingredients from their products. Interestingly, global giants L'Oréal, Revlon, Procter & Gamble and Estée Lauder have not been quick to sign on, although L'Oréal has made substantial strides in reducing its energy and water use, waste products and direct carbon-dioxide emissions through its SHE (Safety, Health and the Environment) initiative.[2] It will be a while before the big cosmetics companies can make themselves green and socially responsible throughout their vast industrial operations. Until then the smaller players can effectively use their "responsible" position to differentiate themselves in the market.

In the fast-food industry, Burger King took an early lead in socially responsible positioning in March 2007. The company announced that in the near term it would source 2 per cent of its eggs from providers that do not confine chickens in cages and 10 per cent of its pork from providers that keep pigs in pens rather than in small crates. The numbers may seem small, but they will rise as more cage-free- and crate-free-produced eggs and pork become available, thanks to Burger King and to consumers' increasing concern about the ethical treatment of animals. I will bet my shirt that Burger King's move will eventually be emulated by other fast-food companies.

• • •

Nike shows how customer preference is forcing companies to make their operations more environmentally friendly and socially responsible. Accusations about sweatshops and exploitation of workers in the Third World affected Nike's reputation badly. It has since made a concerted effort to be seen in a more responsible light.

In the 1970s Nike shoes were made primarily in Taiwan and South Korea. But as economic conditions in those countries improved and workers gained rights to organize, Nike found things more to its liking in Indonesia, China, and Vietnam. It chose these places because wage demands were low and because they had laws prohibiting workers banding together in unions.

The minimum wage in these countries would cover only 70 per cent of the basic needs of one person, and Nike didn't even pay the minimum wage, petitioning governments for exemption citing "financial hardship". In Nike's first year of operation in Indonesia, factory officials were convicted of physically abusing workers and one even fled the country because of investigations into sexual abuse.

But in 2005 there was a massive turnaround. The company commissioned a 108-page independent audit of working conditions at 569 of its factories. It found that as many as 650,000 workers (mostly nineteen- to twenty-five-year-old women) in China, Vietnam and even the United States and Australia are at risk from excessively long working weeks, being ripped off in wages, verbal abuse, and even horrific human rights abuses such as sexual exploitation and not being allowed toilet breaks.

Credit should be given because Nike executives have now publicly acknowledged the problem and promised to clean up their act, and they're seeing massive benefits. Nike appointed a staff of inspectors to go from facility to facility ensuring basic working standards are met, and the company has allowed random factory inspections by the Fair Labor Association. Nike will now also deal directly with organizations that make complaints, rather than just issue denials – which means the days of public street protests are pretty much over because those with legitimate grievances have direct recourse to the company. So it's actually doing real good for their public image.

Nike has also been very smart in sponsorship of Lance Armstrong, highlighting his philanthropic ventures as much as his extraordinary athletic achievement. In conjunction with Lance Armstrong's foundation, Nike has sold more than 50 million yellow wristbands to raise money for cancer research. This move has started a craze, with every charity or "movement" having its own wristband. One of the most visible is the white "Make Poverty History" band.

Fast, good, cheap + beautiful

Dell, another super-performer over the last decade or so, has been suffering recently as its product lines, from desktops and laptops to servers, have become increasingly commoditized. Dell's cost basis has long been the envy of other computer manufacturers. What is truly amazing is that Dell has a better cost basis even than Lenovo and other Chinese manufacturers.

While it remains highly profitable, it knows it must freshen its appeal in customers' eyes. Dell's initial efforts to do so through a new emphasis on design in its XPS range have signally failed, however. Instead it is HP that is gaining in the design sweepstakes on the leader in that area, Apple.

Twenty years ago Samsung was a commodity manufacturer for other consumer electronics companies and had a discount brand image for its own products. Not content with that, the company set its sights on design excellence, and diligently entered every industrial and consumer product-design contest it could. The result is that Samsung has become a recognized global design leader and a premium brand that does joint ventures in LCD panels and other areas with Sony as an equal, not a junior partner.

The power of Samsung's design story has an impact on customers far beyond the technical capabilities of any of their products. *BusinessWeek* calls the lead designers at Samsung "foot soldiers in Samsung's continuing assault on the world of the cool". Jong-Yong Yun, Samsung's chief executive, said he wanted to make Samsung the "Mercedes" of home electronics. Patrick Whitney, the director of the Institute of Design at Illinois Institute of Technology, said that Samsung is a "poster child for using design to increase brand value and market share".

SAMSUNG IS A "POSTER CHILD FOR USING DESIGN TO INCREASE BRAND VALUE AND MARKET SHARE".

The transformation has been happening since 1993, when the then chairman visited a technology show and was frustrated that Samsung products were lost in the crowd. Since then they have revolutionized design practices at the company.

They shifted their design labs to a place that was closer to the best design schools, and started an in-house design school (Innovation Design Lab of Samsung, or IDS) where employees could study under the best in the business. They also started collaborating with design-focused partners, a strategy we will explore in Chapter 7, "To Get Control, Give It Up", such as the US design firm IDEO (their first collaboration was on a monitor in 1994).

Further, they have poured literally hundreds of millions of pounds into updating the look, feel and function of every product from MP3 players to washing machines. Between 2003 and 2004 they upped their design budget from 20 per cent to 30 per cent, and more than doubled their design staff.

This has really paid off. Since 2000 they have received more than 100 citations at the world's top design awards in the United States, Asia and Europe. In 2004 they won five awards at IDEA (Industrial Design Excellence Awards). In 2005, completing more than a decade of reform, Samsung clocked up just over $10 billion in profits, making them the world's most profitable tech company. In his book *Change Begins with Me*, chairman Kun-Hee Lee said of their change from a me-too commodities producer into a leading design-based firm, that in a world where products were fast becoming commodities Samsung would never thrive on scale and pricing power alone. They needed a creative, competitive edge.

A flipstar worth talking about!

Fast, good, cheap + easy

My favourite service in the world is Pronto Valet Parking at Sydney's domestic airport. I board a lot of flights. I also have young children, so I like to come home as much as possible in between commitments. It is not uncommon for me to park my car at the airport three times in a week. I have got to know the guys who park my car, and I can't tell you how much easier they have made my life.

You pull in less than 100 yards from the terminal, leave your car running, give them your ticket, tell them roughly when you will be back, and off you go. I would have missed a dozen flights last year without them, so needless to say they are fast. This service costs an extra $15 for the first twenty-four hours and $5 for every twenty-four hours after that, which considering how much time and stress it saves you would be a bargain at twice the price. So it's cheap, too. I have never had a problem with my car, so I would have to say it is also good. Most of all, though, it is easy. They go out of their way to make it so. The roster is perfectly designed to meet the high-demand spots. They open your boot for you when they return your car. They take all forms of payment. And they are always well mannered. My mate Avril Henry, who leads a similar lifestyle, felt so indebted to the Pronto guys that she bought them a case of beer for Christmas last year.

Airline frequent-flyer programmes, airline lounges and hotel loyalty cards are all examples of ways in which a service provider can make a service easy. There is little doubt that we are feeling a lot of pressure around time. Not only that, though, I would suggest we are feeling even more pressure on our mental space. We feel we just can't take anything more in, not because we don't have the time but because we don't have the mental energy. Increasingly affluent customers who feel increasingly stressed about their mental energy being in short supply will pay a premium for *easy*.

On the topic of being a road warrior, consider the innovative new approach to servicing and selling cars from Mercedes-Benz called Airport Express. Mercedes set up both a service centre and a dealership at major city airports. One compelling reason for doing this is that these are high-traffic areas where exposure is good. And the people who travel regularly are usually professionals and are likely to fit the Mercedes target market. But the real winner is that it makes it much easier for Mercedes owners who travel to have their cars serviced.

But it is not as if they just service the car. They wash it, do the dry cleaning you left on the back seat, and run any other errands they can. Oh, and they drop you at the terminal and pick you up. Clients also get a goodies bag to take on their flight, with chocolate, bottled water, granola bars and loose-leaf breakfast tea. They have introduced flower delivery and gift-buying services, which Belinda Yabsley, my good friend and former manager of the Sydney Airport Express, describes as "things we have time to do but customers don't".

Clearly it's working. Within twelve weeks of opening, the Melbourne operation welcomed its 500th service customer, and sales were running at *twice* the projected levels. But Mercedes-Benz Australia spokesman Toni Andreevski says it's not solely about revenue at each Airport Express location. It's about marketing. Says Andreevski, "It's a way for us to add value to the brand by giving customers a tangible benefit. It's a different form of advertising. We could have spent half a million dollars on a billboard, but instead we're giving people the Mercedes experience, rather than a photo of it." I would suggest that in time it will also prove to be very profitable. It is too good not to be.

Of course it is not just Mercedes that does this sort of thing. As discussed in Chapter 3, "Fast, Good, Cheap: Pick Three – Then Add Something Extra", Lexus was the first luxury-car brand to offer a heightened level of service. Before that, luxury-car makers told the following story to their customers: "You're lucky we sell you our expensive cars, and we and our dealers will bleed you dry at frequent regular service intervals and even more frequent irregular repair visits." Lexus was the first brand to make everything easy for the luxury-car buyer, changing the game for every other manufacturer, as flipstar Toyota has done in every segment of the car business. Toyota has not yet set up a Lexus version of Airport Express, but if they decide to do so they would be a good bet to change the game there, too.

As things stand, Lexus will pick up your car for service at your home or work. They leave a replacement for you to use, and when they picked up my wife's car recently they happened to leave the new model, prompting her to express interest in upgrading. They, too, return the car clean, with Lindt chocolates on the front seat. However, Lexus goes a step further. As part of their brand story (something we will talk a lot more about in a few pages), they align themselves with "high society" establishments, but do so in an unusual way. In Sydney, for example, you get free parking at the opera house. It is not as if Lexus owners can't afford parking, it's just *easy*.

Fast, good, cheap + fun

When you are selling a product or service that has substitutes, and your cost structure prevents you from doing much else, you could always just make it more fun. This is what Virgin Blue has done in the extremely competitive Australian airline industry.

Virgin Blue is not only about fun, of course. The airline is definitely fast, good and cheap, and it is also green. The Virgin Blue website proudly announces that Virgin is "the first airline in Australia to have a comprehensive program for carbon offset".

But in keeping with the cheeky, iconoclastic brand identity of Richard Branson and all Virgin businesses, Virgin Blue pushes the envelope on the fun side of flying. It is not uncommon for the customer-service manager on a Virgin Blue flight to announce a fake destination. You see customers start freaking out, only to hear the customer-service manager say, "Just joking," and move on with the rest of the announcements. On one Virgin Blue flight, I was sitting with a chap who was carrying two boxes of Krispy Kreme doughnuts (which he certainly didn't need, mind you). When we touched down and people started collecting their carry-on luggage, the flight attendant told him that in the state of Victoria you couldn't bring any food or drinks into the terminal from the plane. He was very apologetic and asked where he should leave the doughnuts. She said she would take care of them. A full thirty seconds later, as the doors were opening, she told him she was joking and that he could have his doughnuts back. He was so embarrassed he almost refused them.

While Virgin Blue has not been a runaway, show-stopping success, most suggested it would never last. Since its first flights in 2000 the airline has proven the doubters wrong. Even with the arrival of Jetstar, offering even lower fares, fun seems to be keeping Virgin competitive. In addition, one of the problems Virgin had was that its primary story – "We are the fun, low-cost airline" – didn't attract business-class passengers. Originally they thought it was just that the message wasn't getting through, so they poured money into advertising. But eventually they found that "fun" just doesn't cut it for business-class travellers, who really want to be treated with an extra level of care and to stay connected while in the air. Virgin introduced the Velocity club for frequent flyers and fully flexible fares. These options and the ability to pay an extra $30 to get a front-row or extra-roomy exit-aisle seat make Virgin a viable option for businesspeople flying at times and to destinations that Qantas business-class service doesn't reach.

Now it is not that business-class travellers don't like fun. They do. They just need the travel experience to, above all, be easy. On its transatlantic flights Virgin Atlantic has turned on the pampering style in their business-class offerings. Including an in-flight bar, flat-sleeper seats (like the Qantas SkyBed) and a masseuse, as well as a limousine transfer and a first-class waiting lounge, Virgin Atlantic offers the complete service experience – both at sea level and at 40,000 feet. Anything to help business travellers feel better prepared for that first day of meetings in London or New York.

In-flight extras include dining when you want and eating what you want (rather than the traditional "here it is, eat it now" style). And the amenities kit actually has beauty products as well as basic toiletries, complimentary noise-reducing headphones and extra-large in-chair video screens.

Fast, good, cheap + healthy

Healthy may be the strategy with the most competitive advantage over the next couple of decades. The only thing more important to baby boomers than staying healthy in their retirement years is having the money to enjoy their youthful energy and appearance (bet on the plastic-surgery industry continuing to soar as part of that trend, too). And Generations X and Y are even more fitness-obsessed than their parents.

Let's have a look at some examples.

It has taken just twelve years for Fitness First to grow from a single club in the UK to a sixteen-country, 500-plus gym and 1.2-million-member organization. Sydney was home to the 500th Fitness First gym in 2006. In 2005 Fitness First was acquired by a private equity firm (BC Partners) for more than $2 billion. It is the fastest-growing health-club company in the world; in 2007 Fitness First registered an 18 per cent growth in earnings and was on track to match its 2006 record of forty-nine new clubs worldwide. In the UK the company has enjoyed sixteen consecutive months of impressive like-for-like sales growth (even excluding the impact of new clubs).

Organic food accounts for only 1 to 2 per cent of food sales worldwide, but the organic-food market is growing rapidly. The organic-food market in the United States has enjoyed 17 to 20 per cent growth over the past few years. Meanwhile conventional-food sales grew only at 2 to 3 per cent a year, or in other words about the same rate as the growth in population.

Multinationals are beginning to see the value of these products and to invest in organic produce, leading to increased competition, increasing economies of scale and a subsequent decrease in price and increase in accessibility to fuel the market and force heavily polluting and industrialized agribusiness to clean up its act. Earlier in the chapter I talked about Wal-Mart's green push into practices and products that further environmental sustainability. That has included a substantial increase in organic-food offerings in the grocery sections of Wal-Mart stores.

HEALTHY MAY BE THE STRATEGY WITH THE MOST COMPETITIVE ADVANTAGE OVER THE NEXT COUPLE OF DECADES.

In the UK the market has gone from just over £100 million in 1994 to £1.2 billion in 2006, and will break the £2-billion mark in 2010. Tesco reported a 30 per cent rise in organic sales in 2005–06. In Australia the organic-food market is valued at almost $400 million a year and has enjoyed 25 to 30 per cent growth per year over the last few years.

Vitamins and food supplements (the epitome of self-help and self-medication) are a booming market. For example, the European Molecular Biology Association puts the global food-supplements industry consumption at roughly €125 billion euros a year. In the European Union in 2001 sales of food supplements reached almost €2 billion euros, which was growth of almost 7.7 per cent from the previous year.

In the UK in 2005 vitamin sales alone were valued at over 320 million pounds, which constituted over 15 per cent of total over-the-counter drug sales. This was up from £280 million in 2001 and included a massive 8 per cent jump in 2004. The UK Food Standards Agency places the consumption of high-dosage vitamins alone at between £30 million and £40 million a year, and says nearly 50 per cent of the population takes vitamins.

. . .

Obviously there are more X factors, and the list could probably go on for ever. This is enough to get your mind clicking. What X factor can you offer to set you apart from your competitors?

When you come up with some possible X factors (the only limit on them is your imagination), you need a model to work from as you set about redesigning and repositioning your products and services. And you need to do it from the perspective of the customer. The model I suggest you work from is what I call the Total Ownership Experience.

THE TOTAL OWNERSHIP EXPERIENCE

A few years ago Joseph Pine and James Gilmore published a wonderful book called *The Experience Economy: Work Is Theatre & Every Business a Stage*. The book has been very successful – deservedly so – but sometimes I wonder at how little people seem to have learned from it. I meet estate agents, retailers and even bankers who say they've read the book and who talk urgently about the customer experience. When I ask them what they are doing about it, they say things like, "We brew coffee before we show a new house to stimulate the senses"; "We make sure there is lots of colour in the shops"; or, "We have all our financial products online."

It is not that multisensory stimulation is not a key part of the total ownership experience. It is, but as you are about to find out, it is just one step in building a much deeper connection to your customers. Just ask brand-building legend Howard Schultz, the founder of Starbucks. In a memo Schultz sent to senior management at Starbucks in February 2007 (later leaked to the media) he reflected on the importance of this relationship and criticized the company for losing sight of it:

> Over the past ten years, in order to achieve the growth, development, and scale necessary to go from less than 1,000 stores to 13,000 stores and beyond, we have had to make a series of decisions that, in retrospect, have led to the watering down of the Starbucks experience, and what some might call the commoditization of our brand...
>
> For example, when we went to automatic espresso machines, we solved a major problem in terms of speed of service and efficiency. At the same time, we overlooked the fact that we would remove much of the romance and theater that was in play with the use of the La Marzocca machines.[3]

Schultz noted that the height of the new machines blocked customers' view: they were denied the "intimate experience" of watching the barista make their drink. He also criticized the new streamlined store design. Changes had been made to achieve greater efficiency and ensure that return on investment was satisfactory, but the result was that Starbucks coffee shops no longer had the "soul of the past". They felt like "a chain of stores", said Schultz, as opposed to conveying the "warm feeling of a neighborhood store".

Do you and your people strive to make your service delivery "romantic"? Are your call-centre staff striving to have an "intimate experience" with your customers? When you see opportunities to gain efficiencies in your operations, do you first consider the impact they will have on how it "feels" to do business with you?

As you expand and grow your business you have to hold on to what made you you in the first place. It is exactly this kind of authenticity that makes brands attractive. And as you will learn in this chapter, it is these intangibles, like the "warm feeling of a neighborhood store" that will differentiate your brand, your product, your business from the competitors.

Schultz, however, does not stop there. Later in the memo he says: "Now that I have provided you with a list of some of the underlying issues that I believe we need to solve, let me say at the outset that we have all been part of these decisions. I take full responsibility myself ..."

In a world of corporate executives who usually seem far more concerned about their stock options and golden parachutes than about customers or staff, you've got to love a leader who takes a full share of responsibility for moves that have put his company at risk, relishes the accountability of his position, and then uses it to rally the troops to join him in doing better:

Push for innovation and do the things necessary to
once again differentiate Starbucks from all others.
We source and buy the highest quality coffee. We

have built the most trusted brand in coffee in the world, and we have an enormous responsibility to both the people who have come before us and the 150,000 [Starbucks] partners and their families who are relying on our stewardship.

Let me stop a moment and say with unbridled admiration that these are the words of a true flipstar. Howard Schultz changed how the world drinks coffee and he obviously hasn't lost one iota of his imaginative passion for supplying customer wants as well as needs. And it is not just about the customer, it is as much about the staff, who by the way are not called staff – instead they are called "partners".

I once gave a presentation in Los Angeles about becoming a talent-centric organization, and at the session before me two Starbucks employees shared their experience of what it was like to work for Starbucks. A young man who still works as a barista was in tears as he spoke about how proud he was to be part of Starbucks. In tears, and I was not the only one who noticed – the 400-odd executives in the room did, too, and were clearly moved by the young man's story. And it was not as though the company had rescued him from the depths of despair. He just loved working there that much. But I digress – back to the point …

In regard to "Absolutely, Positively Sweat the Small Stuff", Schultz's memo makes clear that details like the smell of a Starbucks store can only have significance in the context of a total customer experience that is much bigger than using sensory stimulation to trigger emotional responses. In other words the customer experience goes beyond sensory stimulation or

THE TOTAL OWNERSHIP EXPERIENCE

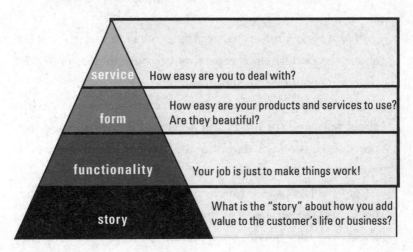

a jazzed-up transactional environment, whether bricks-and-mortar or online. Buying and selling coffee in a way that helps indigenous coffee growers is as much a part of the Starbucks brand story as good coffee. Being able to inject "romance and theatre" into the making of a cup of coffee satisfies much more than customers' need for caffeine and a warm drink. It satisfies their desire to be taken to another place. The "third place" besides home and work or school, as Starbucks calls it. The customer's total ownership experience includes four things:

- service
- form
- functionality
- story

Service is essentially how it feels to *buy* your product or service. It is about store design and layout, the behaviour of staff, the simplicity and ease of navigation on a website, and so on.

Form is how it feels to *use* your product or service. It is less about the performance capability of your product or service than it is about design, appearance and ergonomics.

Function is how it feels to *own* the product or service. It is about how well the product or service integrates into and supports the customer's daily life and lifestyle. It is about both quality and integration.

Story is how it feels for customers to *say* they own the product or use the service. It is the story customers tell themselves about why they bought your product or service and why they have an affinity with your brand. And it is the most powerful of the four elements of the total ownership experience.

Notice the use of the word *feel* in the above descriptions. This is deliberate, considering that emotions drive our decisions, not our rational thought processes. As I said a few paragraphs ago, we tend to seize on relatively superficial qualities to justify our emotional imperatives.

Consider an experience I had with my wife. A few years ago we were shopping on the Gold Coast in Surfer's Paradise, Australia. We were on a street of boutiques for Gucci, Prada, Bally and other high-end fashion brands. In the Gucci shop my wife, Sharon, admired a handbag that cost something near $1,500. I could tell she really wanted it and I also thought it looked nice, as it should for the money.

But something about the bag bugged me. And no, it wasn't just the price tag. It looked strangely familiar. And then it hit me. I had recently seen the same bag in a street vendor's stall in Southeast Asia.

Wise spouses will know that I should have kept my mouth shut. But I couldn't help myself. I said, "I saw the exact same bag last week in Malaysia at a fraction of the price. I will be there again next month and I will bring you one home." (Interesting how a developed-world luxury item generates economic activity in the developing world, too, isn't it?)

"What? I don't want some bag from a street stall in Malaysia. That bag would be a fake!" Sharon said.

"Nobody will ever be able to tell the difference," I said.

"Of course they will. You may not be able to see it, but people who really know about these things will."

"Bollocks. I bet if you put the bags side by side, ninety-nine out of a hundred women and assorted experts who think they know all about Gucci will pick the wrong one as fake. I will bring you back two of those bags in different colours. We will still save a bundle, and I guarantee you, no one will ever know they're fake. I am pretty sure they have them in Chinatown in Sydney as well. Maybe we could look there."

"No way. I want a real one. First, most people *will* know the difference, and even if they didn't, I will. And every time I wear the bag I will know it's a fake. So stop making a fuss and buy me the damn bag."

So we bought the bag. Typically, however, I could not let it rest. "So tell me, darling" – a poor choice of words – "how will people know this is a real Gucci bag?"

"The stitching!" she yelled as we left the shop.

Stitching was her justification. Damn stitching.

"So, $1,450 worth of stitching!" I yelled back as I realized I had made a similar decision some years before based on exactly the same thing – stitching. More on that soon.

Reflecting on that experience now, I have decided we were both right. The bag in Malaysia was quite a convincing knock-off. But buying and owning a fake, and pretending it was real, were not part of my wife's story about herself. She wasn't just buying the bag because of what it said about her to the world, but because of what it said to her about her. This is what I call Aspirational Inside.

Howard Schultz's memo is all about matching aspirational inside with aspirational outside. If Starbucks does something that helps the bottom line in the short term but over the long term undermines the way customers feel about the experience of buying coffee in a Starbucks outlet, drinking it or being seen with a Starbucks coffee cup, the extraordinary success of the Starbucks brand will come undone. This includes not only the smell of the coffee and the look of the stores, but also the coffee having been harvested, packaged and distributed in an environmentally sound, socially responsible way.

Starbucks' ability to offer customers fast, good, cheap at the premium price, plus an X factor of feeling good for, in and about themselves, has recently been extended to sales of specially chosen books and music CDs. Starbucks has achieved great success with exclusive retailing windows for CDs by artists such as Bob Dylan and Alanis Morissette, including outselling all other retail outlets on the late Ray Charles's final CD, *Genius Loves Company*. In 2007 Starbucks formed its own music label, Hear Music, in collaboration with the Concord Music Group, and signed Paul McCartney as the label's first artist. The same year it gave a huge boost to number one on the *New York Times* hardcover bestseller list to Ishmael Beah's memoir *A Long Way Gone: Memoirs of a Boy Soldier,* about being conscripted as a child soldier in Africa.[4]

Note that the crucial thing is not the retailing power of Starbucks. It is how the company uses its hard-earned power to achieve true synergy, choosing musicians and books that fit key customer demographics and resonate with socially responsible themes such as economic justice for coffee growers in the developing world.

As Schultz rejoins as CEO, lets hope he re-creates the authenticity Starbucks so desperately needs. I've already referred to what I call aspirational outside, the conspicuous consumption of something flashy and expensive – such as a ridiculously expensive cup of Starbucks coffee – so other people know you have money, good taste or good values.

You may have said the following things yourself at times:

"A car is just a car. As long as it gets you from A to B."

"You can't tell the difference between a real Gucci bag and a fake one. You are getting conned."

"You would have to be stupid to spend two pounds on a bottle of water when you can get the same stuff for free from the tap."

However, as we gain a deeper understanding of the human mind and how we make decisions, it actually becomes inaccurate to say that such decisions are illogical or irrational. They are not. They are in fact very "normal" ways to behave. The story we tell ourselves about the products we buy and other such decisions we make is so deep to the human experience of the world that "because it feels good" is actually the only rational explanation for why we do

THE STORY WE TELL OURSELVES ABOUT THE PRODUCTS WE BUY AND OTHER SUCH DECISIONS WE MAKE IS SO DEEP TO THE HUMAN EXPERIENCE OF THE WORLD THAT "BECAUSE IT FEELS GOOD" IS ACTUALLY THE ONLY RATIONAL EXPLANATION FOR WHY WE DO ANYTHING.

anything. If it is aspirational inside, the story only has to appeal to me, and who cares what anyone else thinks. If it is aspirational outside, then what is important is the story being presented to other people.

The point is that what we think is rarely what drives our behaviours. It is what we *feel* that matters. I started this conversation by introducing you to the four fundamentals of the total ownership experience, before explaining in some detail why I deliberately used the word *feel* when describing what they were. Let's go deeper into each of these elements now. Please note that even though I have separated them here for ease of understanding, the four fundamentals are inextricably linked – especially the story. The story of a product and why someone would buy it is intertwined through each of the other three fundamentals, as well as being the basis for all PR and marketing conducted by a company (remembering, of course, that this includes you).

THE STORY

No one, least of all my wife, wants to admit that we all shop for things that help tell a good story about us. Through the things we buy and the experience of owning and using them, we tell that story to ourselves and others. This is the foundation of the ownership experience and the most powerful driver of value and premium pricing.

Nothing makes us more loyal and less price conscious than a product or service that integrates into our favoured story about ourselves. You know what I mean. The story that we are popular, hip, savvy, enlightened, successful and socially and environmentally conscious. You fill in the blank, and that's why we're wearing the labels we wear, driving the cars we drive, and so on. The products and services we buy say that we are exactly who we want to be. That we are in with the in crowd. That we are worthy of respect, admiration or envy.

Your job is to find what your story is. The story of your brand, the story of your company, the story of your product, and scream it from the rooftops – or whisper it through the streets, which is usually the more powerful of the two. Notice that I did not say to find out what story the market wants and to yell that story from the rooftops. A story needs to be real, authentic and original.

Let me give you some examples of the stories we tell.

I have a friend who works for a company with an extremely powerful reputation in the market. She hates it. When asked to describe the workplace, she uses words like *toxic, disorganized, small-minded* and *the least friendly place she has ever worked*. So I asked her why she stays there. Her response was: because of how it will look on her résumé. She knows that if she wants to move on to another organization, her next prospective employer will think, *Wow, you worked at ABC company. You must be good*.

Another very close friend recently purchased a BMW, despite saying he never would. He used to say, "Everyone has a BMW," which is why he never would. After his purchase he told me a story that sounded as though he had already related it a few times before. Probably most of all to himself.

"I went to buy a new car and my next-door neighbour made me promise not to buy anything until I had at least test-driven a BMW. I agreed. After test driving a Mercedes, Audi, Lexus and Porsche, I begrudgingly headed to the BMW dealer and took the new 335i coupé for a drive. Omigosh! Dude, it left the rest seriously for dead. I now know why the BMW is such a popular car. Because it is better than all the others."

Now he is not an expert judge of a good car, so don't take this as the hard truth, but this experience had made it OK for him to buy a BMW. If you probe a little deeper, as I did, you learn why he could justify spending the money he did.

"So what makes this car so good?" I asked.

He began to describe the car's many fine features in surprising detail. He capped the story off by saying, "This is my kind of car. And you know what? I work so hard, I deserve it."

Whether you realize it or not, you do exactly the same thing when you make any kind of decision. It may not be as elaborate as this example, but the story is there somewhere.

So the question becomes, *How do we construct a better story so we can build more powerful brands? What makes up the story?*

All good stories have three things:

- detail
- characters
- language

Using the BMW example, consider the following elements of a good story and remember that this is what you need to do for your brand, too.

Detail: My friend knew the BMW 335i went from 0 to 100 kilometres per hour in 5.5 seconds. He referred specifically to its competitors: Audi, Mercedes, Porsche and so on. Plus ATC (Automatic Traction Control) and ABS (Antilock Braking System).

Character: Statements like "no one else has one" are evidence of the identity and character he associates with the car. "My kind of car" and "I deserve it" personalize the purchase, a process that is clinched by calling the piece of metal a "baby".

Language: This bit cracks me up. If you knew this guy, you would think it was ridiculous for him to talk about "twin turbos" and "turbo lag". Less obvious, but more powerful perhaps, was when he described the car as "perfectly understated." I would just bet that the salesperson used that exact language. This is an example of how the story is not separate from, say, the service experience.

Let's look at some more flipstars as we go into a little more depth on these three elements.

Detail

Detail is anything specific you can reference to say why a product is better, more suited, etc. Companies use statistics, competitive benchmarking, surveys, information about the manufacturing process or the history of the company to distinguish their offerings from the competition.

For a recent trip to Las Vegas I asked a travel agent about the best place to stay. I had thought the Bellagio (based on the movie *Ocean's 11,* which is an extreme example of characterization). However, in an attempt to convince me to stay at Wynn's she said that since MGM Grand had taken over the Bellagio, staff-to-room ratios had dropped to 1.5 staff members per room. And that Wynn's, which is owned by Steve Wynn, who previously developed both the Bellagio and the Mirage casino hotels on the Las Vegas Strip before selling them to MGM Grand, Inc, has a ratio of three staff per room. This detail is a powerful piece in the story that will build Wynn's competitive advantage on the Strip.

Or what about American Airlines, whose December 2006 *American Way* in-flight magazine began with a letter from the editor noting the following specific details:

- 120 million passengers
- 1.3 billion miles
- 1.5 million flights
- 100 million bags
- Every twenty-two seconds an American Airlines or American Eagle flight takes off somewhere around the world
- 250 cities in forty countries
- 95 million calls received
- 450 million visits to AA.com
- 100 aircraft

I am not sure this is the kind of detail I would use to build my story. Certainly American Airlines is building a story of a global, regular, experienced airline. As a very frequent flyer I think, *Too many people, just a seat number, and no one really caring about me.* But hey, that's just me.

One more example of detail: Sirius satellite radio tells its story as made up from the following elements:

- over 130 channels
- 69 channels of commercial-free music
- Available 200 miles offshore
- 60 channels of sports, news, talk and entertainment

Characterization

Characterization is what brings a story to life. It does not actually have to be about a specific person, but it must convey human attributes. This is difficult to do, often expensive, but extremely powerful.

In the past the most popular form of characterization was celebrity endorsement. Although it is still very powerful, many would suggest that this technique is losing its effectiveness. Let me share with you some examples of characterization that I like.

Skins Compression Garments are highly styled athletic clothing made with "engineered gradient compression" to improve circulation, minimize soreness from exertion and injury, and speed recovery. Skins are marketed with the constant statement that "We don't pay sports stars to wear our products." This small piece of information is extremely powerful because star athletes and well-known teams in Australia and elsewhere – including all the major Australian Rugby League teams and football players from Arsenal, Chelsea and Manchester United have been seen wearing Skins clothing while training and competing. This is a great story, but it will need to keep evolving.

In the United States, the Under Armour sports clothing line, which includes but is not limited to compression garments, has become a huge success with paid endorsements from major sports teams. If Under Armour matches Skins in technical features, style and price, and both brands are fast, good and cheap, celebrity endorsement could well make the difference in the competition between the two.

There is much debate about whether organizations need a

charismatic leader who is in the public eye. I am decided. *Yes!* It does not need to be the CEO. It could be the founder. The founder could even be dead but have an identity or an image that people can associate with.

I would like to avoid using another fashion example here, and am feeling that you may be bored with my shopping preferences, but it is only fair that I include this example. I have criticized my wife for spending too much money on a handbag; I should at least fess up to doing so on suits.

Many years ago I was looking at the suits in a Hugo Boss boutique. It is important to note that this was in my first year in business and I could hardly afford a suit, let alone one from Hugo Boss.

After looking at a few suits in their entry-level range which were about $800 a pop, I had almost built a powerful enough story in my mind that I needed to buy one of these suits. My story was that if I wanted to be a player I had to look like a player.

Then the sales assistant said, "But you really shouldn't buy any suit until you have seen this range here." It was the over $1,500 range. The sales assistant pulled a $1,700 suit from the rack that, except for being a different shade of black, looked pretty much like the $800 suit I was trying on for size. Neither of them actually looked that good on me. They were a bad fit for my body shape, but I convinced myself, with a lot of assistance from the man serving me, that tailoring could fix this.

I took a good hard look at the two jackets side by side, like a non-mechanical person looking under the bonnet of a car. I couldn't see or feel any difference, and I said so.

"What's the difference?" I asked. "Show me."

The sales assistant said, "This suit has higher-quality fabric and stitching, and it will 'sit' on you better. It will feel like a part of you." (Are you picking up the use of both characterization and language?)

"What does that mean? You can't be serious. It is more than double the price."

The sales assistant repeated himself, more or less word for word, and I said, "Doesn't anyone in the store have a better explanation than that?" At that point, the sales assistant went to get help from the manager. He needed reinforcements, because I had the bit between my teeth.

The store manager walked over, and before he could say a word I asked him, "In addition to the fabric, which doesn't look any better to me, why is this suit worth nine hundred dollars more than the one I'm trying on?"

"Well, if I could just say a word about the fabric, sir, it's what we in the business know as a super 120 and it weighs 280 grams per square metre." (Notice the use of detail.) Looking at me in a way that made me want to punch him in the nose, he continued, 'In layman's terms, this simply means that it is a better-quality fabric and will "sit" better on you.'

"Really?" I wasn't about to give in easily.

"Yes, sir. And then as to the stitching" – remember my wife in the Gucci boutique – "much of this garment is hand-sewn for effect, while the fabric is laser-cut, ensuring perfect shape."

"Uh-huh." It was a good, practised spiel, but I wasn't ready to throw in the towel. "That may be, but is that really going to make a difference to me over the life of the suit? I still can't see any of the differences you're talking about."

"Why don't you try it on?" the store manager said. He got

me to put on the jacket, and repeated some of what he'd just told me about the fabric and the stitching.

I switched jackets a couple of times, looking for a difference in the mirror.

"I still can't tell the difference!" I exclaimed.

"Ah, sir," the store manager said in a mocking tone, "I know you can't tell the difference, but I assure you the people you want to be doing business with can."

I bought the $1,700 suit, not to save face in front of the all-knowing store manager, but because I actually bought into the story that the suit would help me become more successful and respected in my business. I believed it would give me a seat at the right tables, so to speak, in front of the right kind of people. Guided deftly by the store manager, I built a story of myself in my head as a powerful player in the business community.

Language

Finally, on language. We looked at the importance of language in the sections on *detail* and *characterization,* so let me just share two dramatic examples of how language influences our experiences as customers.

One of Australia's favourite sons, Steve Irwin, epitomized a stereotypical view of what Australia is like. For the record, it is nothing like what the overwhelming majority of Australians are like, but the world loved him anyway. The best thing about Steve Irwin was that he wasn't putting on an act. He really was that enthusiastic and he really did use words like *crikey*. This image of Australians is rampant around the world. While I was eating alone at a counter in San Francisco, a road warrior from

New York asked me if kangaroos really hop up and down the main street of Sydney. "Of course not," I said. I would be willing to bet that more than half of Sydney's residents have never seen a kangaroo outside of a zoo. And we don't all talk like Steve Irwin either, but this hasn't stopped people making serious money from the outback "Aussie" story.

The best example of the use of language is when your brand name becomes part of the language:

- "Just Google it," for a search online.
- "I need a Kleenex," when you want a tissue.
- "Get me a Coke," when you couldn't distinguish one brand of cola from another.

And so on.

You may be aware that the founder of Illy coffee invented the first steam coffee machine and coined the term *espresso*. When his grandson recently tried to trademark the word, the powers that be said it was too late, but he had the right idea.

I have spent a lot of time on *the story*. I make no apologies for this. This is fundamental. The story, as superficial as it seems, is anything but. It is the reason why people do what they do. It is also the reason why it forms the basis for the pyramid. The model in this case is also the metaphor.

FUNCTION

Design without functionality will fade. That is, of course, unless the core purpose of the product is simply to look good, as is the case with, say, a piece of art or a collectable for your shelf. I think the best way to market your product is to build a good one. However, when talking about the total ownership experience, I am assuming that you have fast, good and cheap already worked out. What I mean by functionality here is how well the product or service integrates into a customer's life.

Pronto valet parking is a functional service. So is Mercedes-Benz Airport Express. And here are a couple more that were designed purely with functionality in mind.

First Luggage offers on their website that they will "arrange for your luggage to be collected anywhere in the world and delivered to your chosen destination without stress or hassle". Yeah, that's a cool idea.

They note in their FAQs that many companies will ship your luggage for you if you ask, but First Luggage has it as their sole business – so there is no complex paperwork, no weighing of luggage, no boxing of your own goods, nothing like that. You just tell them where you are, where you're going and when you need to be there. Your bags will be there first. They also text you to let you know your bags have arrived ahead of you (ah, peace of mind).

First Luggage has also partnered with British Airways, and offers a 5 per cent discount to passengers who book through BA. The timing for First Luggage could not have been better, as they cash in on increased baggage restrictions caused by terrorism in the UK.

Progressive Insurance has pioneered what they call the Immediate Response System – it's a high-tech network of GPS systems and emergency response vehicles equipped with laptops, printers and wireless net connections. It makes sure claims assessors are on the spot ASAP – sometimes even before the police – and can assess the claim, organize towing if it's required, write out a claim cheque *on the spot* in some situations, and generally provide one hell of a customer experience.

Progressive's Peter Lewis says of this system and his philosophy, "We're not in the car-insurance business, we're in the business of reducing human trauma and the economic cost of auto accidents." Or as I call it, they are in the business of functionality – integrating, in this case during very traumatic experiences, as simply and powerfully into people's lives as possible.

The truth is the Progressive example is driven by cost savings, too, because it cuts out a lot of costly back-office paperwork and administration while vastly enhancing customer loyalty. What a win-win. Save costs, and improve the customer's experience.

Online grocery shopping is another example of an offering based on functionality. Online grocery shopping has soared in popularity – although along its route to popularity there have been a few bumps. In 1999 the US online grocery shopping market was $200 million. By 2004 Forrester Research reported that the market had grown 1,200 per cent to $2.4 billion. The Food Institute predicts that online grocery sales in the United States will reach around $5.4 billion by the end of 2007, and *Key Note* predicts the online grocery-shopping market will continue to enjoy 20 per cent year-on-year growth until at least 2010.

In mid-2006 Amazon.com quietly launched an online grocery shopping service that could deliver to anywhere in the United States. Almost all major supermarket chains in Australia, the UK and the United States now offer online ordering and delivery. For instance, Tesco captured almost 70 per cent of the online grocery market in the UK in 2006 and their sales hit almost £1 billion.

If you don't order your groceries online, you should – at least, in my opinion. It is so much easier than going to the supermarket, it is almost a joke. Given that 25 per cent of our grocery purchases are convenience purchases, it is fair to say that most of the 75 per cent remaining are well-thought-out, planned purchases. In fact, if you are like most shoppers you will do one big shop (weekly, monthly or whatever) and smaller fresh-produce or convenience shops in between. The big shop rarely changes, in terms of the types of items you need and the brands you would normally buy.

ASK YOURSELF, HOW MANY OF YOUR PROCESSES OR POLICIES ARE SET UP TO MAKE LIFE EASIER FOR YOU OR TO MAKE LIFE EASIER FOR THE CUSTOMER? CHANGE THE ONES THAT ARE ABOUT YOU.

Online shopping remembers what you buy, has it all ready in a convenient list, knows your credit-card details and where you live. You then select your delivery time slot, usually in the next twenty-four hours. They deliver outside of normal business hours, which is important for the modern, busy person.

On a different note, the emergence of home services and outsourcing of traditional chores have grown exponentially over the last decade. According to IBISWorld, the average Australian household now spends $14,000 per annum outsourcing things they used to do themselves. Cooking, cleaning, washing, ironing, child care, gardening – you name it, there is someone who can do it for you. This whole industry has emerged to service the needs of people's time-pressured lifestyles. That is, the service integrates into the customers' lives by removing the need for them to do it themselves.

Ask yourself, how many of your processes or policies are set up to make life easier for you, and to make life easier for the customer? Change the ones that are about you.

FORM

Beautiful can be a form of competitive advantage. Apple is beautiful. Well-presented food is beautiful. The choreography of Cirque du Soleil is beautiful. Google's home page is beautiful.

Bang & Olufsen is beautiful, and this Danish consumer electronics manufacturer also understands the often counter-intuitive dynamic of consumer behaviour. Bang & Olufsen products are extremely expensive, but they are sneered at by audiophiles and home-theatre enthusiasts. I would agree with them on the sound, but I think the B&O panels are stunning. But hey, that is just my opinion. It sounds crazy, but whether it is the best audio or video is actually beside the point. Bang & Olufsen's success is built on the superficial areas of design and simplicity.

People don't just buy B&O stereo equipment and flat-panel televisions to listen to music and watch DVDs, they buy them to look good in their homes. The essential functionality of B&O products in customers' lives is as stunningly beautiful interior-design objects. Oh, and so their friends know they can afford to buy B&O products (part of their story).

The company understands this very well. At one point Bang & Olufsen CEO Torben Ballegaard Sorensen wanted designers of B&O's Beomax 8000 television set to include a microchip that would be compatible with future HDTV standards. That would conceivably extend the Beomax 8000's selling life and its annual $10 million contribution to cash flow.

The B&O designers refused to consider the CEO's suggestion, saying it was an "affront" to the design of the television as a sculptural object in its own right. When the new HDTV standards were operational, they would design a new television as a sculptural object from scratch.

I am not criticizing the CEO. He is a flipstar in its purist form, sacrificing what would be potentially more revenue and profits in the short term to stay true to B&O's source of competitive advantage. Form not function. I also love that he was willing to be directed by the design team. He was willing to give up some control, the topic of Chapter 7, "To Get Control, Give It Up".

The very affluent people who spend as much on a Bang & Olufsen stereo or home-theatre set-up as the cost of a well-respected motor vehicle aren't doing it to rock out with killer sounds and images, but so that the products themselves will look fabulous in their homes. Likewise, the equally affluent customers who are focused on audio and home-theatre performance will never buy Bang & Olufsen.

As I said, you can't actually separate form or functionality or service from the story. As Rich Teerlink, the former CEO of Harley-Davidson Motorcycles, once said, "We don't sell motorcycles. What we sell is the ability for a forty-three-year-old accountant to drive through a small town dressed in black leather and have people be afraid of him."

The functional mechanical performance and the distinctive appearance of Harley-Davidson's products obviously combine to make that customer experience possible for communities of Harley-Davidson fans all over the world. But it is equally obvious that for Harleys appearance counts for more than performance. It is the design that enhances the story.

In 2006 Harley-Davidson's net income climbed to $312.7 million from $265 million a year earlier. Revenue rose 14 per cent to $1.64 billion, and shipments jumped 11 per cent, including a substantial 22 per cent jump for their high-end models. Predictions are that earnings per share will rise 11 per cent to 17 per cent by the end of 2009.

There are lots of good motorcycles that cost a lot less to buy than a Harley-Davidson. In every category of product and service, the winning providers, the ones who have the highest profit margins in their fees and prices, are the ones who sweat the small stuff to create a distinctive customer experience, as Harley-Davidson has done with the look and feel of their motorcycles. They go beyond the product or service itself to the total ownership experience that customers have, and they do everything in their power to make that experience truly unique.

Apple, an obvious flipstar, has understood this for a long time. As my Apple mates say to me when comparing PCs to Apple computers, "Apples are beautiful." And it seems as though other computer makers are getting on board, too.

Dell's new cases look much more modern and slick. Asus has teamed up with Lamborghini (an instance of characterization by association with a well-established brand) and produced a leather-bound laptop – not the carrying case, but the actual casing of the laptop itself is leather. Hewlett-Packard has reclaimed the number one PC spot over Dell in large part because they have been faster to jump on the trend that design is a powerful differentiator.

SERVICE

Service usually gets the most attention in discussions of the customer experience. But in many cases product form, functionality and story can trump bad service. That was my experience with an Italian sofa that I bought recently. Actually it only *arrived* recently; in fact I bought it some time ago.

I want to mention the establishment where I bought it by name because the service was appalling, and they deserve to be carpeted, but my publisher's lawyers prevent me from doing so. It was a struggle to get assistance from the staff from the first moment my wife and I walked in the door. And after we had ordered the sofa, they sprang the good news that delivery would take three months. I was thinking more like three days, so we'd be able to start enjoying the new sofa that weekend.

Four months later, *nothing*. No sofa, no phone call, no e-mail, no letter from the shop explaining what was happening. I rang and asked where in blazes my sofa was, and they told me there were always shipping delays from the Italian manufacturer. They assumed I was an idiot and didn't realize the true situation: that they were a small importer of speciality furniture with no inventory except what was on display, and that they minimized costs by shipping only full containers. They had obviously had a slow year, and as the rare customer who had actually bought something I was paying the price.

Half a year after I had initiated the purchase, they called to say that my sofa would arrive the next day. I called back to say that tomorrow was not convenient, but they would have none of that. I asked if they could at least tell me when it would be arriving so I could arrange for someone to be home to receive it. No information there either.

To top it all off, the delivery people refused to take away the cardboard and plastic the sofa arrived in. "Sorry, sir," they said, "that is your responsibility."

I could not imagine a worse service experience. But we absolutely love the sofa. It is both gorgeous and amazingly comfortable. It is a perfect fit for our space. In other words, the service was appalling but the total ownership experience is still awesome. The trials and tribulations we went through to get the sofa only make the story better in the end.

I'm not discounting the importance of the buying experience in general. If a product or service is highly commoditized, then it is the buying experience that may be the only thing that differentiates one offer from another. Such is often the case in banking. In the case of, say, a hotel room, the customer service is the form and function and the primary reason for the transaction. One hotel room is very much like another, and it is the service wrapped around the room that makes the difference.

Like all frequent business travellers, I stay in lots of hotels. Some I visit regularly, perhaps a few times a month. I belong to every loyalty programme, but none of the hotels seems able to remember what my preferences are. Every time I check in, I still have to fill in my details on the form and say I like a non-smoking room with a down comforter and a firm pillow. I am sure any corporate road warriors reading this have similar stories.

Four Seasons, in the words of founder Isadore Sharp, set out to "redefine luxury as service". For instance, they implemented what they call "kerbside check-in" for frequent guests. When you arrive you are literally handed your room keys as you get out of the car. Oh, and how many visits makes a "frequent" guest? As few as *five*.

The "no luggage required" policy is a feature of the hotel to help guests who lose luggage in transit. Lose or forget a tie? No worries – tell them what your suit looks like, they'll fix you up. Wait, what was that? You lost your *whole suit*? No worries – we'll fit you for a new one you can borrow.

Consider the following stories that appeared in a *US News & World Report* article about Four Seasons hotels:

- A concierge donned fins and a snorkel to find a wedding ring lost in a lagoon.
- A hotel telephone operator spent forty-five minutes on the phone directing a lost guest all the way to the hotel's entrance.
- A man asked room service for a martini shaker, only to find a tuxedoed server standing at his door – accessories in hand – ready to do the shaking.

The results speak for themselves. A tiny 2 per cent of guests in 2006 reported problems or registered complaints about service (down from the lofty heights of 4 per cent in 2005 … oh, the shame!) at the hotel. RevPAR (revenue per available room) was up 11.8 per cent in 2006, on the back of a 10.6 per cent rise in room rates, at the same time as a 70 basis-point rise in occupancy. Gross revenues were up 10.5 per cent and operating profits 18.2 per cent. Four Seasons is committing to 20 per cent earnings growth for each of the next five years. Only an unstinting commitment to the customer experience makes this possible.

DESIGNING THE TOTAL OWNERSHIP EXPERIENCE

The Apple iPod is an excellent example of how all four fundamentals of the total ownership experience can come together to create profitable global hits.

When the iPod first came along it didn't sound better than existing digital music players and it cost more. Worse, it had lousy batteries that often failed long before they were supposed to.

But thanks to Steve Jobs, whose brainchild it was, the iPod had a great marketing slogan, "A thousand songs in your pocket", that instantly told the story of what it would do for customers in their daily lives. It had a distinctive look, a pure white rectangle with white bud earphones where other digital music players were all shiny metal and awkward, complicated shapes. And it set a new standard in ease of use and ergonomics on its own and in tandem with Apple's iTunes software. When Apple later launched the iTunes Music Store, customers finally had a compelling, comprehensive answer to their digital-music-player needs and wants. The battery problems, serious though they were and are, have never held the iPod back because of the way the product and iTunes work in customers' lives.

As important to the rise and rise of the iPod is how people think they look when they're carrying their iPods and listening to them. They feel cool and believe they look cool. They are part of a hip community formed around and experienced through a commodity, just like the middle-aged businessmen who buy Harley-Davidson motorcycles and fantasize about riding them with Marlon Brando in the movie *The Wild One* or with Peter Fonda, Dennis Hopper and Jack Nicholson in *Easy Rider.*

Part of the story of the iPod community even came to include the fact that the white bud earphones were a signal to muggers and pickpockets: this person has an iPod. In places like New York City it became a weird badge of honour that the pickpockets on the subway or the bus would focus on you because of your iPod earphones. It meant you were cool enough to have something worth stealing, something hot that everyone wanted. The New York Police Department and the Metropolitan Transit Authority even put up posters specifically warning iPod owners to be wary of pickpockets and other thieves.

Popular retail chains can also engender loyal communities of customers. In the last chapter I spoke about the Uniqlo chain in Japan and elsewhere. In the United States the discount superstore Target has carved out a distinctive brand identity as the favourite discount store of design-conscious, hip consumers in all demographics. Company executives are proud of the fact that the millions who are in on the secret often refer to Target as "Tar-zhay", as if it were a fancy French boutique. This brand identity, summed up in the slogan "Expect More, Pay Less", allows Target to enjoy a price premium over rival retailers such as Wal-Mart and Kmart.

Target's formula for flipping the discount-store brand DNA around and making itself known for high-quality, well-designed products that it can charge a little extra for has two main prongs. One is a product mix that is on the cutting edge of customer trends, thanks to in-house trend spotting and product lines from style gurus such as the fashion designers Isaac Mizrahi and Todd Oldham and the architect Michael Graves. The other is to have superb customer service that would be more expected from a luxury department store than a discounter. Both support the hip design- and value-conscious story that Target customers experience in shopping there.

Target has not yet succeeded in establishing the same brand identity in Australia, but their recent deal with Stella McCartney, Paul McCartney's designer daughter, was a good step in the right direction. In March 2007 Target launched an exclusive Stella McCartney clothing line at its Australian stores and triggered scenes of chaos. Racks in Target stores in Melbourne (where there were lines before opening – unheard of for Target in Australia) were cleared of the Stella garments in as little as forty-five seconds, with security having to be called in to keep the commotion under control. The scenes of women fighting with one another to "steal a bargain" was the stuff of reality-TV programming. One hundred Target stores across Australia opened at 8.30 a.m., only to be emptied of mid-size Stella-range dresses by 9.20. It was absolute chaos. People were actually stripping clothes off mannequins as they cleared the stores of stock.

Target paid McCartney $1.27 million to design the one-of-a-kind range of clothes exclusively for their stores. This is part of their move to position themselves at the "high end" of the discount market. Target US last year teamed up with style guru Isaac Mizrahi for the same reason, and H&M has Madonna designing clothes for them in a similar push.

However, a few weeks after these scenes of mass hysteria, a few articles surfaced that mentioned that the glow had worn off rather quickly. After the initial run on the products, they actually sold really slowly after the hype wore off, with Target only marginally (and sometimes not at all) meeting its sales targets (no pun intended). So while it was a great marketing coup initially, there wasn't really a sufficient follow-through.

Nevertheless, this is a sign of things to come as Target attempts to carry its "cheap chic" story to other countries. In the United States the company is going strong, and in 2006 total revenues rose to almost $60 billion.

Cirque du Soleil is another great example of bringing the four elements together. From its origins in the work of two Montreal street performers, Guy Laliberté and Daniel Gauthier, Cirque du Soleil has become a worldwide phenomenon with multiple touring companies and permanent residencies at Walt Disney World in Orlando, Florida, and no fewer than four Las Vegas casino hotels.

The secret of Cirque du Soleil is nothing other than "Absolutely, Positively Sweat the Small Stuff". Cirque du Soleil takes the traditional elements of circus performance and stitches them together into story concepts such as *Love,* an interpretive stage production done to a musical score of Beatles songs at a specially built theatre in the Mirage Hotel and Casino in Las Vegas; *Kà,* a martial-arts fantasy performed at the MGM Grand in Las Vegas; or *Mystère* at the Treasure Island Resort in Las Vegas, which has as its theme the origins of life in the universe. Cirque du Soleil's other resident companies and touring productions have similar narrative themes that make the familiar circus formula of acrobats, animals and clowns new again.

EVERY DECISION YOU MAKE MUST BUILD THE STORY

In the last chapter I mentioned how Toyota has responded to the fact that all the major car manufacturers in North America,

Europe, Japan and Korea now build good-quality cars. Toyota not only leverages its manufacturing and service expertise to maintain a lead in being fast, good and cheap in customers' eyes, it also adds an X factor with innovations like its pioneering hybrid-engine technology, and thus appeals to customers as "Fast, Good, Cheap+Green".

Toyota has developed another X factor in its Scion range of vehicles for Generation-Y consumers, offering the attributes of "Fast, Good, Cheap+Hip". The Scion is a perfect fit for the customized car culture that has sprung up within the hip-hop generation of consumers worldwide, as evidenced by television shows

> DESIGNING THE TOTAL OWN-
> ERSHIP EXPERIENCE CAN HAVE
> AS MUCH TO DO WITH PRO-
> CESS AS PRODUCT.

such as MTV's *Pimp My Ride*. Toyota acted on this trend much sooner than the competition, just as it did with hybrid engines.

Launched at the end of 2003, the Scion has been a smash hit. Dealers sell Scions as fast as they get them, and they reap significant marginal profit from customers' desire to customize their cars with side-panel graphics, roof racks for snowboards and mountain bikes, and so on. (More on this in Chapter 7, "To Get Control, Give It Up".) These things have absolutely nothing to do with the vehicles' performance on the road and absolutely everything to do with their performance in customers' lives.

At launch, Toyota set a 2006 target for US sales of 150,000 cars. In the early autumn of 2006 Toyota saw that it was on track to sell 175,000 Scions in the United States by the end of the year. Industry analysts said that Toyota could quickly ramp up US sales to 250,000 Scions a year. But instead, Toyota did another flip. It looked at the prospect of those easy sales and huge profits and decided that ramping up sales volume would be foolish in the long run, because it would undermine the Scion's brand identity.

Toyota announced that it would limit Scion production and distribution to ensure that it sold no more than 150,000 vehicles in the United States in 2007. Further, it restricted Scion television advertising, which was never very extensive anyway, to a few late-night television shows that are popular with Generation-Y consumers. It also suggested that it might eliminate Scion television advertising entirely, and concentrate instead on event marketing and branded entertainment. The Scion play already includes a music label for emerging artists and the Scion Release clothing line. Instead of using commonly known sports stars or celebrities to sell their cars, they use DJs.

The way Toyota USA vice president Mark Templin puts it is, "Because we no longer have to focus on brand awareness, we can be even more edgy and more risky." The way I put it is, to sustain Scion's brand awareness as a vehicle that helps customers make their lives into a hip and exciting story, they have to become even more edgy and more risky. They have to do an even better job on "Absolutely, Postively Sweat the Small Stuff", and as the moves I've sketched out indicate, they're well on the way to doing so.[5]

As this and previous examples show, designing the total ownership experience can have as much to do with process as product. In the case of Scion marketing, the medium is the message. DJs instead of celebrities. Edgy shows instead of mainstream. The differentiator in any particular instance depends on the story a product or service tells about customers' lives, their aspirations and their sense of community. The story could emphasize simplicity, ease of use, beautiful design, community, or some combination of these things.

So the big question is:

WHAT'S *YOUR* STORY?

Bang & Olufsen, Toyota and other flipstars understand not just what their customers' desired story is, but what their individual brands stand for. They find the common ground between their own reality and the wants of their customer, and design everything they do to build and tell a story that reflects that common ground. As you consider the competitive position of your company or your hopes for your own career, what compelling story can you offer to your customers, your staff or your employers?

Finally, as you take the flip that you must "Absolutely, Positively Sweat the Small Stuff" to heart, don't lose sight of the previous flip. "Fast, Good, Cheap: Pick Three – Then Add Something Extra" is still the price of entry, and the standard of what constitutes fast, good and cheap is continually on the rise. You must have a solid product or service that matches your competitors' offerings, but to make your own offerings stand out from the pack you must also make magic from the small stuff.

The story changes slightly from customer to customer, and it also changes for each individual customer over time. The point is that if you really want to distinguish your products or services from the competition, you have to give thought to the experiences that they engender or support. The products and services we love the most become part of the story of our lives.

FIVE THINGS TO DO NOW

1. Make a short list of your potential X factors.
2. Think about the sort of activities you could engage in for the social good. How could you leverage these to impress customers and attract more staff, *in an authentic way*?
3. Pick one of your products and develop a story about why someone should buy that product, including detail, characterization and language. Role-play it, pretending you are a customer telling his or her best friend why they spent a premium to buy your product instead of your competitor's.
4. Do an "easy audit". That is, review your "buying" and "ongoing service" experience and decide if they are designed to make life easier for you or for your customer. If they are designed to help you, change them so that they help the customer.
5. Create two compelling lists. One for how your brand appeals to aspirational inside, and another for how your brand appeals to aspirational outside.

5

BUSINESS IS PERSONAL

Ultimately, everything is personal.
– Jonathan Schwartz, President/COO, Sun Microsystems

FROM THE INFORMATION AGE TO
THE RELATIONSHIP ERA

In *The Godfather: Part III,* the murderous Don Licio Lucchesi (played by Enzo Robutti) tries to smooth over a difficult moment by telling Michael Corleone (Al Pacino), "It's not personal, it's only business."

A client recently said the same thing to me in justifying why his bank was offshoring its call-centre operations to Bangalore, India.

"What do you mean, it is not personal?" I said. "Forgetting that you are my client for a second, I am a customer of this bank, and I have to tell you it is very personal to me. I have choices, you know. So do the rest of your customers. Other banks ask for our business every day with credit-card offers in the post and in their advertising. The interest you pay or charge us is no different from what it is at other banks, and you tell me that banking is not a personal relationship. It is now, it was yesterday, and it will be tomorrow. Besides, all business is personal. It is about trust, and when customers call the bank they want to feel comfortable with the people who answer and they want to feel respected by them. Outsourcing the customer service part of your business is insane in my view."

WE ARE FAST EXITING THE KNOWLEDGE AGE AND ENTERING THE RELATIONSHIP ERA.

My protest was in vain. The decision had been made. I bet the decision will be reversed at some point in the future, but by then there is no telling how much damage the bank will have done to its customer relationships and its bottom line.

I'll be coming back to my bank's decision a little later in this chapter, but I want to register the general point that, more than anything else in life, relationships rule. Most pundits in and out of the business world consider this the information age, or its recent fashionable variant, the knowledge age. We hear a lot about knowledge workers being the most important part of the economy, the ones who will reap the greatest benefits from the dizzying pace of technological, social and cultural change.

Sure – but lots of people in developed countries are knowledge workers in some way, shape or form. Being a knowledge worker is not going to offer competitive advantage in and of itself. It certainly won't in a truly global economy. The pundits are living in the past. We are fast exiting the knowledge age and entering the relationship era. The flip in this case is that "Business Is Personal".

I am not talking about the traditional cynical adage, "It's not what you know, it's who you know that counts." It is certainly a part of human nature that people look out for their family and friends and scratch one another's backs to get ahead. But the ideas that what you know and who you know determine your success are both flawed, because they are static rather than dynamic.

In the years ahead, two things will count the most. The first is your ability to unlearn the things that are losing relevance, to flip yourself free of old scripts, and to learn the things that are gaining relevance. The second is whether people come to know and trust you as they struggle to bring their own learning forward. That is, do you really care about and respect them? Sounds soft I know, but especially in Western economies it will be the hardest of business imperatives.

Ben Stein wrote an article in the *New York Times* that focused on a fear that capitalism's success over the last fifty years may not be carried on into the future.[1] Why? Because of a lack of trust. Capitalism is built on trust. Trust that the goods you send to your neighbour will be paid for. Or that the cheque you send to your supplier will be honoured by the bank where you have previously deposited your hard-earned cash, and that your supplier will in turn send you the goods. Goods you bought, by the way, trusting that they will live up to the quality and performance that your supplier said they would. Capitalism is built on trust, and building trust with your clients, customers and staff will future-proof your organization.

In fact, building trust is having a well-deserved renaissance in contemporary business thinking. A comprehensive 2004 study by leading market research company Yankelovich, Inc. – they coined the term *baby boomers* and have the longest continually running database on American consumer attitudes, lifestyles, and buying behaviours – found that "trust increases retention, boosts spending, enables premium pricing, and provides lasting competitive advantage".[2]

Globalization has made knowledge and expertise pure commodities in the same way that goods and services are. In a world as fast changing as ours, no body of expertise, no matter how valuable it may seem, lasts five years, much less an entire career. And no proprietary system is immune to competitors who can cheaply acquire the information necessary to copycat you on quality and beat you on price. Trust cannot be commoditized, and neither can the ability to engage others to believe in your vision, and to inspire them to behave in a certain way.

Any product or service your company offers, any knowledge and expertise you possess, however, can be outsourced and commoditized. And it is not just about people. It is about technology as well. Legal contracts that were once the domain of lawyers charging hundreds of pounds an hour can be downloaded from the internet for £20 a piece. Health care is one of India's fastest-growing industries, and middle-class Americans are going there for their heart operations.

Let me share a personal example of how trust can ensure that your product, service and knowledge remain the favoured choice in the eyes of the marketplace. I recently had laser eye surgery. Two friends had both had it done and raved about the results. One had paid about $6,000 for his surgery at a Sydney clinic. The other had his done in Kuala Lumpur at one-fifth of the price. Both were successful, each having 20/20 vision as a result.

I decided to do a little more research. As it turns out, both places use the same equipment to perform the operation. And as someone who's had it done, let me tell you this is significant. With the exception of administering some Valium (much needed, by the way), putting in some eyedrops and placing a clamp under my eyelid (I am getting freaked out just thinking about it), the doctor basically did nothing. Oh, he did input the appropriate data into his computer based on the pre-surgery tests that I had done, which were also conducted almost entirely by machine.

Furthermore, both surgeons had trained in exactly the same place: Australia. I was heading to KL in a couple of weeks anyway, so it was a simple choice. Did I want to pay $1,200 or $6,000?

I paid the $6,000, and would do it again in a heartbeat. Why? I met the Sydney-area surgeon before deciding to have him do the operation. I even quizzed him on the Malaysia option.

"Pete, I care," he replied, "because my livelihood depends on it. If something happens to you, in addition to my feeling awful about that, my business would suffer a blow that it would struggle to recover from. If something went wrong, the media would be all over it. Do you think the surgeon in Malaysia has that much on the line when he operates on you? Who would you trust with your sight? Me, who lives and works in the same neighbourhood as you and your wife, or someone who lives many thousands of miles away?"

Sold! Why? Because like everyone else in the world, I want to do business with people I know, like and trust, and whom I can rely on for help in the future.

Recall my friend the Plexiglas manufacturer who was struggling with Chinese imports. He eventually sidestepped those imports, and avoided having his business torpedoed by them, through capitalizing on the relationship of trust and confidence that he had built up with his customers. They stood by him as he transitioned his business to concentrate on doing the most profitable special orders and one-of-a-kind displays, rather than fight a losing battle to keep a sustainable share of bulk-order displays. Special orders and one-of-a-kind displays require a deep understanding of the client's business and customer base. You can't outsource that! This does not mean that "Business Is Personal" negates the need to be fast, good and cheap (at the price). As a partner in a law firm said to me recently, his long-term clients were increasingly demanding that he meet the price of his competitors.

> AT THE END OF THE DAY, IT IS PEOPLE – CUSTOMERS AND STAFF – WHO KEEP YOU IN BUSINESS. WHAT APPLIES TO YOUR RELATIONSHIP WITH CUSTOMERS APPLIES EQUALLY TO YOUR RELATIONSHIP WITH STAFF.

At the end of the day, it is people – customers and staff – who keep you in business. What applies to your relationship with customers applies equally to your relationship with staff. Both groups are looking for experiences that give their lives meaning and enhance their sense of purpose in the world. Both want to be treated with respect, and be stimulated to grow and learn. In short, people not only want to do business with, they also want to work for and with, people they know, like and trust.

STAFF AND CUSTOMERS: CO-NUMBER ONES

If there is a disconnection between how you treat staff and how you treat customers, it is going to hurt your business. I don't mean that you can't expect high performance from staff. In fact, treating staff with care and respect supports higher and higher staff performance, especially with regard to meeting customer needs and wants, a subject I'll return to at the end of the chapter.

For now, let me give you an example of how this applies in the legal fraternity, which is definitely dealing with the four forces of change. The Australian market for legal services is a mature one, with most national firms looking to Southeast Asia for new market opportunities. Building market share domestically means stealing that share from the competition. This is as opposed to the organic growth that increased the size of the market for all until recent times. A rising tide lifts all boats. But when that tide turns it's easy to get stuck in the mud.

Australia's big national law firms are now in a nasty fight for market share and profitability. They are all throwing tens of thousands of dollars at the graduate market to woo the best young lawyers, and then spending hundreds of thousands of dollars to develop them. The net result after three years, however, has been a disappointing 50 per cent employee retention rate for many of these firms.

In this regard, Australian law firms are experiencing a common global dynamic. In every category of goods and services, there is global oversupply and global underdemand. At the same time the opposite is true of skilled labour. The world-class talent required to out-innovate and out-market the competition is scarce, and the most talented and best-credentialled individuals are accordingly making demands of organizations that are rocking the foundations of the way business gets done. These circumstances put firms into a squeeze between downward pressure on fees and prices and upward pressure on wages and perks for highly skilled staff.

Recently I conducted a consulting project on recruitment and retention for one of the largest law firms in Australia. This firm has enjoyed an extremely successful commercial practice in Australia, New Zealand and Southeast Asia over the last several years. But upon receiving a prestigious award for market-leading client service, the firm's former chief executive partner said that "the client comes first", that staff "did not have a right to a personal life" and that they must all sacrifice whatever is important to them in order to meet the expectations of clients. The mainstream business media caught on to the story and wouldn't let it go.

The former chief executive partner was not trying to attack his staff. He was trying to say that the law firm's clients were number one. But his comments were not reported that way, nor were they viewed in that light by those the firm needs to recruit, the top Generation-Y graduates who, like all of their peers, are renowned for placing the balance between work and personal life at a premium in deciding which job to accept.

The firm had to start sucking up, and hard. They had to reposition themselves in the talent market, or watch their competitors get the cream of the crop of each year's law graduates. For a firm so used to getting the best of the best, nothing short of a mind-set flip would be required to keep them at the cutting edge of their market.

I advised the firm to go soft. That is, to give their potential new recruits the same world-class service they gave their clients. Or put another way, to make the attraction and recruitment experience more "personal".

Making staff co-number one with customers is a flip that many organizations resist. But if you don't have talented, creative, dedicated staff on board with your thinking and mission, you can't reach clients and customers effectively. A competitor who gives staff higher priority will get there before you.

In conjunction with the partner responsible for staff issues, I presented these ideas to a group of key partners in the firm. As you can imagine, there was some protest from the hardened senior lawyers in the room, most of them ambitious baby boomers and Gen X-ers. All of them had played by the old rules and sacrificed everything outside the job to get where they were. They expected Generation Y to do the same. "Young lawyers should be grateful to work in such a prestigious firm," was the cry. But to their credit they were able to come to terms with the new dynamic in the labour market and *flip!*

Through a series of educational sessions for the interviewing partners and changes to the way recruitment was handled, they made the process much friendlier and more personal. Although I am not at liberty to share exactly what we did, you can use your own team to come up with a strategy to personalize your recruitment process in a way that is aligned with your company's employer brand.

DO NOT TREAT STAFF IN A WAY THAT IS AT ODDS WITH THE WAY YOU TREAT CUSTOMERS.

The result for this firm was a 50 per cent increase in job-offer acceptance. This is an example of a company recognizing that business is personal for both customers and staff, and successfully managing a PR disaster at the same time as attracting more of the best and brightest job candidates. It also illustrates that in today's business world you must flip and "Think AND, Not OR". Conventional business thinking holds that it is an "either/or" world in which customers or staff can be number one, but not both. In fact, as my clients discovered, making both customers and staff number one creates a win-win situation. There's no better evidence of that than the fact that the firm won the same client-service award the following year as well.

Making sure that you do not treat staff in a way that is at odds with the way you treat customers is essential, even if you are a sole proprietor and you are the only staff your business has. The way you treat yourself will inevitably be reflected in the way you treat customers, for good or ill.

With that in mind, let's take a close look at the decisions on outsourcing and offshoring by my bank and numerous other companies throughout the world.

GETTING HIT IN THE HEAD WITH A *BRIC*, OR, GETTING OUTSOURCING RIGHT

Over the next forty years, according to projections by Goldman Sachs, the BRIC economies (Brazil, Russia, India and China) will probably become larger as a group than those of the so-called G6 (the United States, the UK, Japan, Germany, France and Italy). Most of that growth will come in the next thirty years, when China will probably surpass the United States as the world's largest economy. Of the current G6, only the US and Japanese economies will remain among the six biggest.

Many people find this prospect frightening. A study by one of Europe's leading business schools, IMD (the International Institute for Management Development in Lausanne, Switzerland), found that of 1,962 US businesses surveyed, 49 per cent believe they have lost their competitive edge to China, and a further 47 per cent believe they have lost their edge to India as well. These fears are fuelled by the undeniable growth of outsourcing from the developed to the developing world. China and India are now consolidating positions as the world's manufacturing and service-provider destinations, and former Soviet-bloc countries such as the Czech Republic are increasingly doing the back-office work for big companies in France and Germany. For example, General Electric has 48 per cent of its software development done in India, where the engineers earn on average $12,000 a year compared to $72,000 in the United States. It is estimated that salaries rose 17 per cent in India in such professions in 2006, which could quickly erode this price advantage.

Much of the anxiety in developed economies about outsourcing to developing economies betrays a poor understanding of the value chain. It is one thing to make products or do the paperwork for the world cheaply, and it is another entirely to innovate, design and sell goods and services in the world's advanced consumer markets. Own the manufacturing of a product or the back-office part of a business, and you own the links in the supply chain that are farthest away from the consumer and most easily commoditized. They are the least valuable. Own the links that are closest to the customer, however, and you own the links that represent the highest value and profitability. Thus, as Goldman Sachs also projects, per capita incomes in the United States and other currently developed economies will remain higher than those in Brazil, Russia, India and China, even after these economies have grown bigger than the G6.

Doomsayers on the threat of the BRIC economies to the developed world often cite such figures as the numbers of engineering graduates per year in different countries. In 2006, according to multiple media sources, China graduated 650,000 engineers and India graduated 500,000. By contrast, the United States graduated 70,000, Australia, 4,600 and New Zealand 1,500. Even given the vastly larger populations of China and India, this seems like a huge disparity.

But these figures, though often quoted in respected media such as *Fortune* magazine, are in fact misleading. In December 2006 researchers at Duke University reported that in the case of India only 112,000 engineers graduated with a bachelor's degree or higher, and that the higher figure publicized by India's National Association of Software and Service Companies (NASSCOM) was not only wrong but included those with less than degree-level qualifications. In the case of China the correct figure for graduating engineers was more like 350,000 than 650,000. Using the definitions that generate these numbers for India and China, the United States actually graduates as many as 137,000 engineers per year. This places it at 470 engineers per million people, compared to 270 per million in China and just 100 per million in India.

The Chinese and Indian numbers are still impressive, of course, and are growing every day. Consider that according to the UN, 8.5 million regional Chinese citizens move to urban areas every year. So, should freshly minted engineers in the United States, Australia and New Zealand be freaking out? That depends. If you're a new engineer who is betting on applying the rote engineering knowledge you learned in engineering school for the indefinite future, yes, you should be worried. If you're betting instead on a lifetime of learning and unlearning, and of leveraging relationships with valued customers and clients, you should be confident of your ability to make your way.

You might even find it very profitable to go to work in India for a time. India graduates 112,000 engineers a year, but the average quality of these engineers is so poor that Indian business and government officials fear it could be a limiting factor on India's economic growth. To find engineers who can think creatively, Indian firms are beginning to recruit aggressively in the United States and other developed countries.

It is the same if you are an accountant. The big-four accounting firms are beginning to adapt their existing "get them in young, work them hard, pay them as little as possible and charge them out at as much as possible" to the developing world. In 2006 alone, more than 360,000 US tax returns were completed in India at a value of over $40 million. That figure is projected to rise to anywhere between 1.6 million and 22 million returns by 2011. Instead of getting some young graduates in developed countries to crunch the numbers and do the basic work, they found they could get it done cheaper and to a better standard in India.

Again, should you be worried if you are an accountant? Yes, if you believe your value is the left-brain number-crunching skills that are rapidly being replaced not just by some graduate in India for one-fifth of the wage but by software that those same graduates are developing. No, if you realize your value is making your clients feel secure by minimizing their exposure to risk, and remembering the little things about their businesses. And definitely no, if you realize the value of aligning yourself strategically with those clients, building deep relationships that enable you to help them grow and develop their businesses. Skills are becoming commoditized. Relationships are not!

The trend to outsourcing the production of goods and services will continue, as well it should. There are huge cost savings to be had, and companies that do not achieve these savings will be at a disadvantage to companies that do. Successful projects orchestrated by firms such as Accenture are evidence of how powerful such outsourcing activities can be for businesses.

The biggest, most profitable companies in the world are among the most aggressive outsourcers. In the early 1990s, Jack Welch, then CEO of GE, mandated a 70/70/70 rule: 70 per cent of business processes to be outsourced, with 70 per cent going offshore and 70 per cent of that (around 30 per cent of the total) going to India. That policy has been continued by current GE CEO Jeffrey Immelt, and the company has around 13,000 employees in Delhi alone. It's no wonder that according to *CIO* magazine 73 per cent of Fortune 500 companies see outsourcing and offshoring as an important part of their strat-

OUTSOURCE KNOWLEDGE AND EXPERTISE BY ALL MEANS. BUT OWN, NURTURE, AND LEVERAGE THE FINAL LINK IN THE VALUE CHAIN, THE RELATIONSHIP WITH YOUR CUSTOMERS.

egy, and that Gartner estimates the global offshoring market in 2007 as worth around $50 billion.

But if you can achieve short-term savings from outsourcing almost anything, you can also suffer serious long-term costs from outsourcing the wrong things. The right things to outsource, depending on your business, could be manufacturing, process engineering or back-office services. The wrong things to outsource, no matter what your business, are those that touch the customer. Outsource knowledge and expertise by all means. But it is vital to own, nurture and leverage the final link in the value chain, the relationship with your customers.

Let's go back for a minute to my bank's decision to outsource their customer-service call centres to Bangalore. My client at the bank told me, "Don't worry, Pete, your call is unlikely to be answered by someone in India."

"Why not?"

"Well, if you are a low-net-worth customer, then in all honesty you are not that valuable to the bank and your calls will be answered in Bangalore. If you are a medium-net-worth customer we will have your calls answered locally, but most likely by an outsourced provider. But if you are a high-net-worth customer your call will not only be answered by a bank employee here as a priority matter, but you will also be assigned a personal representative and given their mobile phone number."

Every business needs to target its most profitable customers (although as we will discuss in Chapter 7, "To Get Control, Give It Up," the old 80/20 rule may not apply as readily today), but the risk is that some high-net-worth customers were once low-net-worth customers. If my business had not taken off before my bank moved its low-net-worth customer service overseas, I might have moved to another bank before I became a valued high-net-worth customer. Or a low-net-worth customer may actually have plenty of assets elsewhere and be giving the bank a trial run to see how they're treated.

It reminds me of the sequence in the film *Pretty Woman* where the Julia Roberts character goes shopping with credit cards given to her by Richard Gere's character. Julia's character goes into a fancy Rodeo Drive store wearing her own cheap (maybe almost non-existent would be more accurate) clothes and is treated so disdainfully by a sales assistant that she retreats in embarrassment. After getting her courage up and venturing into another shop, where she is treated better, Julia returns to the first shop, wearing beautiful new clothes and carrying bags with thousands of dollars of other purchases in them. Julia asks the sales assistant if she is paid on commission. When the sales assistant says yes, Julia holds up her overflowing shopping bags and says, "Big mistake. Huge."

That moment drew cheers from audiences when the film was first released. And it carries a powerful lesson: All customers have potential, and you'd better be very sure what you're doing before you deliberately treat some customers worse than others.

Just ask Dell Computer, which has spent millions of dollars bringing call-centre operations for North American customers back to North America. Yes, it is more expensive to operate your customer call centre in the United States than it is in Bangalore. But not as expensive as losing thousands of clients who, rightly or wrongly, do not want to deal with a staff member 25,000 kilometres away.

JPMorgan Chase, CapitalOne and IBM have done the same thing. The reason is not necessarily that the outsourced customer service was bad, although in Dell's case it certainly seems to have been, judging from the stories on websites such as crm-lowdown.com. In cases where the outsourced-to-India customer service was actually quite good, North American customers could still feel ill served and condescended to by call-centre staffers speaking English with British-inflected Indian accents. The fact is that North American customers of a company with North American operations want to speak to someone who sounds like them, like a neighbour.

The same thing is true in the UK and the rest of Europe. Citing consumer preference, the Irish arm of the Swedish telecom firm Tele2AG recently switched its call-centre operations out of India and back to Ireland. Lloyds TSB closed all its call centres in India in response to a petition signed by 400,000 customers.[3] One in three respondents in a British survey said they would stop doing business with a bank that relocated its call centres offshore. Another study reported that only 5 per cent of British customers are satisfied with offshore call centres.

If my bank genuinely had customers at the centre of all they did, they would have considered outsourcing something besides their call centres. They would have outsourced the payroll division, the risk assessment division or another back-office function that does not face and touch customers. There is no question that these, or potentially some other functions, can be adequately handled in parts of the world where labour is cheaper.

The bank could then use these cost savings to create better working conditions, increased remuneration and improved training for the staff on the front line. This would improve the bank's ability to attract higher-quality customer-service staff to their call centres (one of the major motivations for offshoring customer service in the first place), which in turn would deliver a better experience to customers. All of which would give the bank a genuine competitive boost against the other banks. After all, there is no competitive advantage to speak of in financial products themselves, which are largely the same in every bank.

That's not mere assertion. Australia's ANZ Bank has already proven it true. ANZ Bank has made customer service a prime focus and has announced a strict policy of not outsourcing or offshoring this function. ANZ does outsource, but nothing that is customer facing. They have about 1,000 employees in Bangalore, but all work in back-office and ICT roles. Customer-facing roles stay in-country.

The bank has also mounted an advertising campaign focused on service rather than product. I do not think it is coincidence that from 2002 to 2006 ANZ saw a 77 per cent rise in share price, beating their nearest rival by 15 per cent and the large-bank average by 25 per cent.

OUTSOURCE EXPERTISE, NOT RELATIONSHIPS. OR TO PUT IT DIFFERENTLY, OUTSOURCE COMPETITIVE NECESSITY, NOT COMPETITIVE ADVANTAGE.

Again, outsource expertise, not relationships. Or to put it differently, outsource competitive necessity, not competitive advantage. It is essential for large organizations to have efficient payroll operations. It is essential to have people who can crunch the numbers. These things are the price of entry, and from a customer point of view offer no real advantage over the competition. Handle them locally, outsource them, or offshore them to the moon, because they have little impact on the customer experience. But don't outsource and send beyond your daily control the part of your business that connects and interacts with the customer. The cost benefits in the short term may be good, but the impact on your brand will be far more expensive in the medium to long term.

A 2005 study by Gartner found that 60 per cent of companies that outsource customer-facing operations risk losing customers. Perhaps that is why 80 per cent of companies that outsource customer service fail to reach their cost-saving targets. The lost customers cost far more than is saved in lower operational expenditures.

In light of all these factors, let me share with you the outsourcing model for – wait for it … an outsourcing company. Syntel, which specializes in advising companies on business-process outsourcing, moved 6,000 out of 6,500 US jobs to Pune, India. But it kept the sales staff – the employees with the deepest and closest customer relationships – in the United States. I think they might be onto something here.

Making the most of your relationships with customers is hard work. Fortunately there are some new technologies that can help.

HIGH-TECH CAN BE HIGHLY PERSONAL: MINING THE POTENTIAL OF NEW COMMUNICATIONS TECHNOLOGIES

Recently I was presenting a master class for clients of CB Richard Ellis, the commercial property giant. During a break, a very senior manager of a listed property trust pulled me aside and said, "Pete, I have a problem with the whole Gen-Y thing."

"What is it?" I asked. "I thought we were making real progress with your managers."

"No. This time it is not a work thing. It is my daughter."

I was not sure I wanted to continue the conversation. But I thought I had better try. "What's the problem?"

"Last night she said she was ready for a boyfriend."

"How old is she?" I inquired.

"Fifteen."

"Were you supportive, or did you remind her that you had a gun collection?" I got a bit of a laugh.

"Of course I was supportive," he said. "I asked if she had met someone. She said no. I asked if there was someone she liked. Again she said no. Finally, I asked if there was someone she thought she would like if she got a chance to meet them. Again she said no. I was like, what's going on?

"Then she told me, "Dad! I don't need to meet them. I am just going to do a search." Some site called Facebook or something like that."

Now I understood the problem. This baby-boomer dad did not know about social-networking websites, and that Facebook is one of the most popular of them, along with MySpace. Even after I described them, he still had difficulty understanding that his daughter could take seriously a relationship she might form on some "stupid website", as he called it.

This same executive used Internet technology every day to connect and stay in touch with colleagues, suppliers, clients, friends and family via e-mail, and he regularly pulled information off websites. In fact the very same sorts of technology had completely changed the way his industry, real estate, advertises, too, and stays in touch with its clients. Despite this, he could not fathom how his daughter could use this technology to start and develop a relationship.

To him that did not seem like a real relationship. But it did to his daughter, and he needed to recognize that not only can such relationships feel real, they can have real-world consequences. In the summer of 2006 a sixteen-year-old American girl tricked her parents into getting her a passport, and then flew to the Middle East to be with a twenty-year-old guy she met on MySpace. The authorities at the airport where her plane landed convinced her to return home to her parents. In December 2006 MySpace announced that it was taking measures to protect MySpace's youngest users from sexual predators who trawl its pages looking for victims whose trust and confidence they can gain online before luring them into a real-world meeting.

FOR GENERATION Y, SOCIAL-NETWORKING SITES ARE NOT A SUBSTITUTE FOR GENUINE PERSONAL CONNECTIONS. THEY ARE INSTEAD AMONG THE BEST CURRENT MEANS OF INITIATING AND SUSTAINING GENUINE PERSONAL CONNECTIONS, EQUALLY VALID AND MEANINGFUL AS AN ENCOUNTER AT A SCHOOL DISCO OR OTHER "REAL WORLD" SOCIAL EVENT.

Facebook and MySpace are part of what has been dubbed Web 2.0. In terms of the evolution of the internet, Web 2.0 signifies the mass adoption of online collaborations and user-generated content sharing, things that have been part of the internet from its inception but that have now moved from being specialist activities to being commonplace ones, at least among Generation Y. For Generation Y, social-networking sites are not a substitute for genuine personal connections. They are instead among the best current means of initiating and sustaining genuine personal connections, equally valid and meaningful as an encounter at a school disco or other "real world" social event.

Also important in the Web 2.0 space are massively multiplayer online games such as EverQuest, World of Warcraft, and Second Life. Owned and produced by Sony, EverQuest is a sword-and-sorcery fantasy world in which groups of gamers as large as fifty to seventy individuals join to complete various quests in nearly 400 three-dimensional zones, including all sorts of geographical terrain and cityscapes. The game is so addictive that it has been called EverCrack, as in crack cocaine, and an online support group, EverQuest Widows, exists for people whose real-world relationships have been affected because of their partners' obsession with it. Lately, World of Warcraft, a similar game with some 8 million subscribers worldwide, has overtaken EverQuest in popularity, although the latter remains a hugely important product for Sony.

Although its current user population is so far only a fraction of that of EverQuest or World of Warcraft, Second Life is an even more interesting phenomenon long term. Owned and operated by Linden Lab, Second Life offers a virtual second world in which all sorts of fantasy activity can take place, but which is designed to look much more like the real world than the EverQuest-type realm. Users of Second Life create an avatar through which they can lead their second lives online, including buying and selling property, building houses and carrying on other economic activity with Linden Dollars, which can actually be exchanged for US dollars in the real world. In early 2007 $655,000 was traded on Second Life every month, and many people earn their real-world livings by designing virtual products and selling them to users who want to spruce up their avatars or their avatars' homes and businesses. The top-ten Second Life entrepreneurs have an annual average income of around $200,000. That's real money.

Multiplayer online games and social-networking sites have become arenas that stimulate creativity and offer opportunities for connection between people and organizations, including businesses and governments, in a way that is becoming an almost seamless extension of the real world. And they are doing so with no regard for geographical boundaries.

The Chicago- and later Los Angeles-based band OK Go were relatively unknown before launching a hilarious video clip on YouTube, a website where people can upload and download video for free. A single continuous shot showing the four band members dancing on eight treadmills, the "Here It Goes Again" video attracted more than 15 million viewings on YouTube and carried the band to stardom. The video was named the most creative video of 2006 on YouTube and won the 2007 Grammy Award for best short-form video.

MULTIPLAYER ONLINE GAMES AND SOCIAL-NETWORKING SITES HAVE BECOME ARENAS THAT STIMULATE CREATIVITY AND OFFER OPPORTUNITIES FOR CONNECTION BETWEEN PEOPLE AND ORGANIZATIONS, INCLUDING BUSINESSES AND GOVERNMENTS, IN A WAY THAT IS BECOMING AN ALMOST SEAMLESS EXTENSION OF THE REAL WORLD. AND THEY ARE DOING SO WITHOUT REGARD FOR GEOGRAPHICAL BOUNDARIES.

Musicians are particularly active users of MySpace, which allows them to upload up to four songs in MP3 format. Music companies in turn pay close attention to MySpace in deciding which new artists to sign. And both music and film companies use MySpace to spread the word about new releases. Given that MySpace has more than 100 million users and is currently the third-most-popular website in the United States and the sixth-most-popular in the world, it is clear that social networking has ceased to be a fringe activity and has become part of the mainstream of popular culture.

In recognition of this fact, politicians are putting their avatars on Second Life. The first woman Speaker of the House, Nancy Pelosi, made her debut in Second Life in the same week that she first brought the gavel down to open a new session of Congress. And Second Life's news bureau filed regular reports from the 2007 meeting of the World Economic Forum in Davos, Switzerland, including interviews with the avatars of attendees such as the American political commentator and blogger Arianna Huffington.

THE KEY IS NOT THAT YOU SHOULD BE IN SECOND LIFE, BUT THAT THE INTERNET AND ITS RELATED TECHNOLOGIES ARE PROVIDING NEW AND POWERFUL WAYS FOR YOU TO CONNECT WITH YOUR CUSTOMERS. BUSINESS IS PERSONAL, AND THE NEXT GENERATION OF COMMUNICATION IS A BIG PART OF BUILDING RELATIONSHIPS THAT CUSTOMERS WILL VALUE.

Some of the most intriguing uses of Second Life and other online communities are in education. Peter Yellowlees, a psychologist at the University of California, has built a practice and hospital environment on Second Life where he takes his students to help them understand what it is like to be a schizophrenic. He has created a chilling experience filled with the types of hallucinations that schizophrenics suffer. People walk through a hospital and mirrors suddenly flash "shitface" at them, or they watch a televised address by a political figure who suddenly starts screaming, "Go kill yourself, you wretch!"

After Yellowlees opened up the virtual hospital to the public on Second Life, 73 per cent of visitors said it improved their understanding of schizophrenia. Many other educational initiatives are popping up in Web 2.0, seeking to harness the immersive experience of virtual worlds in order to accelerate learning.

Harcourts, the New Zealand–founded estate agency, with offices in Australia and Southeast Asia, has set up an office in Second Life. Initially it was to display real-world property, but in time they may find they are able to list and sell Second Life property and make a commission in Linden Dollars that they can convert into real-world dollars. I also have a client in the charity sector looking at how they might be able to have avatars donate Linden Dollars to their charity, in exchange for something that shows they have engaged in philanthropic activity, which again can be converted to real dollars. One of my major banking clients is looking at how they might offer money management, investment and other informational seminars using Second Life as the venue. In June 2007 five companies – Alstom, Areva, Capgemini, L'Oréal and Unilog – held a "neo-jobs meeting" on Second Life, telling job seekers, "In the fantastic Second Life universe, join us for your first 100% virtual interview and discover 100% real positions."[4] The list could go on.

The key is not that you should be in Second Life, but that the internet and its related technologies are providing new and powerful ways for you to connect with your customers. Business is personal, and the next generation of communication is a big part of building relationships that customers will value.

In case you are still not convinced

In November 2006 Toyota launched a virtual Scion City on Second Life, where all of its Scion range can be bought and customized with Linden Dollars. Other companies that have a presence on Second Life include Adidas, Sears and Sun Microsystems. Dutch banking giant ABN Amro has set up a financial consultancy on Second Life. The value of this activity for the companies is twofold. On the one hand it helps stimulate some business in the real world. But more important is that it puts the companies in touch with the leading edge of consumer trends.

Likewise the cleverly crafted MySpace profiles of Wendy's and Burger King each have over 100,000 registered friends, who post suggestions for new meals and funny stories about their experiences at the fast-food chains. They also sometimes post hateful vitriol, which the companies leave untouched. Toyota, Microsoft, Ernst & Young, Apple and EA Games are among the large brands to get actively involved with similar personal/business branding exercises in Facebook, the largest student community site in the world. The CIA has even begun to recruit prospects on Facebook!

Companies, organizations and governments are paying serious attention to developments in online communities because
of hard demographic facts:

- According to the Pew Research Center, 87 per cent of
  US teens are now regular internet users, and *more than
  50 per cent* are daily users.
- Over 81 per cent play games online and almost half
  make purchases.
- With a combined purchasing power of around $139
  billion a year (according to market research firm Harris
  Interactive) and even greater influence over others'
  purchasing decisions, they're not just playing Pac-Man
  any more!

This kind of technology use is clearly not just a fad. It is also no
longer a small enough niche to ignore. In fact, it's large and
powerful enough to warrant serious attention and to be uti-
lized as an extremely powerful new forum for building relationships and brands. But it doesn't have to be massively serious
relationships, nor does the use of technology have to be cutting
edge. What this section is talking about is using the lessons
from high-tech-can-be-highly-personal, and having the courage to apply them to your world.

A car service centre could use it (and some do) very effectively. When a customer's car is due for a service, they can send
a gentle reminder and enable the customer to book any available time slot via text message, and after the service work is
done they can send another text message to let the customer
know the car is ready. This is such a simple, unobtrusive and

useful application of very cheap technology. It simultaneously enhances the customer experience and streamlines the company's operations, making them more profitable.

Or look at other uses of technology to streamline a highly personalized life. The LG internet refrigerator is designed so it can order your groceries through an online grocery gateway. It is also a music player and PDA. The DIVA (among other) air conditioners can be activated via an "I'm on my way home" text message.

First Direct, the online banking subsidiary of HSBC in the UK, sends a text message to its customers when they are approaching their credit limits to save them embarrassment when they try to make a purchase they can't afford, and also to spare them unwanted overdraft fees. In early 2007 the bank estimated that the text-message programme had saved customers around £32 million in overdraft fees.[5] The programme has proven so popular that other banks in the UK, such as Nationwide, have begun to follow suit.

Or you could get slightly more sophisticated in your use of technology in building relationships in the way Amazon.com does. It remembers not only what you have purchased, but what other people who have bought things that you have purchased have purchased, and then makes recommendations that are often very useful of other things you may find interesting. There is no human involved, yet you feel valued and as though the site understands you. At the end of the day, as long as people feel it is relevant and personal, they are happy to listen to your message. This is what Seth Godin discussed in *Permission Marketing,* and also may help explain why a survey of 500 mobile phone users by London PR firm Rainier PR found that 74 per cent of users were happy to receive short-range, location-specific promotional information via technologies such as Bluetooth.

The list of companies that have employed technology in really cool ways to stay in close relationship is getting longer every day, but is still nowhere near as long as it should be. Wireless technology is now allowing personalization based on where you are and what you are doing like never before.

Companies also are now employing high-tech means to empower traditional relationship-building exercises. That is, rather than completely change their marketing to adopt high-tech measures, they are using some new technology in conjunction with their old campaigns. For instance, McDonald's has introduced web access to some of its larger urban restaurants where some clientele (often travellers) want to eat and check their e-mail. Their restaurants and advertising message remain unchanged, but the technology is placed on top. Procter & Gamble tied an extensive print and broadcast campaign for Dove soap to an interactive campaign in Times Square where people could vote in real time for the images they found most attractive.

An Australian example of using technology to connect is United International Pictures' partnering with a number of interactive marketing and technology companies to launch *Mission: Impossible III*. Nearly 10,000 people registered online to use their mobile phones to participate in a huge, citywide

WIRELESS TECHNOLOGY IS NOW ALLOWING PERSONALIZATION BASED ON WHERE YOU ARE AND WHAT YOU ARE DOING LIKE NEVER BEFORE.

puzzle game with clues delivered by text message and "hypertag" technology embedded in bus shelters and signs. This was a far better way than thirty-second television ads to attract a large number of committed fans who would swell opening weekend ticket sales for *MI3* and create an all-important buzz about the movie.[6]

As these examples show, relatively simple interactivity can increase customer participation massively and hence the feeling of a reciprocated relationship with your brand. Not delivering the kind of customer service people expect today is all the more shortsighted when you consider how simple and cost-effective it can be to interact with customers through new technology. Reconnect with one of the governing flips of this book. "Think AND, Not OR", and recognize that high tech can indeed be highly personal.

And for Pete's sake (pardon the pun), start engaging in a dialogue with your marketplace, whether through technology-enabled means or not, instead of talking at them all the time. Monologues are soooooo yesterday!

Finally, if you think social networking is just for people with too much time on their hands, consider that IBM has appointed a vice president for social software. On 24 January 2007, the holder of that new position, Jeff Schick, announced that IBM's Lotus Connections would use text message, blogging, personal profiles and so on to empower employees to

DON'T MAKE TECHNOLOGY YOUR OBSESSION. MAKE CONNECTING WITH CUSTOMERS AND STAFF YOUR OBSESSION. IF TECHNOLOGY HELPS YOU DO THIS, AND IT CAN, THEN USE IT.

establish virtual worlds for mutual brainstorming. This new software – exactly the same thing as teenagers, college students, and others use on MySpace, Facebook and Second Life – will be used within IBM and sold to other companies. IBM's prototype for Lotus Connections contains 450,000 profiles. As Schick put it, IBM believes Lotus Connections will "unlock the latent expertise in an organization". It will do so by making that expertise relational.[7]

(I'll have more to say about business uses of social-neworking software in Chapter 7, "To Get Control, Give It Up".)

In closing this section on high-tech-is-highly-personal, let me say emphatically that *it is not about the technology*. It is about connecting with the customers. Despite what you read about younger consumers, it is not really about the technology for them either. They, and increasingly the broader market, just use technology as their means to connect. *Don't* make technology your obsession – make connecting with your customers and staff your obsession. If technology helps you do this, then use it.

THE REBIRTH OF THE MIDDLEMAN

This chapter's tour of the new relationship technologies would not be complete without a brief look at one of the most interesting business developments in recent years, the rebirth of the middleman. Way back in the late 1990s – doesn't that seem like a long time ago already? – many people predicted that the internet would bring the end of the middleman. No longer would consumers need any intermediaries between them and product or service providers, the argument went. The internet would provide direct connections for everything from A to Z.

And so it did. But in multiplying the connections between customers and a whole world of suppliers it also re-established the value of intermediaries that could sift through all the offerings and sort them in a variety of ways. I say "that" advisedly, rather than "who", because the new middleman may just as well be a technology as a person or a firm.

The most successful sites in the world are in fact middlemen. With the exception perhaps of Amazon.com, the most visited sites are those that connect the supplier to the customer, such as eBay, or people to people in the case of MySpace, or people to content as in the case of Wikipedia and YouTube. Google is no different. As the old saying goes: "When everyone is panning for gold, sell pans."

It is not just about the internet, though. It is about services – be they personal or technologically driven – that help us to sift through the clutter. The phenomenal growth of mortgage brokers around the world is a very good example of what I am talking about.

The home-loan market is becoming increasingly competitive with consumers spoiled for choice, at least ostensibly. However, the variety of sources of home loans, the complexity of comparing them and also the fact that it has to happen in your own time have led to a reintroduction of the importance of the middleman. Mortgage brokers are as a result becoming increasingly popular. In the United States, for instance, mortgage brokers handle more than 80 per cent of home loans.

In fact, the more these places distance themselves from the people who are providing the loans, the more popular they become. In Australia the biggest mortgage broker is Mortgage Choice, which, in the last financial year, boasted a record after-tax profit of $13 million and generated $9.3 billion in housing-loan approvals.

Key to the Mortgage Choice brand story is that they have no stake in which lender provides the mortgage to the home buyer. Their brokers receive the same commission no matter which mortgage you choose, so that effectively they work for you, not the banks. The customer appeal of this brand story is manifest in the steep positive growth of Mortgage Choice's revenues and bottom-line profit.

Companies like Mortgage Choice and eBay demonstrate that there is a business model in just owning the relationship, and not actually selling anything. In the example of Skype in Chapter 3, "Fast, Good, Cheap: Pick Three – Then Add Something Extra", I talked about eBay buying Skype for $2.6 billion. Might I be so bold as to suggest that what made Skype so valuable was in fact their relationships, not their business model, which could easily be duplicated. Although Skype did not yet have profits, it did have a large and growing base of loyal users, and as I mentioned earlier, eBay was making significant progress in monetizing the value of that customer base within a year after buying the company.

> AS THE KNOWLEDGE AND INFORMATION AGE EVOLVES INTO THE RELATIONSHIP ERA, THE ULTIMATE MIDDLEMEN BECOME THOSE WHO CONNECT US TO VALUABLE INFORMATION.

Product review sites are another increasingly popular form of middleman. Sites such as zdnet.com and cnet.com in information technology and consumer electronics – there are similar sites in other product and service categories – have become trusted partners in customers' purchasing. In the same space there are pure price-shopping assistants such as bizrate.com, pricegrabber.com, nextag.com and Google's Froogle. Once you have found exactly which product you want to buy with the help of a review site, you can instantly find out who has it cheapest. Not only that, you can also often see whether a vendor has been found reliable by other shoppers. These sites continue to grow in popularity as people look for advice from people they feel they can trust, rather than people they think are simply trying to sell them something. Again, people want to do business with and take advice from people they know, like and trust.

As the knowledge and information age evolves into the relationship era, the ultimate middlemen become those who connect us to valuable information and people. The internet is full of so much garbage, the middleman has become essential. This is why some of the most valuable property on the net is Google. With a market capitalization of more than $155 billion and with 380 *million* unique users every month, Google is the middleman to end all middlemen. The market has become so oversupplied that being a "trusted adviser", even if it is only in the form of an algorithm, is a very powerful proposition.

Although I have used behemoth brands such as Google to make the point, there is nothing to disqualify local businesses from servicing their markets better than global ones can. In countries like South Korea local search engines have been more popular than Google because customers consider the results to be more relevant. Relevance is key in a world where time and mental energy are scarce resources.

The point here is simple: from the customer's perspective, increasing complexity and the proliferation of choice (partially fuelled by companies mistaking "choice" for "customer service"), in an environment suffering rapid compression of time, have made middlemen attractive again. From the corporate perspective, this could be an excellent opportunity to see if your services can be construed as making you a "middleman". Do you solve complex problems? Do you get people the information or service they need? Are you *saving* them time, or *costing* them time?

Reframing questions about the services and products you provide in this way can help you clarify your position and role, and also may give you great ideas for changes you could make.

TALENT WANTS TO BE "PERSONALLY" CONNECTED TO THE COMPANIES THEY WORK FOR AND THE PEOPLE THEY WORK WITH

You need great people if you want your business to be truly competitive, not just in terms of building relationships with clients, but in terms of being the most innovative, telling the best stories, and having the courage to take the most action. In the talent-scarce environment that we are operating in, this requires a well-thought-out and coordinated campaign to promote your employment brand to attract the best talent. Although building the employer brand is not the subject of this book, I am interested more broadly in what makes a workplace attractive to great talent and how it develops and retains the talent it already employs.

I believe there are two key things that both attract and retain great talent:

1. The work you do
2. The relationships you build with your people

This may seem a little simplified, but it is not. I deliberately leave out things like money and benefits because, as with

"Fast, Good, Cheap: Pick Three – Then Add Something Extra", these are the price of entry. At the end of the day, all other things being equal, people stay at jobs because they like doing quality work and because they like the people they work with.

The quality of the work includes several things. It is about whether people find the work interesting, but it is also about whether the work challenges them and forces them to grow. My attention is obviously going to be on number two, again making my point that business is personal. But before I go on, let me just say that if your organization was a flipstar business, the work would rock. How could it not?

To the point: your ability to acquire, develop and retain the best talent is directly proportional to the quality of the relationship you build with that talent.

Every client I have tells me, "Our people are our greatest asset." They mean it, but most of the time they don't know how to show it. All of my work in companies to date on generational change and workforce trends suggests that this will be one of the most important strategic issues for companies over the coming years.

RELATIONSHIPS ARE SIMPLE, BUT NOT EASY

To finish the chapter, here are five keys to building great relationships so you can profit from a world where people think business is very personal.

Shift your mind-set

Relationships are only as good as you think they are. An insightful study published in the *Journal of Experimental Social*

Psychology found that the single most important factor in determining whether or not a marriage was happy was *not* understanding, sex, love, kids or anything like that; it was whether spouses rated their partners as better or worse than they rated themselves. Couples where each partner rated the other person higher on a list of qualities were happiest.

Relationships work only if you think they can work, and if you think they are worth investing in, because only then will you put in the appropriate effort to ensure they are a success. In other words, relationships are a self-fulfilling prophecy.

Ensure competence

Competence is fundamental to striking up a quality relationship. Simply put, if you are no good at what you do, no one will want to be your friend. To understand what is required to meet basic expectations of competence, think back to Chapter 3, "Fast, Good, Cheap: Pick Three – Then Add Something Extra".

Deliver on what you promise

Once you are comfortable with what you offer, make sure you don't overstretch on what you promise. The only thing worse than a bad job is a bad job that you thought was going to be fantastic. If you can't meet an expectation, be honest with the customer. Don't be like the handyman who came to our house, gave my wife a quote to fix our stairs, and told us when he would be back to do the work, but then never showed up.

Build trust

In many ways, building trust in a relationship is contingent on the three steps above (having the right mind-set, doing a good job and delivering on what you promise), but trust is also established independently of the above. Medical researcher Wendy Levinson found that doctors with good patient relationships were less likely to be sued, *even when they did things wrong*.[8] Patients who trusted their doctors believed they had their best interests at heart. The way patients judged whether their doctors had their best interests at heart were very simple things like:

- Did they "sound" interested
- How "long" they spent in consultation
- How intently they "listened"
- The "tone" of voice

I would like to make the point here that not getting sued and getting return business are different prospects altogether. I may not sue a doctor who misdiagnosed me, but I doubt I will ever go back. So again, competence is still a *huge* part of this equation.

Have good manners

People might think this sounds simple. If that's the case, why is it that websites like crmlowdown.com are *filled* with examples of straight-out rude customer service? And why is it that I can issue you an airtight, money-back guarantee that every single person reading this book can give an example of when they have been treated appallingly by a company? Ensuring that people on your front line (and yes, this includes *you*) treat customers with respect and courtesy (and actually go the extra mile in helping them solve their problems) might seem obvious, but I will talk about it until it actually starts happening!

Consider the following. After buying an expensive phone from a Vodafone store (a brand to which I have been loyal for ten years), I was thrilled to learn that their generous warranty period covered full replacement of my new handset after failure for – wait for it – *two weeks*.

Well, my phone did break (*three* weeks after I bought it), and given that I was about to head out on a five-city business trip to the United States I really needed a functioning phone. So I took it back to the shop hoping they could help me out. After I spent an hour dealing with three different and equally unhelpful people, not only did it become clear that they could not repair the phone in the two weeks before I left for the United States, but I was told that if I wanted a temporary replacement phone I was going to have to pay $100.

They certainly acted as though they didn't value my business and didn't want to help. If this is how you feel, then get out of business! Fast!

The unfortunate thing for Vodafone is that they do not own this shop. It is a franchise, but it still bears their logo. This is outsourcing the relationship you have with the customer. And to make it worse they did not make the phone either. But hey, my relationship was not with the phone manufacturer, it was with Vodafone.

FIVE THINGS TO DO NOW

1. Get a group of key customers in a room and ask them whether they believe your company goes out of its way to build quality relationships with them. Do the same with a group of suppliers, too.

2. Run a focus group with employees and find out whether they think you are a staff-focused organization. Be prepared to do something with the feedback you get.

3. List three new technologies you are going to explore that could be valuable tools to help you stay in touch with existing customers and staff. Might I suggest you start with text messaging, blogs, and podcasts. Then, just for fun, start a personal MySpace profile and visit Second Life and start playing around in these new spaces. Who knows, you might enjoy it.

4. Start one initiative that centres around reconnecting with customers you have lost touch with.

5. Do an audit of your systems and processes and ask if they have positive, neutral or negative effects on your relationships with customers. Ask yourself for each policy, is it helping you or the customer?

MASS-MARKET SUCCESS:
FIND IT ON THE FRINGE

"Generation Y is too small, Pete. No one is asking for it."

This was the response I got from the managing director of one of Australia's leading speakers' bureaux when I introduced her to my area of expertise. I didn't think she was right. So I ignored the advice, and thereby laid the foundations of a profitable consulting business.

"This is every organization's number one problem!" I exclaimed. "They just don't have a label for it yet."

If you do what everyone else is doing and you draw your wisdom from the crowd, you will find yourself just another supplier of the same product, service or skill set. Go your own way. Invent a new wheel. Cirque du Soleil did. The Apple iPod did. Burton Snowboards did.

Let's go back for a minute to one of the dominant parameters in today's business world: global oversupply, and global underdemand, in every category of goods and services. In these circumstances you can putter along doing what everyone else is doing, and if you're more or less industry standard in your offerings and practices you'll probably do OK. But if you want to

"WHEN YOU FIND YOURSELF ON THE SIDE OF THE MAJORITY, IT'S TIME TO REFORM." – MARK TWAIN

stand out from the crowd you have to differentiate yourself in one of two ways. You can either differentiate your approach to an existing market, or you can differentiate the market you're operating in by dis-

covering or creating a new market. If you want to be a flipstar, you've got to zig when all your competitors zag (kill me if I use another cliché).

This is not to deny that there is a kind of wisdom in crowds. "The wisdom of crowds" has become a popular notion lately, as studies have shown that patterns of behaviour among large groups of people can be self-organizing in an optimal way. For example, pedestrian traffic on a crowded street will naturally flow in the most efficient way possible, and the stock-market picks of millions of investors determine very accurate share values over time. Likewise, large groups of people responding instinctively to various options can reveal the best product among competing alternatives and give important clues to emerging trends. This is the kind of risk-averse, largely unconscious wisdom that James Surowiecki, the "Financial Page" columnist of the *New Yorker* magazine, celebrates in his recent book called *The Wisdom of Crowds*. (I'll be talking about some of the same phenomena from my own perspective a little later in this book in Chapter 7, "To Get Control, Give It Up".)

Notice, however, that crowds do not make something new

on their own. Crowds don't create innovations, they validate them. In a global marketplace the crowd will recognize and celebrate the best innovations. But those innovations don't come from the centre of the crowd. They come from the fringe, from bold companies and individuals who are willing to risk doing something different from

YOU CAN EITHER DIFFERENTI-ATE YOUR APPROACH TO AN EXISTING MARKET, OR YOU CAN DIFFERENTIATE THE MARKET YOU'RE OPERATING IN BY DISCOVERING OR CREAT-ING A NEW MARKET.

what competitors are doing, and to offer something different from what the crowds are currently embracing.

Let me put it another way. Crowds are where the big profits are, no question. You don't make money with unpopular goods and services. But market-changing and market-making products don't come from a crowd. They cannot be designed and developed by committee to the crowd's existing

CROWDS DON'T CREATE INNOVATIONS, THEY VALIDATE THEM.

specifications. Market-changing and market-making products like the iPod, ING Direct, Progressive Car Insurance, Cirque du Soleil, Starbucks, Virgin Blue or Callaway Golf's oversize Big Bertha drivers spring from the minds of maverick companies and individuals who have the guts to gamble on attracting the crowds that will eventually validate them.

One thing crowds are definitely wise about is in telling whether something is a true innovation or a tarted-up version of the same old thing. Crowds have a nose for things that are really new and exciting. The best way to differentiate your offerings from the competition is therefore always to take the route least travelled. *Flips* are the way to locate those routes, and speed from the fringe to the mainstream. Or, to adopt some language from Kim and Mauborgne's insightful book *Blue Ocean Strategy,* flips are the course to adopt to discover entirely new markets – blue oceans – and leave behind mature, overcrowded markets – red oceans.

FROM THE FRINGE TO THE CENTRE

Say you're looking at the iPod and thinking, *If we come up with a better MP3 player with a better link to the home computer, the internet and the home-entertainment system we can take the iPod's place.* Even if you could do it right away you are probably still too late. With sayings like "iPod therefore I am" being bandied about, you are likely to get slaughtered. In reality it will take any organization a while (Samsung, Sandisk and others are trying), which may actually mean that by the time you have built a better MP3 player the world may well have left MP3 players behind in favour of a totally new way of getting, carrying and enjoying music, pictures and other things.

When Apple introduced the iPod in 2001, the MP3 market was still a blue ocean, despite the presence of a number of MP3-player manufacturers, because no one had yet created a total customer solution for managing digital entertainment. The market is a red ocean now – red with the blood of Apple's shark-bitten rivals, you might say – thanks to the iPod–iTunes combination. It will take an entirely new blue-ocean strategy to supplant the iPod with something else.

The market-changing power of the iPod is manifest not only in its huge sales, but in Apple's decision to change its name and start trading as Apple, Inc, rather than as Apple Computer, Inc. In 2007 Apple extended the iPod line with the iPhone, a combination of a wide-screen iPod with a mobile phone, a camera, and a wireless touch-screen internet communicator for web-browsing, e-mail and text messaging.

The last feature led a friend of mine to say, "Hey, now might be a good time to short shares in RIM," the makers of the BlackBerry. I don't think so. As initial sales showed, the iPhone is unlikely to be a BlackBerry killer, as long as the only way to input text is via a clumsy virtual keyboard on the iPhone's touch screen.

But that doesn't make me any less excited about Apple's phone. The iPhone is not a short-term threat to the BlackBerry as a business device, because that's not what the iPhone is trying to be. Instead the iPhone is the culmination to date of Apple's efforts to make the iPod the first "infotainment" device, a multipurpose gadget for talking to friends, listening to music, looking at video and still pictures, and surfing the web, all with the characteristic ease and simplicity of the Apple interface. It marks a journey from the one-time fringe of MP3 players to the centre of consumer culture.

The iPhone's initial price showed that Apple does not worry about hitting the centre of the mass market when it launches a product. Instead it uses what I call market gravity, which Apple has steadily acquired over its innovative history, to pull the market to its new products and their unusual mix of appealing design and seamless functionality. At $499 or $599, for four or eight gigabytes of storage respectively, the iPhone was priced well above the mass market in mobile phones in the United

ACTING ON THE FRINGE AND
TAKING A RISK WILL ALWAYS
FEEL UNCOMFORTABLE. IN
FACT ALL OF THE FLIPS WILL.
THEY ARE COUNTERINTUI-
TIVE AND CAN CREATE A
SENSE OF FEAR (I WOULD
RATHER THINK OF IT AS
EXCITEMENT).

States, just as the original iPod was priced well above other MP3 players. Obviously this shows Apple's love of fat profit margins, but it also shows its confidence that launching the iPhone on the fringe of affordability, so to speak, would help fuel the product's long-term popularity. And again, just as it did with the iPod, Apple lowered the price of the iPhone in due course, but still maintained a price premium over competitors.

Acting on the fringe and taking a risk like this will always feel uncomfortable. In fact all of the flips will. They are counterintuitive and can create a sense of fear (I would rather think of it as excitement). It takes guts to take action without a fully formed plan or a sense of certainty about your success. It takes guts to invest heavily in becoming fast, good and cheap. It takes more guts to get to the heart of who you are and to yell that story from the rooftops as you build a total ownership experience. It takes even more guts to know who you are and not yell it from the rooftops, allowing people to discover you. And it takes guts to venture from the known, from the crowd. This is why it is a *flip*. But even if the iPhone had not taken off, Apple would have learned from the process. That is why Apple is, well, Apple!

The benefits of shuttling between the fringe and the mainstream show up plainly in Apple's bottom line. In the final quarter of 2006 Apple reported a 78 per cent increase in profit to $1 billion on sales of $7.1 billion. During those three months the company sold 21 million iPods, an increase of 50 per cent over the same period a year before. It also sold 1.6 million computers, an increase of 28 per cent over the same period a year before, showing how the iPod cast a halo of enhanced desirability over the entire Apple range. As Apple CFO Peter Oppenheimer said, "This one was for the record books."

Apple would never have boosted its bottom line so much without making big, bold bets. In a study of new product launches by 108 companies, 86 per cent of the "new" products were actually line extensions and they accounted for only 39 per cent of total profits. The 14 per cent of remaining launches that involved genuinely new products accounted for 61 per cent of total profits.[1]

Toyota took the route less travelled by making an early bet on bringing a mass-production hybrid-engine vehicle to market with the Prius. Now it's leveraging the success of the Prius throughout the Toyota and Lexus product range. Making the part-electric and part-internal-combustion-powered Prius hatchback a viable mass-market product is one of Toyota's most notable achievements. All the major manufacturers had developed some form of hybrid technology. But General Motors and Ford, despite losing dominance to Toyota in almost all categories, sat on that technology and did nothing. Toyota, already winning the game, took action to change the game in a way that could have backfired.

Some may argue they didn't need to do this, as they were already dominating the market. Well, that's why they were dominating. They were prepared to innovate. To try new things. To challenge the conventional paradigm that "if it's not broken, don't

TODAY'S BEST PRACTICE IS TOMORROW'S BAD PRACTICE.

fix it". Toyota has not only positioned itself favourably in an increasingly "green" developed market, but sales of the Prius have been so successful that the company cannot meet demand in many countries, with waiting lists up to nine months in some.

The Prius's sales are limited to some extent by the greater up-front cost to the consumer of hybrid technology. Toyota has accordingly extended hybrid technology from the volume-car business to their luxury line, Lexus, whose affluent purchasers will find the additional cost less significant. The strategy doesn't depend primarily on the performance of the car, however, but on its appeal to a segment of affluent purchasers who want to be seen as "green".

In March 2007 the Prius sold almost 20,000 units in the United States, a 133 per cent increase from the previous year, and the competition is feeling the pinch. Toyota experienced an 8 per cent rise in demand for its hybrids last year, at the same time as GM felt an 8 per cent drop in demand for their cars. On Wall Street, Toyota's stock price rose 38 per cent and GM's fell 20 per cent.

Many attribute Toyota's pioneering foray into hybrids to rising oil prices and growing concern over global warming. The truth is, however, that Toyota had moved far ahead of the crowd long before these issues took centre stage as they have in the last couple of years.

Perhaps the biggest hybrid-related flip on Toyota's part is that instead of trying to keep a proprietary lock on their technology they are licensing it to all comers, creating a new income stream for technology that is already ten years old. The companies that are buying this technology will probably achieve Toyota's 2007 "best practice" only in 2010 or 2017. Current business advice is to benchmark your efforts against winning companies' best practices. But the flip is that today's best practice is tomorrow's bad practice. In ten years' time there will be much better ways to build a "green" automobile, and Toyota's competitors should be racing it to that new benchmark, not plodding along in Toyota's footsteps. (More on this in Chapter 7, "To Get Control, Give It Up".)

What is your company's or industry's version of the Prius? Are you doing enough to develop this potential new market opportunity?

Again, Toyota was the first to identify and act on the mass-market potential in the fringe custom-car culture. As I discussed earlier, Toyota scored an instant hit with the Scion and then demonstrated its ability to flip perspective by deciding to limit production, selling many fewer Scions over the short term than it could, in order to protect its hip, edgy brand story over the long term. Toyota knows exactly how to sell to the masses without losing the fringe characteristics that spell innovation in the marketplace.

When Toyota was developing the Scion, the other car companies' marketing research – they all spend millions of dollars a year on trend spotting and consumer surveys – undoubtedly told them that customizing small cars was a growing phenomenon among young urban customers. But only Toyota had the guts to bet that what was still a fringe activity could generate a high enough volume of sales to support an entire new range of vehicles like the Scion.

After the Scion scored a huge hit with young customers, Honda and Nissan rushed out copycat vehicles, but they had missed the chance to establish themselves as cutting-edge brands for Generation Y. The Detroit three were even further behind the curve. Toyota performed a similar market-changing flip from the fringe into the mainstream with the Prius.

More recently, other carmakers are trailing Toyota down the electricity–petrol hybrid path. Not BMW. The most successful of the European car brands over the last decade, BMW is going against the grain of the hybrid-engine technology Toyota has popularized and is instead developing hydrogen-powered cars.

Like Toyota, BMW took serious alternative-energy action long before it was cool to do so. First demonstrated at Expo 2000, the BMW 750hL is the culmination of three decades of research into hydrogen-powered vehicles. BMW sees the use of hydrogen as the answer to many environmental problems, since there are no harmful emissions, no depleting of resources and no danger to the atmosphere.

The heart of the 750hL is a hybrid, twelve-cylinder combustion engine with two independent electronically controlled fuel-induction systems. These systems allow the 750hL to run on either petrol or hydrogen. Now, before you get too cynical about this high-priced twelve-cylinder beast, BMW has also developed a Mini Cooper using the same BMW clean energy system.

Working with Shell Oil Company, BMW has developed a technology for dispensing hydrogen from a petrol station's pumps into a car's fuel tanks. The world's first fully automatic hydrogen filling station was opened in May 1999 at the Munich Airport.[2]

My hat is off to both Toyota and BMW – and Honda has been aggressively developing similar technologies, too – for investing long before the market demanded that they do. Markets may be efficient, but in this case they would not have driven innovation soon enough.

Or consider the snowboard. In 1966 an American entrepreneur named Sherman Poppen bolted two pairs of children's skis together to make a stand-up sledge for his daughter. As soon as they saw it, all the neighbouring kids wanted one. Mrs. Poppen combined "snow" with "surfer" and dubbed the contraption the Snurfer. The Poppens licensed it to the Brunswick Company, a sporting-goods manufacturer, which sold more than a million Snurfers through sporting-goods, toy, and department stores.

The Snurfer was a toy that couldn't be used on more than a gentle hill. But in the mid to late 1970s, a handful of entrepreneurs who had been exposed to it as teenagers began trying to develop what became the snowboard. One of the handful was Jake Burton, who in 1977 began shaping snowboards in a barn in Vermont and selling them out of the back of his Volvo.

The proto-market seeded by the Snurfer kept Burton's business alive, but snowboarding remained an underground sport confined to sledging hills. It took five years of lobbying on Burton's part before the first ski resort, Suicide Six Resort in Vermont, opened its slopes to snowboards. Throughout the 1980s and early 1990s snowboarders struggled to reverse bans against them at major skiing areas.

By the mid-1990s ski-resort operators were finally waking up to the flip: snowboarding didn't threaten their businesses, it brought a populous new, young demographic to their facilities, an infusion of fresh blood that they desperately needed.

IS YOUR COMPANY AS ACTIVE A MEMBER AND PROPONENT FOR ITS MARKETPLACE AS JAKE BURTON IS FOR SNOWBOARDING? IF NOT, HOW COULD YOU BECOME AN AUTHENTIC PLAYER IN THAT COMMUNITY?

Snowboards appealed to young people who loved surfing and skateboarding, cost a lot less than skis, and were much easier to learn to use. As the snowboard express gathered speed, ESPN mounted the first Winter X Games in 1997, scoring big ratings, and in 1998 snowboarding competition came to the Winter Olympics, where it has become as high profile as alpine skiing and figure skating.

Today snowboards and related products are a $3-billion-a-year industry that continues to grow by leaps and bounds. And at the centre of it all, reaping a substantial per centage of the business, stands Jake Burton, whose entrepreneurial portfolio includes both snowboard equipment and clothing companies.

Is your company as active a member and proponent for its marketplace as Jake Burton is for snowboarding? If not, how could you start to be an authentic player in that community?

For a digital example of the success of a product that started on the fringe and went mainstream, consider Stephen Cakebread, who designs games for the Xbox. While the rest of the market was looking for the next Doom, Halo or Project Gotham Racing, he pioneered the online download of small, retro-styled games for consoles. Ironically, his most successful release is Geometry Wars: Retro Evolved, which began while he was working for Bizarre Creations on the hit game Project Gotham Racing. With more than 200,000 trial versions downloaded, and 45,000 paid downloads, this is impressive for a game that took one person less than three months to write as a hobby.

Although these numbers are dwarfed by the sales of "on disk" games, including the disk version of Project Gotham Racing, what Cakebread has started with downloadable games for consoles seems to be the next big trend. Downloadable gaming as an idea is not new. Publishers small and large have been developing and distributing small games over the PC for years via services from Yahoo and Real Networks with great success. But offering downloadable games on a console through things like Xbox Live Arcade is new.

Wired magazine has reported that from 2004 to 2005, console disk sales in the United States dropped by $700 million, according to market research firm NPD Group. Meanwhile, game companies earned $143 million from online console gaming in 2005, a figure JupiterResearch predicts will grow to $2 billion domestically by 2011.

Take this old-is-new-again style of gaming, couple it with the power of new technology to create new results (think back to complexity as a force of change), and you have a new trend starting on the fringe and heading to the mainstream.[3]

On the topic of console gaming, a really cool innovation from Nintendo has taken the market by storm. While Sony and Microsoft battle it out for supremacy with the hard-core gaming community, Nintendo's Wii is proving to be a huge hit with a target demographic of families and females. If that is not a departure from the gaming crowd, I don't know what is. Most notable is the use of the one-handed controller, about the size of a TV remote, with motion sensors that allow the gamer to use body movements rather than a joystick and half a dozen buttons.

It is so simple that grandparents can do it. In early 2007 many of my clients were talking about how fun it was to play Wii over Christmas with their kids and actually be competitive. I think some of them are even a little addicted. It helps that the Wii landed at half the price of the PlayStation 3, which was released around the same time (a good example of "Fast, Good, Cheap: Pick Three – Then Add Something Extra").

This "simple and easy to use" strategy has also fuelled the phenomenal success of Nintendo's handheld gaming device, the Nintendo DS. The DS has a touch-screen function that allows users to navigate menus with a stylus rather than a kepad. Sales of the DS in 2007 are likely to hit 20 million.

The bottom-line impact is compelling. In the nine months following the release of the Nintendo DS in January 2006 and in anticipation of the release of the Wii, Nintendo's share price jumped 71 per cent. And these investors' hopes have been more than met. The Wii became the fastest-selling console in history, selling more than 600,000 in the first eight days following its release. As a comparison, Sony's PS3 sold around 200,000 units.

In the year ending 31 March 2007, Nintendo increased its revenue and profit forecasts three times. In advance of final results for the year, Nintendo said it expected an operating profit of ¥185 billion and net profit of ¥120 billion. Nintendo also said it expected a foreign-exchange-related profit of ¥20 billion, rather than its previous forecast of a ¥10 billion loss. Finally, the stock nearly doubled over Nintendo's 2006–07 fiscal year, while the Nikkei remained virtually flat.

In the words of Nintendo itself, the success of the Wii is that it has broad appeal as a "family-oriented game". Its success globally was reflected in Australia with sales of 32,901 units in the first four days, beating the Xbox 360 record of 30,421. In North America, Nintendo expected to sell 4 million Wii units by the end of 2007, compared with 1 million for Sony's PS3.

I have said little of the Xbox 360, also about twice the price of the Wii when it was released, which was sold at a loss for Microsoft in an attempt to "win the war for the living room". Nintendo's flip – ignoring the conventional wisdom of the gaming crowd – catapulted it to a market-leading position in less than twelve months, and in August 2007 it exceeded the life-time sales of Microsoft's Xbox 360. To think that before the Wii's release pundits were suggesting it was all over for Nintendo.[4]

> ASK YOURSELF, ARE YOU SO BUSY COMPETING ON FAMILIAR STANDARDS AND ASSUMPTIONS THAT YOU ARE MISSING A BRAND-NEW MARKET SEGMENT AS A RESULT?

Ask yourself, are you so busy competing on familiar standards and assumptions that you are missing a brand-new market segment as a result? What would happen if you stopped competing in the way you always have and went in a whole new direction? What direction might that be?

OUT ON A LIMB

To be a flipstar, you've got to venture out onto a limb. You can make OK money doing what everyone else is doing, but that's not the way to put a dent in the universe, as Steve Jobs puts it. Although the odds against immediate success may be daunting, the more you are willing to keep trying new things the more the odds change in your favour.

Let's briefly look again at Progressive Car Insurance, which I discussed in Chapter 4, "Absolutely, Positively Sweat the Small Stuff". In 1996 Progressive Car Insurance was the thirteenth biggest insurer in the US market on the basis of serving a limited population of high-risk drivers. A change in California state law that limited the insurance premiums Progressive could charge threatened its entire business model. So it found a new one.

TO BE A FLIPSTAR, YOU'VE GOT TO VENTURE OUT ONTO A LIMB.

Progressive figured out that not all high-risk drivers were the same. The telltale factor was customers' credit ratings. High-risk drivers with good credit ratings were much less likely to have expensive accidents than high-risk drivers with poor credit ratings. Pushing the analysis further, Progressive found that the relationship between a customer's credit rating and the cost of serving that customer held for drivers at all risk levels.

With this customer understanding, Progressive saw that it could shift from offering insurance only to high-risk drivers at high premiums to offering insurance to all drivers at widely varying premiums. The company could become a low-cost provider and undercut every other insurer in the marketplace.

The brilliance of Progressive's play was that it didn't stop its analysis there. Progressive understood that if it gained enough market share, the biggest automotive insurance providers in the US market – State Farm, Allstate and Geico – could easily lower their own rates. In a price war alone, these three had deeper pockets and could beat Progressive at this game.

But remember the need to "Think AND, Not OR". Progressive did. Along with offering the lowest prices, Progressive ramped up its claims-adjustment service to match the capabilities of the big players and it staked its brand story on being the easiest insurer to do business with as well as being cheap and offering good service. That led to innovations such as offering prospective customers rate quotes from competitors (they became the middleman), even when the competition was offering a lower quote than Progressive itself was, and – in states that allowed it – enabling customers to register their vehicles with the state motor-vehicles department from the Progressive website.

Progressive gained immediate traction in the marketplace. Although State Farm, Allstate and Geico all emulated Progressive's innovations, Progressive had successfully established its brand story in customers' minds as the insurer that would save them time, money and mental energy. The result is that Progressive has jumped from thirteenth place to become number three in the US market behind State Farm and Allstate, largely on the strength of its "easy to use" brand identity, including sending claims adjusters to the accident site or the customer's home or office and writing claims cheques on the spot. From the fringe, Progressive has moved right into the centre of the mass market.[5]

While on the topic of insurers, how about AAMI in Australia? While their competition is pushing towards "efficiency of operation" with push-button this and voice-recognition that on all of their customer "help" lines, AAMI refuses to let a machine do the talking. They have real people answering your call, and from recent experience provide one of the most friendly and helpful services I have ever received anywhere. It was almost a pleasure to have crashed my wife's car so I could make a claim. Well, that's an overstatement, but my experiences with AAMI and their customer service have been outstanding. They not only understand that business is personal, but they are prepared to stake their competitive advantage in this area even though no one else is. Not only that, but they have been the most competitively priced insurer for the three cars I have insured in the last couple of years.

ING Direct is following a similar path in financial services. Instead of trying to compete with the traditional banks in the traditional way, ING has created a new banking brand story by offering savings accounts online at higher rates than those available at your local brick-and-mortar bank. Appealing especially to younger customers who are comfortable with the internet and love the ease of use of online banking, these accounts give ING a chance to achieve impressive long-term growth by offering new services to these young customers as they progress through the life cycle, develop in their careers and become more affluent.

The traditional banks eventually wised up and began making similar offerings available. But the advantage in online banking lies with ING Direct, the company that was willing to go out on a limb and be the first to offer the customer a simpler, easier, more rewarding way of doing business. It helped that their product was also fast, good, cheap and *easy*!

At the same time ING never forgot the fundamentals of the consumer financial-services market, and made sure that customers associated the company with security and reliability as well as innovation. In this regard it's interesting to see the stumble that

Virgin, one of my all-time flipstars, made recently with the Virgin Superannuation Fund. As in most Virgin-branded businesses except the airlines, Virgin holds a relatively small stake in the enterprise, which is offered by Virgin Money but is operated by Macquarie Bank's Macquarie Fund Manager.

On the face of it, a Virgin Superannuation Fund makes great sense as a logical extension of the Virgin credit-card and Virgin mortgage services. But there was an embarrassing disconnection between Virgin's hip, edgy, risk-taking brand story, which reflects the persona of Richard Branson himself, and the overwhelmingly "old" advertising and marketing. Under the Virgin logo, known worldwide for being youthful and cutting edge, there were the same images of sixtyish couples walking on the beach as in every other retirement-fund marketing campaign. It was a disconnection both for the young customers using Virgin Money's credit-card and mortgage services on their first important purchases, and for baby boomers approaching the end of their working lives and wanting to make sure they had enough money to stroll worry-free on the beach.

Virgin may well ultimately succeed with its retirement fund. The company continues to be a flipstar precisely because of its willingness to keep on taking chances to enter and create new markets, and its successes far outweigh its failures. Richard Branson's R&D process is reportedly to listen when someone brings in an interesting idea and then put that person

YOUR INNOVATIONS HAVE TO BE IN LINE WITH THE FUNDAMENTALS OF YOUR OWN BRAND IDENTITY.

in charge of developing it. But here is a case that shows that your innovations have to be in line with the fundamentals of your own brand identity. So far, that is not true of the Virgin Super-annuation Fund, at least not in my opinion.

Given the mention of Macquarie Bank as we talked about Virgin, I thought it useful to include an example of going out on a limb in your employment proposition. *Everyone* is talking about work–life balance, so much so that companies traditionally known for punishing hours are starting to talk about work–life balance (even when it is a lie) when trying to recruit good talent. Not Macquarie Bank. Sure, there may be some discussion of this at the HR level, but when you are being interviewed by a director at Macquarie, he or she will tell you in no uncertain terms, "Say good-bye to your friends, say good-bye to your family. You are not going to see them for ten years. But when you do, you will be rich! Interested?"

Having worked with Macquarie and knowing some senior people there, I can tell you that this is not entirely true. The people I know don't think they have sacrificed anything to be at Macquarie. They feel as though their work is an integrated part of their life, and they love how Macquarie celebrates success, develops its people and promotes from within. Most of all they love that they are given "freedom within boundaries", to steal an old Macquarie phrase. Macquarie Bank gets more unsolicited applications than any company I have worked with in Australia (not as many as Google in the United States, but a lot by Australian standards) and they have very low attrition rates. Phenomenal when you think about how "off trend" their positioning is.

It is not surprising really that Macquarie would carve its own path in the employment landscape because they have a worldwide reputation for innovation in deal-making models and banking in general.

In the consumer financial-services market, Prudential Financial has shown how even a giant company can be a flipstar. When the technology bubble that burst in March 2000 was still expanding, Prudential's competitors such as Fidelity were all running advertising that emphasized dramatic growth in wealth. But Prudential was sending a different message: grow and protect your wealth. This was in keeping with Prudential's "rock solid" brand identity and its long-time logo featuring the Rock of Gibraltar.

Refusing to follow the herd of competitors, Prudential kept its eye squarely on affluent baby boomers who were middle-aged or nearing retirement. When the tech bubble finally burst, the company's "grow and protect your wealth" message resonated even louder with the most desirable customers. It also resonated with the competition, who all migrated sooner or later to a copycat positioning with some variation of the "grow and protect your wealth" promise to customers. Prudential was a flipstar because it took a divergent path from the competition. Then the market flipped in the direction Prudential was already pointing, and the competition had to flip their messages. But the copycats' messages don't resonate with customers like the original flipstar's do.

KEEP EXPLORING

Going out on a limb is not something you do once. Suppose you fall and never take another chance? Then you'll never get anywhere exciting. Flipstars go out on a limb many times in the course of their careers or their existence as companies. Richard Branson and

FLIPSTARS GO OUT ON A LIMB MANY TIMES IN THE COURSE OF THEIR CAREERS OR THEIR EXISTENCE AS COMPANIES.

Steve Jobs are the guiding risk-takers at Virgin and Apple respectively, and all four are flipstars.

Chapter 2, "Action Creates Clarity", speaks about the importance of risk-taking in terms of an action orientation in general. A key element in a successful action orientation is contact with fringe areas within society where new ideas percolate. Many, if not most, of these ideas will turn out to be fizzles, or just a case of old wine in new bottles, but a few of them will set an agenda for the centre. They represent the future of the mass market in embryonic form.

This is why Nike assiduously tracks trends within minority urban communities, striving to identify what suburban consumers will later buy in even greater quantities. Retailers such as Uniqlo in Japan, Sportsgirl in Australia and Target in the United States do the same to maintain a hip, cutting-edge identity in customers' eyes.

Nike has become such a big company, with 2006 revenues of $15 billion, that it is easy to forget that it started out on the fringe. In 1962 University of Oregon track-and-field coach Bill Bowerman visited a fellow coach, Arthur Lydiard, in New Zealand. Today movie fans across the world know New Zealand as the place where Peter Jackson filmed the *Lord of the Rings* trilogy, but in 1962 the country was definitely on the fringe of awareness for most North Americans and Europeans.

Bowerman was fascinated to observe that many people in New Zealand regularly engaged in an activity they called "jogging" for fun and fitness. Even though Bowerman was an ex-competitive runner and coached runners, he had never seen ordinary people running for pleasure. He joined Arthur

Lydiard's jogging club for out-
ings, kept jogging on his return
home, and legend has it that it
took four inches off his waistline.
More important, he had wit-
nessed a fringe activity that he
thought had enormous potential

A KEY ELEMENT IN A SUC-
CESSFUL ACTION ORIENTA-
TION IS CONTACT WITH
FRINGE AREAS WITHIN
SOCIETY WHERE NEW
IDEAS PERCOLATE.

for an increasingly health- and fitness-conscious population in
the United States and elsewhere.

Back home, Bowerman teamed up with cardiologist Waldo
Harris to write a twenty-page pamphlet entitled "Jogging".
The pamphlet morphed into a book that sold more than a mil-
lion copies. It also gave impetus to a handshake deal between
Bowerman and an ex-athlete he had once coached named Phil
Knight. Their enterprise, Blue Ribbon Sports, was eventually
renamed Nike, and the rest is history, as they say.

Let me highlight one milestone in that history, the 1978
signing of tennis bad boy John McEnroe to a Nike endorsement contract. Those with long tennis memories might say
that Nike would have gone after Björn Borg if he hadn't already been signed to Fila. But I doubt it. Picking a renegade
from the mainstream like McEnroe has typified all of Nike's
marketing, right up to the present, including its controversial
1987 use of the Beatles song "Revolution" in an ad (Nike
apparently had the permission of EMI/Capitol Records and
John Lennon's widow, Yoko Ono, but not that of Apple Records and the other Beatles), its 2004 Chinese martial-arts-
themed advertising featuring NBA superstar LeBron James
(some thought it was racist), and the 2005 use of a slightly
modified but easily identifiable Minor Threat album cover in

a promotion for Nike skateboarding shoes (easily identifiable by Gen Y, that is).

Consistently innovative companies like 3M recognize the need for regular visits to the fringe. There is a long-standing mandate at 3M that research staff should spend 15 per cent of their time on whatever interests them. Most of what results from this are harebrained failures, but it also gave 3M the Post-it note, structured abrasive belts, new lenses for computer-monitor manufacturing, and other products. Following much the same practice, although it credits Stanford University's PhD programme in computer science as inspiration, Google got its Froogle shopping service, Google Earth and Gmail from this practice. 3M goes so far as to arbitrarily demand that a certain per centage of its revenues in a set number of years should come from products or services that currently do not exist at 3M.

UNIQUE

Learning to innovate on the fringe and then carry the fruit of your innovations to the mass market makes you unique. Though all of the companies we've looked at in this chapter are not without competition, they each have distinctive brand stories that can never be mistaken for those of competitors.

It is possible for several companies in a single industry to be unique in customers' eyes. Think of the luxury-automobile market, where BMW, Ferrari, Lexus, Mercedes-Benz and Porsche have unique brand identities and tell unique stories to customers.

I mentioned the example of Generation Y and my work at the start of this chapter. A few people were talking about

Generation Y when I decided to publish my research in this area. But more than one person told me I would need to position myself more broadly than Generation Y, and even

though I had some expertise in other areas I knew this would be bad advice. To be perceived as unique you really have to go out on a limb.

I took action. By action I mean I spent three years (seriously) writing a book, even before I had a publisher. I knew this generational shift was a cause of many challenges facing businesses today, from both a staff and a customer point of view, and I knew over time businesses would come to recognize that.

They did, and the result for me was a very successful (meaning fun and profitable) consulting business that takes me all over the world, and has allowed me to work with some of the most powerful businesses and people on the planet. Through my work in this well-defined area I have been able to build my expertise in other areas.

Of course I am not the only person in my category any more, and there are plenty of me-toos in the market. The truth is I was not the first into the market either, but I was the first to be focused primarily on Gen Y and I was able to tell a story that people remembered and passed on, and this rising tide has raised all of our ships.

Peter Switzer, a well-known finance commentator in Australia, is changing the way financial planning is done. Switzer Financial Services offers investment advice but makes a point of taking no commission and having their consultants paid by the hour to ensure absolute impartiality. Any commissions paid by the institutions that receive investment at their advice are actually *paid back to the client*. This is a Virgin-like assault on the margins of the financial planning sector.

Even though Switzer is not the only advisory business with this fee-for-service model, it is certainly a fringe model in the industry. Gaining in popularity, it goes against the product-centric, commission-driven model that has built this industry to date. Imagine it was you. Think of how your adviser buddies would have felt about you "undercutting" their pricing model as you went out on your limb. Might I suggest that not only were they not agreeing with you, but there was no love out on that fringe either.

Interestingly enough my own advisers, Ark Financial, have gone in the other direction. They not only charge a fee for service, they also charge commission plus a yearly retainer. They are staking their positioning on what they call "Beyond Wealth". They regularly coach and educate their clients on how to enjoy their wealth, and get more out of life while at the same time helping to grow their finances. It is more like going to see a life coach than just a financial planner. The point is that both approaches are unique and both are being endorsed by growing numbers of customers.

Two other Aussie examples of companies that bucked industry wisdom and started whole new trends are Boost Juice and McGrath real estate.

While accompanying her husband, Jeff, on a trip to the United States, Boost founder Janine Allis saw a hole in the Australian market for a healthy fast-food alternative. Upon returning to Australia, she developed a business plan and raised $250,000 start-up money by recruiting her friends as investors.

The first store opened in Adelaide in 2000, and since then more than 170 stores have opened throughout Australia, with the first international franchises in Chile, Indonesia, Kuwait and Singapore. With revenues expected to exceed $100 million in 2007, this is a great achievement in just six years. So much of what Janine has done at Boost has been against the crowd. The staff are the most obvious. Unlike so many retailers, the staff at Boost more often than not are having fun. Boost deliberately hires some of the wackiest and weirdest people who apply. They want that kind of edginess in their stores.

Their PR activities have included giving away a franchise at Sydney's Manly Beach through popular local radio station TodayFM. Not to mention Janine being the charismatic leader and voice behind so much of this PR activity. Instead of running a typical radio ad, Janine would instead give motivational advice to

DIFFERENT IS COOL JUST BECAUSE IT IS DIFFERENT.

listeners, building the Boost story of a healthy lifestyle through proper nutrition. Although there has been some debate as to how healthy Boost juices really are, few could argue with their phenomenal success. It is cool just because it is different.

McGrath real estate is another of my favourite examples. During the property boom of the late 1990s and early 2000s John McGrath turned McGrath Partners into a force in the Sydney property market. They were among the very first agencies – along with Ray White Double Bay, Di Jones and others – to raise the bar in the industry. Their advertising was clean, modern and of the very best quality. Their signs used colour and images and matched the high standard of their print advertising. They moved away from private treaty sales and helped spur the auction culture that drove Sydney property prices to dizzying heights. They motivated vendors to make significant improvements on their homes before listing them for sale, including renovations and renting furniture to make a better presentation.

This market leadership enabled McGrath Partners to charge a commission 1 per cent higher than the industry average, which on sales exceeding $1 billion is a handy, full-profit premium. Today, many agencies have raised their standards, and with a flat market McGrath will need to become faster, better and cheaper, as well as easier and more inspiring to deal with if they want to continue to be a leader in their industry. Innovation never ends!

On the flip side in the property business is long-time friend of mine and flipstar Pete Gilchrist. He recently established an estate agency in New Zealand called The Joneses. It sets out to totally reinvent the way property is sold. Their biggest changes from the usual model? A flat fee rather than commission, and team members with dedicated tasks (rather than a single agent who does the whole thing end-to-end).

The absence of commission has been calculated to save up to $6,000 on a $300,000 sale, $10,000 on a $500,000 house sale and over $21,000 on a million-dollar sale. The team structure means that instead of having a "jack of all trades" (who has to manage the whole thing because her commission rides on it) doing everything from photographs to booking

INNOVATION NEVER ENDS!

advertising space, a dedicated professional is assigned to each task.

This turns the real estate model on its head, and it's being met with very positive reactions from consumers who have long felt that the traditional model wasn't giving them very good value for their money.

For companies and individuals the flip that mass-market success is found on the fringe has two implications. Either differentiate yourself from competitors within an existing market, or differentiate the market you operate in by creating a new market. Or for best results, do both; but in any case, start exploring.

Ten things to do when you finish this chapter

I know I have been finishing each chapter with five things to do, but in the spirit of being a little different, here are ten.

1. Start an innovators' club. Pull together a group (or multiple groups) of high performers in your company and host a meeting with them once a month where you look at fringe activities, new market opportunities and your current competitive strategy.
2. Keep a journal of fringe stuff. Not just fringe stuff in your market but any market. If your bank does something new and unique, write it down, give it some thought and then present it at your innovators' club.
3. Do something random at least four times per year. Visit an art gallery. Buy a different magazine than the ones you normally read. Or maybe even take a new course in something that does not relate to your job.

4. Surf the net. If a new activity, product or service is becoming popular, the first signs of it will appear on the internet. Spend some time regularly looking at MySpace, Facebook, YouTube and other popular sites to see what's becoming hot – or not.

5. Check out what teenagers are doing at the local shopping centre. What are they wearing? How are they talking? What are they talking about?

6. Block out three hours at least four times a year and ask yourself: If I was going to build this company from the ground up, what would I do? Or if I was going to redesign this product, or develop a different product for this same need, what would it look like? What else could this product or service be used for?

7. Hire someone a little wacky. If you are big enough and have the resources, employ someone in marketing with an industrial-design background. Or as Google does, hire an actuary to work in HR.

8. Don't attend your industry conference this year. Attend some other industry's conference instead. Or at least attend both.

9. Apply the 3M test. For example, demand that 20 per cent of your revenue in three years comes from a product or service (or many of them) you don't yet have.

10. Stop being such a wimp! Do something new, different and cool with your product or service. Something that has never been done before.

TO GET CONTROL,
GIVE IT UP

You don't own your brand, you don't own your customers and you don't own your staff. These days you have less control and influence over them than ever before. If you are smart, you will flip this negative into a positive, and use it to tell a better story, add more value and turn your business into an awesome place to work. This is the only way you will get significant control. And even then it won't really be control, just influence.

This is the hardest flip to master. Human nature makes us want to expand the territory we control, whether as companies or as individuals, and at the very least hold on to the power we already have. But some of today's biggest success stories are being written by companies and entrepreneurs who have learned to give up control.

This chapter will describe some companies that are struggling to let go of the business models that have made them successful. This is understandable. Take for example the music industry, which – it is no secret – is struggling with the onset of digital music downloads, peer-to-peer file sharing and a host of technologies that are completely changing the way music is made, distributed and listened to. You can hardly blame the music executives who have made their careers, and their companies' profits, with a tightly controlled selection and distribution model for clinging to the only way of doing business they have known.

I don't say this because I think a music executive reading this chapter will be surprised to hear that his business model is under threat. Nor will a chief marketing officer be shocked to learn that the customer owns his company's brand. What I do hope is that these executives, and you, feel inspired by the possibilities these changes present rather than crippled by them. Specifically, this chapter will suggest you do the following things:

> YOU DON'T OWN YOUR BRAND, YOU DON'T OWN YOUR CUSTOMERS, AND YOU DON'T OWN YOUR STAFF.

- Stop resisting and learn to embrace the changes forced upon your business model and distribution networks.
- Connect and interact with your customers, not just so you can build valuable relationships with them, but so you can benefit from their expertise for better product development.
- Let go of your desire to control the research-and-development process, and tap into the pockets of individual brilliance that can be found when you open your doors to a wider community.
- Resist the urge to own and hold on to everything. Explore new business models where money can be made

in relationship with suppliers, and even competitors, that
your organization cannot or will not exploit in isolation.
* Empower your staff to do their job.

THE POWER SHIFT

The four forces of change have shifted power from the organization to the individual. Technology like the internet, increasingly affluent customers, oversupply in customer markets and
extremely tight labour markets are putting the individual in
the driver's seat. This is forcing businesses to be more accountable for what they do, and it is also undermining some of the
most successful business models on the planet. Read on to learn
what flipstars are doing about this new centre of power.

Winning through losing

Change is like a wave. You either ride it, get pummelled by it,
or you sit on the beach and watch it run its course. For a while
in the early 1990s Microsoft decided to watch the internet wave
from the beach. That was until 1994, when two twentysome-
things who were still wet behind the ears – J. Allard, a pro-
grammer, and Steven Sinofsky, a technical adviser to Bill Gates
– sent separate memos to senior managers at Microsoft. Their
memos said: get into the water, the internet is huge, and it is
here to stay.

In effect they were saying that the internet was no ordinary
wave, it was a tsunami that would consume even those sitting
on the beach. These memos were enough to get Microsoft off
the sand and into the water. A little more than twelve months
later Bill Gates himself issued a memo aptly entitled "The internet Tidal Wave". He exclaimed, rightly, that the net was the

"most important single development" in the computer industry since the IBM PC. "I have gone through several stages of increasing my views of its importance. Now, I assign the internet the highest level," he wrote.[1]

The battle began to develop the ubiquitous browser for the internet. Microsoft, among a few others, wanted to be the gateway to the World Wide Web. Or more technically, the facilitator of people's web experience. The battle, mostly with Netscape in the late 1990s, was won by Microsoft – first, because they built a better browser, and second, because they embedded Microsoft Explorer into the Windows operating system, which created problems with antitrust regulators in the United States and Europe, but not before it had won the company market dominance in internet browsers.

The cool thing is that the internet wave is still coming in, and some would argue it has not even started yet. Are you riding the wave, getting pummelled by it or standing on the beach? No one is immune. The internet is redefining distribution networks and consumer power, at the same time compromising the "trust" and property rights that the capitalist system is built on. And it is not just the internet either. For Microsoft the next tidal wave, apart from perhaps Google and online applications, is probably China. The battle there is twofold, with the software pirates and with Linux, a free open-source operating system.

In the United States, Europe and Australia the battle for the computer desktop was won by Microsoft with more than 90 per cent of all PCs using Windows as their operating system. While piracy is still alive and well in these markets, it is nothing compared to what happens in China. According to the

Business Software Alliance, piracy in the United States hovers around 22 per cent, the UK 29 per cent, and Australia surprisingly a little higher at 31 per cent. This sounds high, but it is estimated that 90 per cent of all software in China is pirated.

In China piracy seems to be a way of life. It is in everything from pharmaceuticals (making Viagra rip-offs using ancient Chinese herbal ingredients) to aeroplane and automobile parts.[2] There was around \$2.2 billion worth of software, films and music piracy in China in 2006. China accounts for roughly two-thirds of the world's pirated goods and is the point of origin of around 80 per cent of counterfeit goods seized at U.S. borders.[3]

Add to this equation that Linux is basically a free operating system that can be customized to your company's needs. Despite being a model of "open source", which I will discuss later in this chapter, Linux has done little to dent the phenomenal market share that Microsoft has in the developed markets mentioned above. In China it is a different story. Although it is believed that Microsoft is ahead, Linux is not far behind in what is obviously a more immature and rapidly growing market, including deals with the Chinese government and education system.

It is likely there are more illegal copies of Windows than there are legitimate ones. It may seem obvious to someone in Australia, the United States or the UK to put a stop to this piracy and instal controls on piracy in China like those imposed in Western countries. But it could be argued that this is the opposite of what Microsoft should try to accomplish. To win this war, Microsoft needs to lose the battle. For now anyway, some industry experts have suggested that Microsoft turn a blind eye to the piracy that is rampant in China for two main reasons. Once you build your IT infrastructure around Windows, it is highly likely you will want a number of add-on applications, many of which are made and sold by Microsoft. And it will be easier to enforce anti-piracy measures when China's own nascent computer and software industries begin to value a more "respectful" relationship with intellectual-property-rights advocates, and when Linux no longer poses a significant strategic threat.

This may seem like a very audacious thing to suggest for a company that has profited hugely from exercising strict control of their product, but winning by losing is actually a strategy Microsoft knows well. The Xbox 360 is built on this strategy. Microsoft and others see the next big market opportunity in becoming the operating system and hardware vendor of choice in the living room, as people increasingly receive and store their home-entertainment content digitally. In an attempt to gain the dominant position over its main rival, Sony, and more recently Nintendo, Microsoft sells the Xbox 360, which ironically is still very expensive, at a loss.

> IT MIGHT SOUND AUDACIOUS, BUT WINNING BY LOSING IS A STRATEGY MICROSOFT KNOWS WELL. THE XBOX 360 IS BUILT ON IT.

It seems that Microsoft has been doing this in China for longer than we may think. In a 1998 presentation at the University of Washington, Bill Gates remarked, "Although about three million computers get sold every year in China, people don't pay for the software. Someday they will, though. And as long as they are going to steal it, we want them to steal ours. They'll get sort of addicted and then we'll somehow figure out how to collect sometime in the next decade." That decade is basically up, and Microsoft has yet to collect. However, any attempt to control piracy in China is likely to be ineffective. In this case Microsoft will get some control only if it is willing to give it up for a little longer.[4]

If the internet is the main power shifter, it would be remiss not to examine the company that has probably best worked out how to profit from the democratization the net has created: eBay. This book's second chapter is about the flip that action creates clarity, and eBay is the ultimate "action creates clarity" business. Pierre Omidyar began eBay as a "thought experiment". He was interested in finding out if people could trust one another enough to buy and sell items without being controlled by some third party. Obviously it worked. In terms of the preceding chapter, Omidyar brought his innovation in from the fringe of his own mind and had it validated by the wisdom of crowds. Not only that, but even the name was not part of some grand master plan. Prior to starting eBay in 1995, Omidyar owned a business consultancy called Echo Bay Technology Group and tried to register EchoBay.com, but it was owned by Echo Bay Mines. So he abbreviated it to eBay.

To grasp the power of eBay, consider the following numbers:

- Since its launch in 1995, eBay has grown from nothing to a $6.35-billion-a year business. Not bad for a company barely a decade old.
- More than $52 billion worth of goods were sold on eBay in 2006.
- Approximately 1.3 million people around the world used eBay as their primary or secondary source of income in 2006, including almost 13,000 in India.

- There are more than 222 million members of eBay who trade in over 50,000 categories of goods. More than $729 is spent on eBay every second.
- There are more than 100 million items on the site at any given second, with 6.6 million added per day.
- Last year, more than £2 billion worth of goods were sold on eBay in the UK alone (a car was sold every two minutes), and eBay claims that as many as 70,000 Britons now make their living from eBay.

The cool thing about eBay is that it is not a middleman in the same way Mortgage Choice is a middleman. In my mind it is not a middleman at all. It is simply a marketplace, a platform with very limited controls, policed mainly by the users (the wisdom of the crowd), where buyers and sellers meet and transact.

Pierre and eBay still kick Yahoo Auction's arse because they moved fast, had a simple and fast procedure, and gathered a critical mass of users that makes it seem crazy to buy or sell anywhere else. As a result they are able to charge a premium for listings and sales that is three times that of other competitive online auction sites. And it is not just eBay that wins. By removing the layers of control (all the people trying to skim dollars off the top), the eBay buyer gets a better deal and quite often so does the seller because of the excitement of the auction and the absence of high-rent retail space.

EBAY OWNS, STORES AND SHIPS *NOTHING*! YOU DON'T HAVE TO OWN EVERYTHING!

Best of all eBay owns, stores and ships *nothing*! You don't have to own everything!

The next big frontier for eBay

is in the Chinese market, where they have had little success to date. After pouring tens of millions of dollars into China, eBay recently announced a partnership with Chinese company Tom Online Inc.

FREE MUSIC ANYONE?

Until recently the recorded music business was very resistant to the changing nature of their marketplace. The entire industry is being dragged kicking and screaming into letting customers purchase and download individual songs online rather than buy an entire CD. The record companies are still wasting time and money suing illegal downloaders in court. But that war is already lost to the overwhelming force of consumer action. Some day an economics student will make a nice PhD thesis calculating how much money the record companies lost in refusing to face reality.

One of the hall-of-shame examples in that thesis will be Sony's misguided attempt to copy-protect its CDs with a computer virus. Sony secretly implanted two types of viruses on around 100 different CD titles that it sold to consumers.

When CD owners played their CDs on their computers, the viruses installed themselves on the computer operating systems and started making changes to the media player to ensure the CD could be played only on that one computer. The program automatically installed itself, and the user was never informed about its presence. The changes it made to the computer also rendered it susceptible to other viruses and hackers. And the program communicated personal information to Sony about the computer on which it was installed, including the user's IP address (enabling Sony to identify each user).

This was seen by many, justifiably, as a massive breach of

privacy and trust. Eventually, Sony had to recall the CDs from distribution. They also faced legal action over the copy-protection programs, due to breaches of privacy and damage to personal computer property.

Sony Pictures Entertainment senior vice president Steve Heckler said this in 2001: "The industry will take whatever steps it needs to protect itself and protect its revenue streams ... Sony is going to take aggressive steps to stop this. We will develop technology that transcends the individual user. We will firewall Napster at source – we will block it at your cable company, we will block it at your phone company, we will block it at your ISP. We will firewall it at your PC... These strategies are being aggressively pursued because there is simply too much at stake."[5]

As music-CD sales continue to fall because of downloading, music-industry executives are understandably worried, but the position outlined by Mr Heckler is not a winning one, as Sony's copy-protected-CD fiasco shows. Illegal downloading is wrong, but when asked, many who engage in this activity have said that if it was easier and less restrictive to download legally they would. Obviously iTunes and a host of other such sites have now made it easier to download, but still make it restrictive to use.

Digital music sales from legitimate downloading have not yet offset the decrease in CD sales. But they are getting closer to doing so. Legitimate downloads increased 89 per cent in 2006 over 2005, and global digital music sales over some 500 legitimate downloading sites reached $2 billion. Total music sales were down 4 per cent from 2005 to 2006, but the trend is clear: music customers want to pick and choose the songs they buy, not be locked into the music company's, or the artist's, album offerings.

Not only do customers value control over the songs

THE MUSIC INDUSTRY IS BEGINNING TO RECOGNIZE THAT IT IS BETTER TO ADAPT TO, RATHER THAN FIGHT, GLOBAL CUSTOMER BEHAVIOUR.

they buy, but buying online is faster and easier. The simplicity builds on the power of ideas presented in Chapter 4, "Absolutely, Positively Sweat the Small Stuff".

There are signs of the music industry beginning to recognize that it is better to adapt to, rather than fight, global customer behaviour. The *New York Times* reported from the January 2007 meeting of Midem, the music industry's annual trade fair, that the major recorded-music companies are feeling their way towards joining independent labels in selling digital downloads in MP3 format without copy-protection, based on the realization that hackers will quickly work out a way around any copy protection software and on the expectation that these unrestricted file formats will serve as a form of advertising.

Customers' demands to access music however they want will also put pressure on Apple's digital-rights management model, which makes iTunes available only on the iPod. Fuelled by customer frustration, legislative proposals to mandate interoperability are being made in France and other European countries. Throughout its history, Apple (like Sony) has made things that work only on its proprietary platforms. The first important signs of moving away from this were making iTunes compatible with Windows and using Intel chips in the latest Macs.

The introduction of an Intel chip into Macs and Apple laptops was a major reason for the strong growth in Apple sales in very recent years. iTunes will need to follow a similar path. Sooner rather than later, I hope. Considering the rate of downloads, Apple will probably find more money and better margins selling digital music than they did selling digital music players.

Meanwhile the musicians who have embraced free downloading have vastly broadened their potential markets. This is not surprising considering that, until such technology came along, their ability to access the market was very low without a record label, and in effect they had no control.

The Arctic Monkeys are one of several bands to use MySpace to attract the interest of record labels. But some now argue that in a downloadable world bands no longer need a record label at all. January 2007 was the first time a band hit a major music chart without being signed to any record label. The "unsigned" rock band Koopa, from Essex, hit the UK Top 40 with a single called "Blag, Steal & Borrow" that was available only as a downloaded MP3 file.

Unfortunately the PR frenzy that surrounded Koopa being the first "unsigned" band on the UK charts was a little misleading. You technically can't be on the UK charts without being signed, because you need what is called a Catco ID for royalties to be paid. So in truth Koopa was actually "signed" with a company called Ditto Music, owned by brothers Lee and Matt Parsons. The key differentiator is that a deal with Ditto Music is non-exclusive and is only for distribution and promotion. In other words, Koopa retains the rights, whereas with a "traditional" music label this is usually not the case.

The real example of getting control by giving it up is in fact Ditto Music, not the band. Ditto managed to get their second "rights-retained artist" (which they spin as being an "unsigned" artist) onto the Top 40 charts in the UK in March 2007 when Midas entered the UK charts at number three. According to its website, Ditto Music has hundreds of artists as clients. It has these clients because it doesn't want to "own" the rights for its clients' music. Sure, it is not a multibillion-pound giant like EMI or Sony Music, but it is certainly a sign of a new business model emerging – a model that seeks to get control (distribution of new music) by giving it up (rights).[6]

As television-executive-turned-internet-entrepreneur Jordan Levin puts it, 'Ultimately these big media companies are all wrestling with the same thing – the power is being taken out of their hands. This is an industry that for its entire history has imposed its model on consumers. They've always said, "We'll tell you when you'll watch our TV show or see our movie." But that's fundamentally changing. The whole structure of people who control content is being supplanted by the content users themselves.' And according to MGM executive Harry Sloan, "We've got to get the creativity to stand against user-created content, because that's what people are watching at my house." In an interview with *Variety*, Sloan described his seventeen-year-old son with the television on behind him and "two screens in front of him, one connected to friends and one to play World of Warcraft".[7]

> CURRENT TRENDS DO NOT SPELL THE END OF THE MOVIE AND TELEVISION COMPANIES BUT THE END OF THE MOVIE AND TELEVISION COMPANIES CONTROLLING WHEN AND WHERE WE WATCH WHAT WE WATCH.

I don't think these current trends mean the end of the movie and television companies, just the end of movie and television companies controlling when and where we watch what we watch.

YouTube has become an arena for copyright-protected content uploaded without the copyright holders' consent as well as user-generated content. Thanks to its $1.65 billion purchase of YouTube, Google can demonstrate that advertising tailored to each individual user's viewing habits, like the advertising on Google Search that changes depending on what you're looking for, can adequately compensate copyright holders for the loss of control over their intellectual property. Google will also be making advertising-based payments to the amateur video makers who upload their own creations to the YouTube site. No doubt the most successful of these amateurs, who may as well be film school graduates as self-taught, will face the same quandary as the rock band Koopa: if there is profit without them, who needs the movie and television companies or the record companies? Personally I think YouTube is a holding yard for a collection of garbage. Organized garbage, for sure, but I am astounded daily at not only how many clips get loaded up, but worse, how many hours people spend downloading them.

I am more of a fan of the News Corporation, AOL and NBC deal that will use the internet to distribute quality content.

This shows that despite some who suggest the "end of TV", the industry will not die. They just need to flip some of the paradigms that until recently had made them phenomenally successful. It is time to take some action, and have the courage to explore new business models. For example, despite the movie studios' and cinema owners' resistance, simultaneous release of movies in cinemas, on pay-per-view television and on DVD is coming soon, because that's what the public wants. The maverick entrepreneur Mark Cuban, who coincidentally owns the NBA team the Dallas Mavericks, has staked out an early lead in this arena.

Together with fellow entrepreneur Todd Wagner, Cuban has assembled a vertically integrated media and entertainment company that includes a film-production studio, a film-distribution company, a chain of cinemas and an all-high-definition digital television network "to experiment with a 'day-and-date' model in which films will be released simultaneously across theatrical, television and home video platforms, thus collapsing the traditional release windows and giving

AUTHORS WHO HAVE MADE THEIR WORK AVAILABLE AS FREE DOWNLOADS HAVE SEEN INCREASES IN THE SALES OF THEIR PRINTED BOOKS.

consumers a choice of how, when, and where they wish to see a movie". The model received its trial runs with two high-profile projects: George Clooney's *Good Night, and Good Luck* and the documentary *Enron: The Smartest Guys in the Room*.

Book publishers have also struggled to come to terms with the world of downloads. Interestingly, book publishing shows perhaps the clearest benefits to both companies and intellectual-property creators in making downloads freely available. Listening to a downloaded file is no different from listening to a CD (sorry to all of you audiophiles). The best file formats can offer CD-quality sound, and video and film downloads will surely follow the same upward quality curve. But reading a book on a computer is not as enjoyable and practical as reading an actual printed book. Dedicated electronic-book readers have not yet bridged the gap in terms of the quality of the reading experience. At the same time, making part or all of a book available for free downloading as an electronic file can actually trigger hefty sales of a conventional print edition, a business model that the marketing commentator Seth Godin and the science-fiction writer Cory Doctorow have successfully pioneered.

For example, Seth Godin made chapters of his most successful book, *Permission Marketing,* available for free online before it was available for sale in bookshops. And Cory Doctorow says on his website:

> I've been giving away my books ever since my first
> novel came out, and boy has it ever made me a
> bunch of money... I believe that we live in an era
> where anything that can be expressed as bits will
> be... Me, I'm looking to find ways to use copying to
> make more money and it's working: enlisting my
> readers as evangelists for my work and giving them
> free ebooks to distribute sells more books."[8]

PROFITS THROUGH PARTICIPATION AND PERSONALIZATION

I opened this chapter by saying that your brand does not belong to you. While this is not news to anyone, it is worthwhile to remind ourselves. The identity of your brand and its fate in the marketplace ultimately rest with your customers. Likewise, the identity of your employment brand and its fate in the marketplace ultimately rest with your staff.

What customers think and say about your products and services determines whether they will be profitable and for how long. And what staff think and say about your business determines whether you can attract, develop and retain the best and brightest to work for and with you. For good or ill, nothing beats word of mouth.

NOTHING BEATS WORD OF MOUTH.

Nothing beats it, that is, except for word of *mouse*. What has changed with the internet and the new communications technologies is the speed with which perceptions of your brand can spread, infecting people with an enthusiasm for contact with your brand, or with a disdain for it, as the case may

NOTHING BEATS IT, THAT IS, EXCEPT FOR WORD OF *MOUSE*.

be. The old rule of thumb was that whereas a satisfied customer might tell one person what was great about a product or service, a dissatisfied customer would tell eight people what was wrong with it. Nowadays there is no limit to how many people dissatisfied customers can communicate with via the internet. And although there may also be no limit to how many people satisfied customers can communicate with, human nature still means that people get more fired up about complaining when something goes wrong than they do about enthusing when something goes right. A 2006 *BRW* article cites research by Melbourne Business School that notes a correlation between negative word-of-mouse publicity and a company's performance. There was no corresponding correlation between good feedback and good performance.

Let's briefly consider Dom in my office, who not so long ago had an ordinary experience with his local Australian bank. It was so bad it prompted him to start a user group on Facebook.com called "I hate banks: let's start a consumer rebellion". Within one hour sixty-four of his "friends" had joined. Interestingly enough, a significant number of them were from Western Europe, so obviously we are talking global here. Now assume that, like Dom, his first-degree connections also have dozens of "friends" independent of Dom's network. Before you know it hundreds of people, many of whom Dom has never met, have joined his club. They then ask their contacts, who in turn ask their contacts, and so on until this user group has thousands of members beating up the banks.

After I gently reminded Dom that the banking sector is one of our best sources of clients, and that I like those clients very much, and so should he, given that they pay his bills, the growth of the user group was stemmed (or should I say halted) but not before showing me a live example of just how powerful word of mouse can be. By the way, my behaviour here goes against the flip I am putting forth in this chapter, and had I been the bank I would have been more interested in learning from the experience, knowing full well I had no ability to shut it down.

A search by industry on the website my3cents.com can show you how powerful customers banding together can be. A search about the banking sector brings up posts like "Bank XYZ –

Not like all the other banks – WORSE!" And another that reads "Big banks need to follow rules too."

According to their website:

> My3cents.com is a leading source of real consumer advice. Visitors come to learn, interact and voice opinions regarding companies, products and services in our open community. Learn from other consumer experiences, and help others learn from your own personal consumer experiences. Join the revolution today and start being heard!

My3cents is not a popular website, but there are hundreds just like it, such as CRM Lowdown, which I mentioned earlier and which gives people an opportunity to vent, or more important, find out about certain products and companies. Such sites are evidence of the increasing transparency and accountability I have been talking about, which is one of the four forces of change we face daily. The result of this and other changes discussed in this book is that the power of customers and staff is increasing, and the power of companies is decreasing.

The explosion of the blogosphere, platforms like MySpace and user-generated content are all part of the consumer voice. It is easier to be heard (or read) now than ever before, and search technology makes it simpler to find specific information on what you need. More and more consumers, and businesses, too, will do a search before making a purchase or a decision about a product or service. Job applicants are Googling a company to see what other people say about it, and giving more weight to these opinions than to what may be on the company's own website.

I say embrace the transparency. Once upon a time it would have cost hundreds of thousands of pounds to truly find out how a customer felt about your product. Now it takes a few hours and a free internet search. If I was a senior leader at Bank XYZ, I would want to know what happened to the customer who is now complaining on My3cents. If I was the Aussie bank that Dom was complaining about, I would want to read his post, and all the comments, to find out how I could improve my services.

I personally know this experience well. Every week I present to an audience, sometimes as small as six and at other times as big as a few thousand. As disturbing as feedback can be, you need to suck it up and learn from it, both the good and the bad. When I first launched my blog, I disabled comments. Why? Because it was integrated into my commercial website, and the last thing I wanted was a client engaging me in their business to read things other people say about my ideas and work. Talk about missing the point. It is about dialogue these days, not monologue. It is a conversation, not a dictation. I have since changed my approach, and with the exception of the odd inappropriate link (I think you know what I mean) that some computer-generated program has placed there, my blog leaves all comments exactly as they were posted.

Such public dialogue is not to be taken lightly. General Motors ran a competition where anyone could make their own commercial for the new Chevy Tahoe (in conjunction with Donald Trump's television show *The Apprentice*). It should be noted that GM's foray into viral marketing was incomplete from the outset. Even within the strictures set out by GM (they provided the videos that users could use, so it wasn't *entirely* user-generated), there was still a significant consumer backlash that made the whole campaign backfire.

A slew of global-warming-based criticisms and anti-SUV vitriol whipped around the web in the wake of the appeals for consumer involvement. GM was quick to remove some of the "offensive" content, although to their credit they left some of the more benign critical ads online.

GM had an opportunity to learn from this backlash. As one blogger noted:

> … instead of chocking this up to a bad marketing decision, they could really use the information here. There are a growing number of people who believe that the proliferation of SUVs is getting ridiculous. Does everyone need a vehicle that can climb snowy mountains?
> But what SUVs solve for many is a "cooler" alternative to minivans for their growing families.[9]

Their decision to remove some of the ads just created more controversy and backlash. As another blogger responded:

> Dear Chevy: Gas mileage, the environment, and big cars are not exactly a new issue. Hell, I got 32 miles per gallon on a 1967 Toyota Corolla! What did you think the public would do, given the chance?[10]

The company, however, claims they left all the ads online with the exception of vulgar and offensive content. Chevy general manager Ed Peper commented on his company blog:

> We at GM are not culturally unaware; we realize
> that there are people who would never purchase an
> SUV. That's why we make more vehicles that get
> over 30 miles-per-gallon than any other
> manufacturer...
>   Anyway, it sure got people talking about the
> Tahoe. Which was the whole idea, after all.[11]

That's a cracking response from GM. So they got it about half right, I guess.

What is most exciting about this trend is that while Web 2.0 is about user-generated content, Web 3.0 and Web 4.0 are going to add *huge* value to the consumer, and companies that do a great job will tap into the power of word of mouse for the positive. The word will spread loud and clear who the market leaders are, and what products and services you should buy, and what the best companies are to work for.

Here is what the evolution might look like. The idea comes from Tim Berners-Lee, who is widely credited with inventing the World Wide Web, and is what he had envisaged it to be like all along. Web 3.0 is often referred to as the *semantic web*. This means it is about ordering and giving meaning to content and information. It refers to both a *philosophy* for future web design (that the content should be readily searchable and understood by software programs so it can be ordered, sorted and accessed) and also to *technologies* that enable that philosophy to be borne out.

At the moment you can use the internet for a whole lot of

useful stuff, but you can't just have a machine do that for you because web pages are designed to be read by people, not machines. Semantic web is a vision of an internet where computers can understand the information. Talk about fast, good, cheap and easy. Web 3.0 is not really here yet, but a visit to the Media Labs at MIT would suggest it will come.

While Web 2.0 is user-generated and social-networking content, and Web 3.0 is about a learning, semantic web, some already look ahead to what Web 4.0 might be. Marketing guru Seth Godin, whom I mentioned in connection with book downloads, has an interesting idea that is worth sharing: that Web 4.0 could be about forming an intense and close connection with a small and intimate group of people.

Consider this flash into the future, found on his blog:

I'm typing an email to someone, and we're brainstorming about doing a business development deal with Apple. A little window pops up and lets me know that David over in our Tucson office is already having a similar conversation with Apple and perhaps we should coordinate.

Google watches what I search. It watches what other people like me search. Every day, it shows me things I ought to be searching for that I'm not. And it introduces me to people who are searching for what I'm searching for.

I'm late for a dinner. My GPS phone knows this (because it has my calendar, my location, and the traffic status). So, it tells me, and then it alerts the people who are waiting for me.

I visit a blog for the first time. My browser knows what sort of stories I am interested in and shows me highlights of the new blog based on that history.

Web4 is about smaller, far more intense connections with trusted colleagues and their activities. It's a tribe.[12]

According to Godin, for Web 4.0 to become a reality we need:

- an e-mail client who is smart about what I'm doing and what my opted-in colleagues are doing. Once that gains traction, plenty of vendors will work to integrate with it.
- a mobile phone and mobile-phone provider that is not just a phone.
- a word processor that knows about everything I've written and what's on the Web that's related to what I'm writing now.
- moves by Google and Yahoo and others to make it easy for us to become non-anonymous, all the time, everywhere we go.

People, companies and governments are watching what we do; our computers and the search engines we use are recording what we look for, read and say — why not use this information in a way that adds power to our lives? It might scare some people, but it certainly excites me.

LET THE CUSTOMER PLAY

Sony stumbled over this chapter's flip when players of its Ever-Quest game created a black economy via PayPal to buy and sell virtual assets in the game's alternative online world. Sony told its customers in effect, "We want to control those game features and any income stream associated with them." Sony's customers said, "Back off. It's our game now." In the face of massive customer resentment, Sony had to back down. In doing so, it allowed Ever-Quest to continue to grow and continue to pour profits into its corporate coffers. Sony won loyalty and profits by losing control.

In a different version of events, some companies have set out deliberately to exploit the desire of the audience to partici-pate. Reality TV is one example, and its most successful fran-chise is the *Idol* format, which includes *American Idol,* the original British show *Pop Idol* and more than thirty other *Idol*

franchises around the world. The *Idol* shows not only star am-ateur talent, but the results of the shows' talent competitions are determined by viewers' votes. Viewer choice also deter-mines the outcome on other extremely successful reality shows such as *Survivor* and *Big Brother.* It is no longer enough to pas-sively watch a TV show. We want to participate, and vote off the people we don't like.

In addition to making the actual shows extremely popu-lar, driving up traditional advertising revenue, the reality for-mat lends itself perfectly to be more integrated with other mediums – such as the internet – which also drive revenues. Perhaps the most significant spin-off, however, is the revenue from voting itself. It is no secret that the voting format is a big cash spinner.

To get some idea of the power of this new format, which perfectly taps the desire of the audience to have more control over their experience, check out this information that appeared in a white paper on the *Idol* format by interactive marketing specialist SMLXL:

- Over 3.2 billion viewers over the past six years.
- The thirty-plus countries the format is aired in cover a total of 560 million TV households.
- There were 215 million unique viewers for the final alone.
- During the past five years *Pop Idol* viewers have generated 1.9 billion votes.
- The fourth *American Idol,* which took place in 2004, was at the time the biggest texting event in the world, with 41 million text-message-based votes cast. What is more remarkable is that 30 per cent of those texters had never sent a text message before.
- The 2004 figures turned out to be only the beginning, with the spring 2006 run of *American Idol* attracting 64.5 million text-message votes.
- New applications include trivia, sweepstakes entries, text message chats, a fan club, a vote number reminder and downloadable ring tones.
- It just keeps getting bigger – 680 million votes in the last twelve months.
- So for a typical twenty-episode run, viewers have about fourteen opportunities to vote.

Consider that there is about a 90 per cent profit margin on each text message, and you see what an enviable income stream this generates for *Idol*'s producers and broadcasters, not to mention the mobile-phone service providers.

Today's viewers want to customize their viewing experience in the same way Starbucks has been customizing their lattes. It is no longer enough to just watch people on television; I need to have some control over who stays on what shows and for how long.

Interestingly, it took a music-industry man (not a TV producer) and a gutsy UK television station to try the reality format, and to add voting capability to it. This was not a "crowd" initiative. Fremantle Media and 19 Management are reaping the rewards of a concept popularly credited to one man: Simon Fuller. Fuller, who founded 19 Management in 1985, was previously known as the manager of the Spice Girls and S Club 7. The Spice Girls and the birth of the *Idol* format in 1998 make Simon Fuller a world-class flipstar.

The most interesting iteration of the *Idol* format came in 2005 in Finland. They ran side by side with the show proper an uncontrolled version called *Jokamiehen Idol* (*People's Idol*), where anyone and everyone could post to the internet their own "Idol" performance, whether they had auditioned for the show or not, and whether they were any good or not; 150,000 Finns listened to the amateur posts and cast 1,950,000 votes, which according to SMLXL was more than actually voted for the televised "real" *Idol*.

Australia did the same with Telstra in 2006 when they allowed users to become the "Street Idol", winning $20,000 and a trip to the Grammy Awards.

What is cool about this is that it is an example of the producer giving up even more control. It is the same participation that has driven the phenomenal success of YouTube.

CUSTOMERS WANT WHAT THEY WANT

Formerly of the MIT Media Lab, Nicholas Negroponte famously said, "Customers don't want choice; they want what they want." This is true, but a limited and controlled set of choices allowed companies to spread their risk, and get closer to giving what the customer wanted to a broad enough market to maintain some level of economies of scale so they could deliver their "almost right" products to the market in a cost-effective way. Digital distribution, global markets, better production technology and more sophisticated supply chains giving the ability to the customer to more easily declare what he or she wants are just some of the things allowing companies to move from "almost right" product choices to "mass personalization".

But customers generally don't really know what they want. Many times a product is successful when the company is able to convince consumers that they want something that previously they did not. Or in extreme cases like the motorcar, the digital watch or more recently the digital music player, convince them they want something that previously did not even exist. Remember there is no wisdom in crowds when it comes to innovation, and maverick innovators are still required here.

A SUCCESSFUL PRODUCT OFTEN CONVINCES CONSUMERS THAT THEY WANT SOMETHING THAT PREVIOUSLY THEY DID NOT.

Let's revisit the Scion. Although the brand story and styling of the Scion are closely controlled by Toyota, part of that story is that this can be "your" ride. Just how you want it. The Scion has been designed to be personalized. This is the trend to which I am referring – the desire of the consumer to have products that they feel are uniquely theirs. This is why the story is so powerful, as talked about in detail in Chapter 4, "Absolutely, Positively Sweat the Small Stuff".

James Farley, vice president of the Scion at the time of its unveiling, said, "Scion is about personalization. It's about providing buyers with a personalized dealership experience, a personalized ordering process, and personalized vehicles."

The Scion team developed almost forty accessories that could be fitted to the car to meet the customer's exact wants, including fog lamps, rear spoilers and auxiliary interior light kits. Scions also lend themselves to post-purchase customization, with a whole market of non-Toyota companies springing up to offer various types of customization, including additions of subwoofers, superchargers and non-Scion decals.

The Scion FUSE concept car unveiled at the New York Auto Show in 2006 takes this to the next level. Another Scion executive, Mark Templin, says that as well as pushing the "creative envelope" the Scion also demonstrates "boundless personalization" potential. Everything from the customizable multicoloured headlights to the different options for in-car WiFi access, video consoles and televisions can be tailored down to the individual tastes of the customer.

Your company's version of personalization does not need to be as sophisticated as the Toyota Scion. Perhaps you could start by giving your customers a wider choice of payment methods. Maybe it is more delivery options. I am willing to bet you have all had that experience of buying a piece of furniture only to then be told it will need to be delivered in a few days (or months) as they keep no stock on hand. I can understand this, knowing how expensive retail space is, but your average consumer gets annoyed by it. If this is not bad enough, the retailer then tells you on what day it will be delivered, regardless of whether this suits you or not. So you arrange to duck out of work for an hour or so, but then they only give you a window of about six hours. And then they refuse to call you one hour before they are due to arrive. So basically you, the customer, end up having to take half a day off work, which probably costs you more in lost productivity than your initial purchase was worth, and you sit around waiting for the delivery van to arrive. And if they are anything like the furniture shop I referred to earlier, they will leave their rubbish in your living room because "this is not their responsibility".

Probably the best and most successful example of "mass personalization" around the world is IKEA. The build-it-yourself model that IKEA embraces comes from their desire to constantly drive down prices but not sacrifice quality. They sell all their furniture disassembled (in "flat packs") so costs of construction are passed on to the consumer (that is, the price is lower but the cost in effort is higher). The idea came from when Gilles Lundgren was struggling to fit a table into the back of his car, so he took the legs off it and it fit "in five easy pieces".

People like this model for a few reasons. First, they understand that their personal effort is part of the model that secures them lower prices, so they are happy to have a hand in building what they buy. But second, the fact that many IKEA products can be assembled in a number of ways (desks that can have a few hutches or be just plain, cupboards that can have multiple shelves in a few different layouts) means that consumers can assemble furniture that they feel is uniquely theirs – both *functionally* and *aesthetically*.

It obviously works. IKEA had an annual revenue of over $26 billion to March 2007 and employs over 100,000 people. Profit margins are 18 per cent and sales have trebled in the last decade, while at the same time prices have come down.

I have to be honest here. Until very recently I hated IKEA with a passion. The thought of having to take down my own order, load my own shopping trolley and car, and then not be able to pay with my preferred credit card was enough to drive me mad. Paying extra for some service is what I prefer. (Perhaps IKEA should consider a premium service, where you get a one-to-one service for sixty minutes for a per centage of your purchase, with a minimum charge.) However, a recent experience has changed my view, and now I am a huge fan. Redoing a playroom for my kids, I found that IKEA's myriad furniture options can indeed create a customer experience that is fast, good, cheap and (mass-) personalized.

The point: where possible give your customers what they want, and not what you think they want. Or worse, what you want. Do an audit of your product choices, delivery options, and payment methods. Ask yourself, are they set up to favour the customer or to favour you?

THE TRUE WISDOM OF CROWDS

It may come as a shock to you, but the smartest people in the world don't all work for you. But you still want to access their brains and creativity, and these days that is easier than ever before. Consider the Chicago T-shirt manufacturer Threadless.

It makes all its T-shirts to designs that its customers post on the company website and that other site visitors can rate on a scale of one to five. Each week the company puts the most popular new designs into production, paying each winning designer $1,500 in cash and $500 in merchandise. On an average day well over 100 designs are posted on Threadless.com, and in an average month the company sells almost 80,000 T-shirts at $15 a piece.

According to Threadless co-founder Jacob DeHart, "We've got four rules we follow. We let the [Threadless customer] community create the content. We let the community build itself – no advertising. We let the community help with the business; we add features based on user feedback. And we reward members of the community for participating."

Similarly, on the website of Seattle's fast-growing Jones Soda, which sells a range of organic teas and carbonated beverages, customers post and vote on photographs, with the winning images becoming incorporated into Jones Soda bottle labels. Founder and CEO Peter van Stolk says, "We founded this company with the philosophy that the world does not need another soda. That forced us to look at things differently: How could we create a new kind of connection with customers, let them play with the brand, let them take ownership of it? Everything at this company is about sharing ownership of the brand with our customers. This is not *my* brand. This is not *our* soda. It belongs to our customers."[13]

Although the crowd itself is not wise in the sense of generating new ideas, it contains a lot of insanely talented individuals who have the ability and desire to contribute in meaningful ways to the brands they love. Sometimes, purely for love. Consider LEGO.

In 2003 LEGO suffered its greatest-ever loss, $238 million. In response, rather than keep doing the same thing and hoping it would turn around, LEGO adapted. It tore up the detailed blueprint it had been operating under and became a flipstar. The company folded its game-software division, as well as a number of underperforming LEGO kit designs, and decreased the number of unique LEGO blocks and other kit pieces it manufactures by over 40 per cent. Fairly normal cost cutting, but a bold, aggressive start to the action.

LEGO followed that by deciding to reinvigorate one of its most successful recent products, the Mindstorms LEGO robot kit. Costing $199 at retail, the Mindstorms kit had sold almost a million units since its 1998 release and by 2003 was still selling around 40,000 units a year with no advertising. But the kit was too complex for most children, and many of its most loyal fans were adults.

After some initial development of a new Mindstorms prototype in-house, LEGO decided to invite a small group of adult users who had become celebrities in the Mindstorms world to become a top-secret Mindstorms Users Panel (MUP): Steve Hassenpflug, an Indiana software engineer; John Barnes, the owner of a firm that manufactures ultrasonic sensors; Ralph Hempel, author of several Mindstorms how-to books; and David Schilling, co-founder of a Mindstorms user group called SMART, the Seattle Mindstorms and Robotic Techies. Working on the project without pay, and even buying their own plane tickets when they visited LEGO headquarters in Denmark, the MUP-sters influenced every aspect of what became Mindstorms NXT, a runaway bestseller for LEGO at a list price of $249 since its 2006 release, in exchange for a few free prototypes and other LEGO kits and the satisfaction of being involved in creating the new version of something they loved.

Assembling the MUP was a huge break from LEGO's tradition of controlling every aspect of design and production in-house. A flip, no less. To create Mindstorms NXT, they also went outside for software programming. But they had already taken an important step in this direction with the original

Mindstorms product release in 1996. When a hacker quickly broke and published the Mindstorms software code, LEGO considered legal action against him. Then it took a far more profitable legal action: it altered the Mindstorms software licence

THE OPEN-SOURCE MODEL IS THE ANTITHESIS OF THE COMMAND-AND-CONTROL SYSTEMS OF PRODUCT DEVELOPMENT AND EXPLOITATION THAT MOST BUSINESSES STILL FOLLOW.

by inserting a "right to hack". As fanatical Mindstorms hackers published code for making Mindstorms robots that could deal blackjack, scrub toilets and perform a host of other functions that had never been in LEGO's product brief, LEGO became one of the first manufacturers to reap the benefits of open-source software development.

On a final note, LEGO has started to use this same approach to sell more of its innovative new products. LEGO enlisted influential consumers as online evangelists. After a new locomotive was shown to the 250 most hard-core LEGO train fans, their word of mouse helped the first 10,000 units sell out in ten days with no other marketing.[14]

The open-source model is the antithesis of the command-and-control systems of product development and exploitation that most businesses still follow. In command-and-control R&D, the company sets all the parameters at the top executive level, and a research-and-development department attempts to execute accordingly. Attempts, because as history amply demonstrates there is no effective way to dictate specific discoveries in a closed system.

In Chapter 6, "Mass-Market Success: Find It on the Fringe", I argued that you have to be open to ideas from the fringe. You have to be open to serendipity, to finding things you weren't looking for. The open-source model does this by recruiting the energies not of a proprietary research force whose resources are limited even in the largest companies and organizations, or even the most powerful governments, but of anyone who cares to contribute. This ensures that new ideas will have a chance to emerge from the fringe. It's a flip on a flip. The true wisdom of virtual crowds is that people will be pursuing their individual interests and agendas. It's a market of the mind, which winnows out the good ideas from the bad in an uncontrolled, Darwinian survival of the fittest.

> THE TRUE WISDOM OF VIRTUAL CROWDS IS THAT PEOPLE WILL BE PURSUING THEIR INDIVIDUAL INTERESTS AND AGENDAS.

Nothing demonstrates the potential of the open-source model better than Linux. Linux itself grew out of two earlier open-source projects – Unix and GNU. Unix, the free-time pet project of two AT&T Bell Labs researchers in the late 1960s, was initially quite successful but quickly became heavily protected by patents. In response, GNU emerged as an open-source alternative to Unix, but lacked some central elements of a viable operating system, such as a microkernel.

Linux, the brainchild of Finnish computer scientist Linus Torvalds, was released in the public domain in 1991 and was a fully viable operating system. Today, only 2 per cent of the Linux kernel is directly attributable to Torvalds, but it is hugely successful. IBM and other large IT corporations use Linux as an operating system, and there are numerous small companies selling Linux software, which runs on everything from supercomputers and servers to mobile phones and PDAs. In 2008 the global Linux market is projected to reach $35.7 billion a year.

None of this could have happened cost-effectively within a single company's, or even a consortium's, proprietary software development. To compile the millions of lines of source code in Red Hat Linux – the first important, but now discontinued, product from Red Hat – would have taken 8,000 man-years of conventional development time at a cost of $1.08 billion a year.

I said that open-source development represents the true wisdom of crowds, and the thousands of contributors to Linux certainly make up quite a crowd. But this does not actually contradict Chapter 6's flip, "Mass Market Success: Find It on the Fringe". To appreciate this, we have to look closely at the development of the Linux kernel, and consider the concept of *lead users,* people who innovate solutions for their own specific needs in advance of similar general needs.

Only 2 per cent of the current Linux kernel is directly attributable to Linus Torvalds. But by functioning as, in effect, a lead user of the Unix-like concepts and designs that he drew on to create the first Linux kernel, Torvalds put his stamp on everything Linux and pointed out a direction for its future development. By the same token, LEGO's Mindstorms User Panel, recruited from outside the company, served as lead users for the development of Mindstorms NXT. By definition, lead users are to be found on the fringe of mainstream activities, or to put it another way, on the cutting edge of developing trends.

Lead users act like fringe ideas that attract mainstream interest. As I said in Chapter 6, innovations don't begin in crowds, but crowds are necessary to validate innovations. There may be no *I* in team, but there definitely is an *I* in innovation, and lead users put it there. An article published in *BRW* in Australia cited research that looked at fifty projects in development over about a year and found that products using the lead-user approach generated returns that were on average eight times greater than products developed the conventional way.

In his book *Democratizing Innovation,* Eric von Hippel shows that lead-user product development can be a far more effective means of innovation than conventional product development within a closed system. At 3M, for example, von Hippel and his research associates found that lead-user development resulted in five major new product lines with annual sales forecasts of $146 million per product, whereas conventional solely-within-the-company product development over the study period resulted in forty-one incremental improvements to existing product lines and only one major new product line with an annual sales forecast of $18 million.

Von Hippel says of the lead-user product-development

process, "This is not traditional market research – asking customers what they want. This is identifying what your most advanced users are already doing and understanding what their innovations mean for the future of your business."

Some of the most interesting new branding and product development today are being done by companies that use social-networking technology to solicit contributions from lead users and/or validate innovations by seeing what customers in general think of them. For example, the Vancouver-based shoe designer John Fluevog, who has boutiques in several North American cities and distributes his shoes to high-end shops around the world, practices what he calls "open-source footwear" by inviting design submissions from customers. Although only a few such submissions become actual products, Fluevog says, "Even submissions we can't make add to the stimulation. Our customers get more involved, and we get insight into who they are and what they're doing."[15]

Consider a slightly different version of the same phenomenon – the InnovationXChange. I had the pleasure of meeting John Wolpert, who developed the BRIDGE methodology, which instructs professional intermediaries on how to help companies share intent and find mutually beneficial collaborations without exposing secrets to one another directly.

Less than four weeks later I serendipitously bumped into InnovationXChange CEO Grant Kearney boarding a plane to Sydney. IXC is a not-for-profit company that helps companies, universities and research institutions collaborate and share information in the midst of highly complex international intellectual-property laws, while still maintaining strict confidentiality. In their own words, they "make it safe for organizations to 'talk'".

They have dealt with everyone from food makers to pharmaceutical companies, in one case linking a pharmaceutical company working on a partially finished drug with a nanotechnology company on the other side of the world that revolutionized the drug's delivery mechanism. IXC is a fascinating organization, adding real value to Australian businesses.

This trend is global. For instance, the website Global Ideas Bank (www.globalideasbank.org) is a public forum where people can post ideas at any level of development (from a small inkling of an idea to a well-progressed idea that is hitting stumbling blocks), and people can comment and contribute.

SOME THINGS ARE (STILL) WORTH PAYING FOR

Innovation contests and prize challenges are another means of open-source, lead-user product development. The pharmaceutical giant Eli Lilly recently incubated and spun off a new enterprise called InnoCentive, which acts as a middleman between companies ("seekers") and a worldwide community of self-selected scientists and engineers ("solvers"). Seeker companies post challenges with cash awards for the development of new products and processes, and scientist solvers post their suggested solutions by a specified deadline.

In early 2007 InnoCentive's open challenges included an award of $140,000 for new pressure-sensitive adhesives and $1 million for a biomarker for the disease ALS (amyotrophic lateral sclerosis), as well as $15,000 each for a novel method of dust control and packaging to limit the breakage of potato crisps. Successful solutions to past challenges include a new method for assessing the risk of breast cancer, UV-resistant coatings and a next-generation paper binder, among several dozen others for companies such as Procter & Gamble, Du-Pont, Dow and Boeing.

Contests to spark innovation have a long history. In the eighteenth century the British government offered £20,000 pounds, an enormous sum then, for the solution to finding an accurate longitude on the open sea. The solution didn't come from highly credentialled astronomers of the day, but instead from a clockmaker. His name was John Harrison. After four different incarnations of his longitudinal chronometers, he finally built one that worked extremely accurately. For petty political reasons he was initially refused his reward! He fought it and fought it, and finally — *years* after building a properly working device that could measure longitude at sea — he was granted his reward. He was *eighty,* and lived only three more years. Thankfully, today such contests are known for paying up more reliably. Can you imagine the PR and word-of-mouse frenzy that would follow if they did not?

Netflix, the DVDs-by-post service, which operates on a lending-library subscription model, asks customers to rate the films they watch and then uses an algorithm to make recommendations of new films based on over 1.6 billion total customer ratings. As with similar algorithms that lie behind Amazon.com's customer recommendations and Google's search-tailored advertising, the more accurate Netflix can make its "Cinematch" algorithm, the more customer satisfaction and loyalty it will engender and the better positioned it will be against competitors, including coming digital download services.

In October 2006 Netflix announced a $1 million prize and a five-year submission deadline for an algorithm that would increase the accuracy of Cinematch in predicting customer responses to films by at least 10 per cent. According to the *New York Times,* the company, which did not expect quick results, "underestimated the power of an open competition". Less than six months after the start of the competition the model of the leading contenders, a team of Hungarian scientists, was "already 6.75 per cent better than Cinematch".

Incidentally, showing that it knows how to "Think AND, Not OR", in January 2007 Netflix introduced a new feature to its DVD-rental subscription plans. For no additional charge, Netflix customers got the capability to watch streaming films from Netflix, as well as continue to receive and return DVDs through the post.

On a side note, Netflix sounds a little bit like a nascent kind of Web 3.0, but it probably falls a bit short. It is certainly an example of organizing information. But to truly be a part of the semantic web the data would have to be ordered and stored in such a way that machines could understand what the data *meant* so they could parse it for useful information. It would need what information specialists call a *metalanguage*.

Netflix really is just a good database with a good search algorithm. If it was really Web 3.0, you should be able to ask the database, "I want to see a funny film, but I want it to be dark humour, not slapstick, and I want it to have a serious edge."

The only way of doing that with Netflix would be to wade through all the user comments. In Web 3.0, the computer could understand qualitative judgements and comments.

Summing up the benefits of innovation contests at Netflix and elsewhere, the *New York Times* noted the "two essential features of prizes. They pay for nothing but performance, and they ensure that anyone with a good idea – not just the usual experts – can take a crack at a tough problem."[16]

Procter & Gamble adopted a strategy called Connect and Develop as part of its fightback following its market slump in 2001. It employed a network of scouts to look for (connect) new ideas, and then to develop them. Procter & Gamble has an internal R&D operation with a nearly $2-billion-a-year budget, but they are smart enough to still "Think AND, Not OR" and look outside, too, by using InnoCentive's 8,000 independent, self-selected "solvers". It's like an R&D version of e-lance.com, where the company posts R&D projects and people can contribute. Procter & Gamble's decision to move away from just traditional in-house R&D and combine it with this new outsourced variety has led to a 60 per cent increase in R&D productivity and the launch of more than 100 successful products, including the hit Olay Regenerist.

Cisco Systems has an outstanding internal culture and empowered staff, but another vital factor in their long-standing success is an "acquire and develop" strategy: they buy up small, innovative companies and use their resources and market clout to realize their potential. Rather than create an open competition, Cisco will let fringe entities develop an idea in their own time and with their own money until that innovation looks ready to be integrated into existing technologies or commercialized in its own right. Cisco will then buy the company, ideas and talent both, and take it to market.

Or for another favourite, Intel has built "lablets" in strategic universities to work closely with researchers and graduate students to publish research that Intel will not own. The goal is to build the amount of innovative activity in the areas that Intel works in. In the future they could adopt a connect-and-develop or even an acquire-and-develop approach to some of the innovations created from these relationships.

These strategies make more sense when you consider data published by the National Science Foundation showing that between 1981 and 2001 the percentage of total R&D expenditure that can be attributed to large businesses has shrunk from 70.6 per cent to 39.4 per cent. This is especially telling because the per centage that can be attributed to businesses with fewer than 1,000 people has grown from 4.4 per cent to 24.7 per cent. It makes sense to connect, acquire and develop when smaller firms are where a significant chunk of the action is.

THE FASTER YOU MOVE THE LESS LIKELY YOU ARE TO TAKE THE TIME TO FIND AND EVALUATE EXTERNAL OPTIONS. YOU NEED TO GET OVER THIS NATURAL FOCUS, AND GET OUT AND SEE WHAT IS HAPPENING.

The other advantage of these approaches by companies such as Procter & Gamble, Cisco and Intel is that these smaller entrepreneurial ventures are putting everything on the line and have already taken the risk. They are generally more nimble organizations, able to move quickly when the market changes, and in reality their success depends on getting it right. If a large company fails to innovate in one product area, there are a few thousand others to absorb the loss. If one of these smaller companies fails to stay on trend, it will find itself out of business fast.

As a side note, of the four forces of change, compression of time is the most likely to prevent you from embracing the opportunities that open-source and lead-user development present. As you try to keep up with change, you are forced to move more quickly. The faster you move the less likely you are to take the time to find and evaluate external options. You need to get over this natural focus, and get out and see what is happening.

The whole idea of open source, like rewards for ideas, is not a new one. Although the term *open source* is alleged to have come out of a strategy session held at Palo Alto in response to Netscape's decision in January 1998 to release its source code (think "open" source code), its origins are older, and the concept as it is being presented here is far more broad in application than simply source code.

Let me give you a great Australian example. CAMBIA is a not-for-profit research centre founded in 1992 by Richard Jefferson in Canberra. Focusing on plants and biotechnology, CAMBIA was an acronym for the Centre for the Application of Molecular Biology to International Agriculture.

These days CAMBIA has evolved into more broad lifescience applications but retains the name CAMBIA, which in Italy and Spain means "change". CAMBIA develops new methodologies and technologies for plant improvement and then provides that information to the wider market. In effect CAMBIA is an open-source biotechnology research centre and a driver for much innovation.

The key goal of CAMBIA is to promote open-source innovation in the wider arena of biotechnology. They see open source as an enabler of innovation, and have developed a suite of technologies, patents and licences that in their view will give innovators greater freedom to develop and market new biotechnologies. CAMBIA makes specific reference to helping smaller businesses and ventures who, without assistance in what can be both scientifically and legally complex space, would not gain sufficient access to the market. In

> TAP INTO THE BRILLIANCE THAT INDIVIDUALS WHO DON'T WORK FOR YOU HAVE, WHETHER THEY BE CUSTOMERS, BORED SCIENTISTS IN ACADEMIA OR TEENAGE KIDS WITH AN IDEA ABOUT HOW TO ADVERTISE YOUR PRODUCT BETTER.

a way, CAMBIA helps to create and spread innovation by removing control from the hands of the wealthiest companies.

I am not suggesting you give everything away for free, nor am I suggesting you expose your competitive advantage. This would make no sense unless it made your business more profitable. You should, however, tap into the brilliance that individuals who don't work for you have, whether they be customers, bored scientists in academia or teenage kids with an idea about how to advertise your product better.

INVISIBLE PROFITS: SUCCESS THROUGH CO-OPETITION AND PARTNERSHIP

I had the pleasure of sitting next to a senior engineer from Maunsell, Australia, on a flight from Perth to Brisbane. His name is Richard Jackson. Richard now claims that one of his great achievements in life is to sit next to me for more than four hours in a confined space and survive. It was the start of a relationship with Maunsell, and now AECOM globally, a company that ranks among the most exciting I have ever worked with. In that conversation one thing stood out and has influenced my thinking greatly.

In the development of huge infrastructure projects, competitive firms are often engaged simultaneously to get the project finished on spec and on time. Apparently these "partnerships" have traditionally been hostile ones. When I asked Richard to describe the biggest change facing his industry, he said it was a move towards win-win relationships with suppliers and traditional competitors, away from the older-style hostile partnerships.

Recently I was listening to a podcast of a presentation by Bill Clinton at the annual TED conference in Monterey, California, in which he used the word *interdependent* repeatedly. This idea of teaming and partnership even with traditional competitors seems to be gathering real momentum.

A 2000 Booz Allen Hamilton Consulting report notes that more than 50 per cent of business alliances in the "new wave" of business collaborations (which refers to the massive increase of business partnerships since around the year 2000, facilitated by technology and spurred on by an increasingly crowded market) are between *competitors,* and lead on average to a 7 per cent higher return than traditional collaborations.

Toyota realizes that sharing their hybrid technology has real benefits for them. They already have technology-sharing agreements with Nissan and Ford (who use Toyota technology in the popular Ford Escape). Toyota not only enjoys licensing fees and royalties from other companies using their technology, but the more people who use their technology the higher their output volume, so the lower their per-unit production costs become. It's win-win.

Apple recognized that the best way to achieve their goals lay in cooperating with other established companies in partnerships where they could ride each other's innovations. In 2006 they partnered with Intel to deliver Mac computers running off Intel chips. The companies' faith in the power of collaboration is clear when you look at the way they described the venture in a joint press release on 6 June 2005.

> JUST BECAUSE YOU HAVEN'T FIGURED OUT A WAY TO MAKE AN IDEA WORK, IT DOES NOT MEAN SOMEONE ELSE CAN'T.

Apple CEO Steve Jobs said, "Our goal is to provide our customers with the best personal computers in the world, and looking ahead Intel has the strongest processor roadmap by far ... we think Intel's technology will help us create the best personal computers for the next ten years."

Intel CEO Paul Otellini said, "We are thrilled to have the world's most innovative personal computer company as a customer. Apple helped found the PC industry and throughout the years has been known for fresh ideas and new approaches. We look forward to providing advanced chip technologies, and to collaborating on new initiatives, to help Apple continue to deliver innovative products for years to come."

Just because you haven't figured out a way to make an idea work, it does not mean someone else can't. Sell it, license it, partner on it. Stop keeping it hidden, especially if you are getting no return on the asset. You wouldn't leave a huge piece of real estate or a factory doing nothing. You would work that and your other physical assets as much as possible. It is time we started thinking of our intellectual assets the same way.

According to Ron Sampson, secretary of the not-for-profit National Institute for Strategic Technology Acquisition and Commercialization in Manhattan, 90 to 95 per cent of all patents are idle. Procter & Gamble only uses about 7,000 of their 36,000 patents, according to company spokesman Jeff LeRoy.

Companies will patent any meaningful advance but only work on the ones that fit into their immediate R&D. The worst for this are pharmaceutical companies. The phenomenon is called "the tragedy of the anticommons" – that is, patents keep knowledge in the hands of just a few people (monopoly on knowledge), which is bad for innovation. In fact, in the European Union, a report by a group of Italian academics found that as many as 18 per cent of patents were "blocking" patents, which are patents taken out not so you can develop them into something, but to make sure someone else doesn't. That's not cool, and that is not progressive enough for the flip world.

THE ULTIMATE POWER TRIP: LEVERAGING POWER BY SHARING IT

The antiquated 1950s view of business is the boss walking around trying to squeeze every last bit of work out of employees, worried they are ordering Christmas presents online. I actually worry about the opposite, getting my people to take all their vacation time. We have a system that notifies me when someone is about to lose vaca-

tion days because they haven't SMART PEOPLE WORK
taken them in time. Every one of FOR YOU. USE THEM!
my direct reports is in danger.

– Jonathan Schwartz, President/COO,

Sun Microsystems

Smart people work for you. Use them! One of the biggest complaints that my own research, and that of companies such as Gallup, has found is that one of the most frustrating things about
work is when your company doesn't fully utilize your skills.

Technology can help

The same technology that is putting the power back in the
hands of the consumer can also help you to generate collaboration and knowledge sharing within your own workforce. Consider the following example that appeared in an *Australian
Financial Review* article in 2007.

Geek Squad, the computer-repair company started by University of Minnesota IT graduate Robert Stephens, uses a whole
suite of electronic collaborative software to keep teams all across
the United States working in sync with one another. Geek Squad
wikis are accessible and editable by all of their almost 12,000
employees, so they provide *useful* and *up-to-date* information all
the time. Some evidence suggested that appropriately deployed
in-house wikis could cut company meeting times "in half" and
decrease e-mail traffic volume by 75 per cent.

While some are sceptical about those figures, the direction is
right. It's interesting to note that the *AFR*'s source for the Geek
Squad story, a book called *Wikinomics: How Mass Collaboration*

Changes Everything, by Don Tapscott and Anthony D. Williams, is supplemented by a wiki that readers can contribute to and edit online. Recognizing that the book's information could quickly become obsolete, the authors say a wiki is the only way to keep it relevant.

The *AFR* article also cited Xerox, where CTO Sophie Vandebroek flipped the whole R&D strategy on its head: instead of the strategy emanating from the boardroom and filtering downwards, she started a company wiki where researchers in the R&D teams could collaboratively define the entire R&D strategy.

Perhaps the most extreme example is IBM's InnovationJam in 2006. The event brought together over 100,000 IBM employees in a moderated series of online discussions over seventy-two hours, where they brainstormed potential new products. Nothing was out of bounds for discussion. Such is IBM's commitment to the project that chief executive Sam Palmisano has committed $100 million to develop ideas with the most social and economic potential.[17]

IBM's first jam took place in 1998 and was a single, full-day collaboration between R&D labs. It was so successful that it was turned into a three-day extravaganza and eventually put online. An enormously detailed website for the 2007 jam includes "tips for successful jammers" that lead off with, "Don't be shy – you're the expert." This encapsulates the philosophy of "To Get Control, Give it Up".

Also, the jam has now gone way beyond just innovating in products (traditional R&D). Now every one of the 330,000 IBM employees has been explicitly given licence to offer suggestions and "riff" on everything from new products and services ideas to new business processes and business models. It really is an innovation free-for-all.

ON TOYOTA'S ASSEMBLY
LINES THE LOWEST-LEVEL
WORKER CAN SHUT DOWN THE
LINE FOR ANY REASON, EVEN
IF IT'S JUST THE SUSPICION
OF A PROBLEM.

I feel like I am overdoing the Toyota examples, but here I go again. The truth is the company is a flipstar in many ways. Toyota became admired first and foremost for its quality manufacturing system. Ford, GM and Chrysler have all sent high-level staff to observe Toyota's assembly lines, and in recent years the Detroit Three have greatly improved the quality of their own vehicles, in large part by copying the Japanese companies that once copied them.

But one feature of the Toyota manufacturing system seems to be too tough for Detroit to emulate. On Toyota's assembly lines the lowest-level worker can shut down the line for any reason, even if it's just the suspicion of a problem. In fact, Toyota's managers start to worry if the line doesn't shut down

IF YOUR STAFF ARE SO BORED
THEY ARE SPENDING HOURS
DOWNLOADING JUNK FROM
THE INTERNET, THEN YOU
SHOULD LOOK AT YOUR STAFF
SELECTION PROCESS, AND
MORE IMPORTANT AT THE
WORK YOU ARE ENGAGING
IN AND THE CULTURE THAT
EXISTS. BUILD A MORE
EXCITING PLACE TO WORK!

frequently, because it probably means quality problems are slipping through without being fixed. Yet despite all these stops and starts, Toyota produces vehicles in a shorter time than any other car manufacturer in the world.

What a flip! Empowering the lowest-level worker to shut down an entire assembly line lifts the entire workforce's dedication, performance and morale. Meanwhile, the Detroit Three, trapped in the bunker of a command-and-control mentality, re-coil from distributing such power down to the factory floor, even as their market shares erode and their losses mount. With Ford reporting its biggest-ever loss of $12.7 billion in 2006, it's no won-der CEO Alan Mulally went to Japan in December of that year to discuss a possible partnership with Toyota.

I would like to give you some simple day-to-day examples of managers trying to hold on to power, and it having a poten-tially adverse impact on results. Even though these examples seem quite insignificant, they represent a much deeper chal-lenge in businesses today.

I confessed earlier to not being a fan of YouTube, and men-tioned how I can't understand why people spend so much time downloading what I consider garbage from this and other sites – but remember, regardless of whether you or I do it, millions of others do it every day. And they are both your customers and your staff. It is this kind of attitude that leads to companies try-ing to ban sites like YouTube from being viewed by their staff at work. And herein lies one of the lessons of "To Get Control, Give It Up". If your staff are so bored they are spending hours downloading junk from the internet, then you should look at your staff selection processes, and more important at the work you are engaging in and the culture that exists. Build a more exciting place to work!

Or consider the insurance company that doesn't give the ma-jority of their call-centre staff access to the internet or even e-mail. Imagine not having e-mail at work. I know for some of you this sounds more like heaven, but seriously e-mail is a ubiquitous busi-ness tool and one way that we keep in touch. Oh, and they also banned mobile phones. Imagine doing this in a workplace filled with young people, who can't go to the toilet without phoning five of their friends. The result was that the staff continued to use their phones, they just had to hide them. And staff attrition rose to very expensive levels. This is when I was called in.

My favourite example comes from the airline industry. A senior safety engineer at a leading airline had a problem with his trainee safety-inspection officers (or whatever their official title was). They were listening to their iPods while doing routine safety checks on the planes. On first hearing this, being someone who boards literally hundreds of planes each year, even I was disturbed.

When I said I could understand why it would be a problem if customers saw this, the manager looked at me blankly. "I had not thought of that."

"What are you worried about, then?"

"Customer perception is not my area, I was simply worried that mistakes would be made."

Fair enough, I thought, and asked, "So what did you do?"

"I banned iPods."

I asked him how that went. Badly, was the answer. The young trainees started to put their iPods in their pockets and run the headphones under their uniforms, up and out of their collars, and into their noise-protection earmuffs, leaving only a small indication of the recognizable white iPod headphones.

"What did you do next?" I asked, grinning.

He employed an independent consultant to come in and do random accuracy checks on the trainees. This is not an uncommon activity, as the airline does things like this to benchmark its safety performance anyway, and has been doing so for a long time. What he found was that there was no correlation between listening to the iPods, albeit hidden, and inaccuracy.

"What happened next?" I asked.

"They bought me an iPod for Christmas."

I laughed. Just because he couldn't work effectively while listening to music, it doesn't mean someone else couldn't. In life we perceive the world through the lens of our own experience. Then anything that does not match our personal experience we think is wrong, and attempt to bring that person or thing back into alignment. The problem with this is that we usually attempt to do it by "controlling" it and using our positional authority. Are you married, or in a relationship? If so, let me ask you, have you ever tried to change your partner by controlling them? How did that go for you?

I thought so.

This experience reminded me of the financial adviser I met who was struggling with some of his staff, again younger staff, who refused to wear ties. He asked that they do, but they simply ignored him. Over time it got worse, to the point where some stopped wearing suits altogether. When one of his team came to work in jeans and flip-flops, he completely lost it.

He conducted a survey of his key customers about staff dress and the impact it had on their experience. He had expected to see a compelling response demanding that the staff wear more formal attire. Instead he found the opposite.

MANAGERS HAVE FAILED TO GIVE SPACE, RESOURCES AND, MOST IMPORTANT, TRUST TO THEIR STAFF TO DO THEIR JOBS.

Almost 75 per cent of the respondents had not even noticed the more casual attire of these advisers and para-planners. A further 20 per cent actually said they preferred it because they felt more relaxed, and only 5 per cent said they preferred more formal attire. He has since changed his "rules".

These examples are superficial, but are evidence of a much deeper problem in workplaces around the world: a failure on the part of managers to give space and resources and, most important, trust to their staff to do their jobs. They micromanage everything, from whether they wear a tie, to what time they arrive, down to what they say in their e-mails. This all leads to frustration for the staff, and lost productivity and profitability as a result.

According to Gallup, there are twelve questions – each of which relates to a specific need – that indicate whether someone is fully engaged. Of the twelve, the first two relate directly to the idea of letting go of control:

> "A COMPANY WILL GET NO-
> WHERE IF ALL THE THINKING IS
> LEFT TO MANAGEMENT ... WE
> INSIST THAT ALL EMPLOYEES
> CONTRIBUTE THEIR MINDS."
> – AKIO MORITA

- Do you have the materials and equipment you need to do your work right?
- At work, do you have the opportunity to do what you do best every day?

Akio Morita, the founder and former chairman of Sony, has this to say about listening to staff: "A company will get nowhere if all the thinking is left to management. Everybody in the company must contribute and for the lower-level employees their contribution must be more than just manual labour. We insist that all our employees contribute their minds."

START HERE

The old mantra of a job for life and the "loyalty" companies want so desperately from their employees also bespeak trying to keep control. Now, don't get me wrong, retention is extremely important. Crunching some numbers recently with a law-firm client of mine, the net return per person more than triples between the second year and the third year for professional legal staff.

However, expecting them to stay for very long periods these days is probably unrealistic. Some will, but most will not. This is why Ernst & Young has adopted a "start here" approach to its graduate recruitment. Instead of sweating bullets trying to keep the best and brightest from leaving, the company wishes them well and gives them every support in moving out to move up. It has built its graduate-based employment brand on the tagline "start here". The company does this for a few reasons. One is the departing staff might come back, assuming of course they had a pleasant exit experience. Secondly, they may move into non-accounting-firm employment and later become clients. But most of all because the company believes that if employees want to leave, let them. There is no point having someone unhappy at work.

Rather than try to keep the employees, the company strives to keep a relationship with them as they move to other companies and advance in their careers. When the best and brightest of these young workers have become senior executives and CEOs, they'll remember Ernst & Young as the great place where they got their start and they'll be inclined to send their consulting work to their old friends rather than to one of Ernst & Young's competitors.

More to the essence of "To Get Control, Give It Up" is the example of a "tailored taste" being implemented by the Australian Defence Force. In research I helped conduct for the ADF, we found that the younger generation shied away from the forces not just because of the work, the risk of war, or even some ideological opposition, but because they would be "locked in" for a set period of time. They were not at all keen on being controlled in this way. One of the recommendations made to combat this was the gap-year programme. A "gap year" is becoming a sort of rite of passage for young Australians after they finish high school. They head to the UK, the States or somewhere else in the world for twelve months as a gap between high school and university. Some, however, don't have the cash to head overseas, and would love to take a year off but want to grow and learn at the same time. Enter the ADF gap year.

Defence believes they have a superb product. They believe that if people at least try it they will enjoy their time in Defence and join longer term. Defence is putting in place a two-year programme as a gap-year option. It's "try before you buy". That is, students finishing year twelve can enroll in one of the forces for two years only, get trained, develop some leadership skills, stay fit, and travel overseas on at least one operation while there for the year. They can then leave and pursue their other interests, and at worst the army or navy or air force had a committed soldier for a couple of years. Or in the best case, they could leave and spread the word on how brilliant their time was in the forces. Some of these gappers will love the experience so much that they will enrol for full service, attend the Australian Defence Force Academy or something similar, and become fully fledged members of the ADF. This is at least the theory. Markets call this a tailored taste.

GET OUT OF THEIR WAY, AND LET SMART PEOPLE DO WHAT SMART PEOPLE DO.

The way I look at it, particularly the Ernst & Young "start here" positioning, is that if your employees know you have no illusions about them staying for life, they will converse with you actively about their plans because they don't feel threatened. This helps you better prepare, better retain knowledge, and better orient their replacement.

Empowering your staff works when you have hired good staff. Once you have them, you really need to use them. Get out of their way, and let smart people do what smart people do.

FIVE THINGS TO DO NOW

1. Ask yourself if your current business model is under threat, or if it could be if technology continues to develop rapidly. Start now to consider how you would exploit such forced change so you are not on the defensive when it happens.

2. Come up with ten ways you could tap into a broader population to stimulate ideas for you and your business.

3. Start a structured programme within your company that brings your best and brightest people together regularly to work on new ideas or existing problems. Give it a cool name and start using it to attract and retain talented people.

4. Come up with five ways you could collaborate with your existing competitors to bring a product to market, enhance an existing product or service, or even crack open an entirely new market.

5. Does your business have IP that is very valuable to the marketplace, that you are not benefiting from because it is hidden or overprotected? How could you better exploit this asset? In other words, how could you win through losing control?

conclusion:
GET MOVING!

Getting inspired while reading a book is the easy part. Talking to yourself and getting yourself psyched about a new idea for your career and company take little courage. Sure you should be commended for picking the book up in the first place, and you should be celebrated for making it to the end. However, this is the catalyst, not the action. You have to get stuff done.

When you put this book down and head back to work, you will be met by people who have not yet been *flipped*. They won't see the world through the same ideas as you now do. They will be entrenched in out-of-date and inefficient practices, which have made them successful to date.

You should not reject, ridicule or try to "fix" these people. At least, not right away. Nor should you develop a sense of superiority because you now "get it". You will need these people in order to flip your organization.

What you must do now is exercise finesse, generate real and impressive results, and develop an inspiring view of your business's future.

Finesse because people will want to reject you and your ideas. New can often scare people. Your job is to "play the game" and win these people over. Going head-to-head is usually not the best approach. Although, if you get no love – go hard!!! You might as well go down fighting. Then start your own company and kick your old organization's arse in the marketplace.

Results because at the end of the day in business this is what matters. No point having cool ideas, as flipped as they may be, if they don't get results. Being different for different's sake is no different from change for change's sake. If all it does is keep you interested and add some variety to your life, get a hobby. Play a little, take some risks, too. Just remember business is about getting results.

And finally *an inspiring view of the future* because people can and will change if they believe it is for the better. They want to know you have their best interests at heart, and deep down I think they just want to be inspired by the possibility of a better future.

My hope is that *Flip* has given you an inspiring view of the future. I wanted to provide some clarity about the changes we are dealing with daily, and most of all I wanted to give you an empowering mind-set for meeting those changes head-on.

Get off the sidelines and into the ring. Throw some mud at the wall and see what sticks. No one really knows the answers. Not today, and certainly not tomorrow. But this is no excuse not to get in the game. Play a hand or two in the new world of business and see how you fare. Or in closing, consider these words of a flipstar from days gone by:

> It is not the critic who counts: not the man who points out how the strong man stumbles or where the doer of deeds could have done better. The credit belongs to the man who is actually in the arena, whose face is marred by dust and sweat and blood, who strives valiantly, who errs and comes up short again and again, because there is no effort without error or shortcoming, but who knows the great enthusiasms, the great devotions, who spends himself for a worthy cause; who, at the best, knows, in the end, the triumph of high achievement, and who, at the worst, if he fails, at least he fails while daring greatly, so that his place shall never be with those cold and timid souls who knew neither victory nor defeat.
>
> – Theodore Roosevelt, "Citizenship in a Republic",
> a speech given at the Sorbonne, Paris, 23 April 1910

Or put more simply:
Get up off your arse and do something!!!

acknowledgements

Thanks first to my wife, Sharon, for not killing me when I wake up in the middle of the night to write down a new idea and most of all for being a great mum to our beautiful kids as I traipse around the world from hotel room to hotel room.

Second, to Dom Thurbon in my office. Dude, you're a flip-star no doubt. This book would not have been written without your help. And to Hilary Hinzmann in New York, this book would be nothing more than ordinary if it had not been for your wisdom, prose, and basically keeping it real.

Also to my agent, Mary Cunnane, who persevered for liter-ally eighteen months as *Flip* was, well, flipped again and again and again. We made it.

To Henry Ferris and the team at William Morrow, thanks for having the vision to see this was a book the market needed. It may have been a little ahead of its time when you first saw it, but now the world is ready. Thanks for your support, and for the guidance and for trusting me back then.

Finally, to all of my clients. Without you, why write the book? Thanks for your support and I look forward to hanging out some more in the future.

notes

Chapter 1. The Four Forces of Change

1. Pankaj Ghemawat, "The Myth of Globalisation", *Australian Financial Review,* "Review" section, 16 March 2007.

2. The *Time* magazine article where I found this information is no longer available online, but the main findings of the original report it references, produced by technology research firm IDC, are summarized by the Pakistan Software Export Board in its March 2007 online bulletin, available at: www.pscb.org.pk/bulletin/mar07/Bullet_details_march07.htm#test2.

3. Pew Research Center, "Luxury or Necessity? Things We Can't Live Without: The List Has Grown in the Last Decade", 14 December 2006, available at: pewresearch.org/pubs/323/luxury-or-necessity.

Chapter 2. Action Creates Clarity

1. Spencer Reiss, "His Space", *Wired,* 14 July 2006, available at: www.wired.com/wired/archive/14.07/murdoch.html.

2. T. Gilovich and V. H. Medvec, "The Experience of Regret: What, When, and Why", *Psychological Review* 102 (1995), 379–95.

3. David Gray, "Wanted: Chief Ignorance Officer", *Harvard Business Review,* November 2003, 22–4.

4. Bain & Co, "Change or Die", *Fast Company,* May 2005, 60.

5. Daniel Gilbert, *Stumbling on Happiness* (New York: Alfred A. Knopf, 2006).

Chapter 3. Fast, Good, Cheap: Pick Three – Then Add Something Extra

1. Michael Arndt, "McDonald's 24/7", *BusinessWeek,* cover story, 5 February 2007.

2. Kasra Ferdows, Michael A. Lewis, and Jose A. D. Machuca, "Rapid Fire Fulfillment", *Harvard Business Review* 82, no. 11 (November 2004).

3. Noel Capon, *The Marketing Mavens* (New York: Crown Business, 2007), 177–9.

4. Saul Hansell, "EBay Profit Rises 52 Per cent", *New York Times,* 19 April 2007.

Chapter 4. Absolutely, Positively Sweat the Small Stuff

1. Marc Gunther, "The Green Machine", *Fortune,* 7 August 2006; Michael Barbaro, "Home Depot to Display an Environmental Label", *New York Times*, 17 April 2007.

2. L'Oréal 2005 Sustainable Development Report, available at: www.loreal.com/_en/_ww/group_new/pdf/LOREAL_RDD_ GB.pdf.

3. Howard Schultz's original memo can be viewed online at: starbucksgossip.typepad.com/_/2007/02/starbucks_chair_2.html.

4. Jeff Vrabel, "McCartney to Anchor New Starbucks Label", www.billboard.com, 21 March 2007, available at: www.billboard .com/bbcom/news/article_display.jsp?vnu_content_id=1003561098.
5. Gina Chon, "A Way Cool Strategy: Toyota's Scion Plans to Sell Fewer Cars", *Wall Street Journal,* 10 November 2006.

Chapter 5. Business Is Personal

1. Ben Stein, "The Hard Rain That's Falling on Capitalism", *New York Times,* 28 January 2007.
2. Yankelovich Partners, "A Crisis of Confidence: Rebuilding the Bonds of Trust", 2004, available at: www.compad.com.au/cms/ prinfluences/workstation/upFiles/955316.State_of_Consumer_ Trust_Report_-_Final_for_Distribution.pdf.
3. "Building Trust at Home in a Global World", *Australian Financial Review* 19 (March 2007).
4. www.neojobmeeting.com.
5. Finextra Research, "First Direct Hails Text Banking Milestone" 11 February 2005, available at: www.finextra.com/fullstory.asp?id= 13225.
6. Australian Interactive Media Association, "Campaign Success for Mission Impossible 3 and Expansion of Hypertag Solution into New Zealand for AURA and Adshel", available at: www.aimia .com.au/i-cms?page=2263.
7. Laurie J. Flynn, "IBM to Introduce Workers' Networking Software", *New York Times,* 22 January 2007.
8. Meredith Levine, "Tell the Doctor All Your Problems, but Keep It to Less Than a Minute", *New York Times,* 1 June 2004; Wendy Levinson *et al.*, "Surgeons' tone of voice: a clue to malpractice history", *Surgery*, 132, no. 1 (July 2002), 5–9; Wendy Levinson, "Doctor–patient communication and medical malprac-

tice: implications for pediatricians", *Pediatric Annals*, 26, no. 3 (May 1997), 186–93.

Chapter 6. Mass-Market Success: Find It on the Fringe

1. W. C. Kim and R. Mauborgne, *Blue Ocean Strategy: How to Create Uncontested Market Space and Make Competition Irrelevant* (Cambridge, MA: Harvard Business School Press, 2005), 7–8.

2. "BMW 750hL: The Ultimate Clean Machine", available at: www .bmwworld.com/models/750hl.htm.

3. Stephen Totilo, "No Ruler Required for Xbox 360's Cost-Effective Geometry: Trial Version of Game Has Been Downloaded More than 200,000 Times", 12 January 2006, available at: www.mtv.com/news/articles/1520696/20060112/index.jhtml ?headlines=true; Tom Bramwell, "Reshaping the Past", 2 February 2006, available at: www.eurogamer.net/article.php?article_id= 62715; David Kushner, "The Infinite Arcade", *Wired,* August 2006, available at: www.wired.com/wired/archive/14.08/nintendo .html.

4. "Success of Nintendo's Wii Hinges on Games, Not Hardware," FoxNews.com, 12 October 2006, available at: www.foxnews.com/ story/0,2933,220299,00.html.

5. Joseph B. Treaster, "One-Stop Car Insurance Service: Body Work Included", *New York Times,* 26 May 2007.

Chapter 7. To Get Control, Give It Up

1. Kathy Rebello, "Inside Microsoft (Part 2): The Untold Story of How the internet Forced Bill Gates to Reverse Course", *Business-Week,* 15 July 1996, available at: www.businessweek.com/1996/29/ b34842.htm.

2. "Intellectual Piracy in China", *News Hour with Jim Lehrer,*

13 October 2005, available at: www.pbs.org/newshour/bb/asia/july-dec05/china_10-13.html.

3. Bloomberg News, "Piracy in China of Music, Software Draws Ire of US", *Seattle Times,* 10 April 2007.

4. Charles Pillar, "How Piracy Opens Doors for Windows", *Los Angeles Times,* 9 April 2006.

5. M. A. Anastasi, "Sony Exec: We Will Beat Napster", New Yorkers For Fair Use, 17 August 2000, available at: www.nyfairuse.org/sony.xhtml.

6. Andrew Dubber, "The Real Reason Koopa Is Important", 27 February 2007, New Music Strategies, available at: www.newmusicstrategies.com/2007/02/27/the-real-story-of-koopa.

7. Patrick Goldstein, "Hollywood Is Seeing Fans Pull a Power Play", *Los Angeles Times,* 23 January 2007.

8. For more information on Cory Doctorow's work, see his website: www.craphound.com.

9. Tara Hunt, "Chevy Tahoe's First Mistake", HorsePigCow (blog), 3 April 2006, available at: www.horsepigcow.com/2006/04/chevy-tahoe-first-mistake.html.

10. B. J. Ochman, "Won't It Be Funny When Chevy Tahoe Sends Cease & Desist Letters to Bloggers!", whatsnextblog.com, April 2006, available at: www.whatsnextblog.com/archives/2006/04/post_49.asp.

11. Ed Peper, "Now That We've Got Your Attention", GM Fast-Lane (blog), 6 April 2006, available at: fastlane.gmblogs.com/archives/2006/04/now_that_weve_g_l.html.

12. Seth Godin, "Web4", Seth Godin's Blog, 19 January 2007, available at: sethgodin.typepad.com/seths_blog/2007/01/web4.html.

13. William C. Taylor, "To Charge Up Customers, Put Customers in Charge", *New York Times*, 18 June 2006.

14. Brendan I. Koerner, "Geeks in Toyland", *Wired*, February 2006.

15. Taylor, "To Charge Up Customers, Put Customers in Charge", *New York Times*.

16. David Leonhardt, "You Want Innovation? Offer a Prize", *New York Times,* 31 January 2007.

17. "All Profit in the Wiki Workplace", *Australian Financial Review,* 29 March 2007, 57.

index